Progress in
Computing

KS3

Ben Barnes # Mark Clarkson # Graham Hastings #
Tristan Kirkpatrick # Lorne Pearcey # George Rouse

Editors: Lorne Pearcey, George Rouse

Orders: Please contact Hachette UK Distribution, Hely Hutchinson Centre, Milton Road, Didcot, Oxfordshire, OX11 7HH. Telephone: +44 (0)1235 827827. Email education@hachette.co.uk. Lines are open from 9 a.m. to 5 p.m., Monday to Friday. You can also order through our website: www.hoddereducation.co.uk

ISBN: 978 1 3983 2345 2

© Hodder & Stoughton Limited 2021

First published in 2021 by

Hodder Education,

An Hachette UK Company

Carmelite House

50 Victoria Embankment

London EC4Y 0DZ

www.hoddereducation.co.uk

Impression number 4

Year   2024

Cover illustration © olegberesnev – stock.adobe.com

Typeset in India by Aptara

Produced by DZS Grafik, Printed in Slovenia

A catalogue record for this title is available from the British Library.

Contents

Why study computing?

Computers and the internet are integral aspects of modern life. From governments and multi-national businesses to local enterprises and individuals, we rely on computer networks and software to keep the global economy running. Studying computing will enable you to develop a range of knowledge and skills necessary for success in the modern world.

This course combines key concepts related to computational thinking, information technology and digital literacy to provide you with skills and knowledge across the main elements of computer science. At its core is computational thinking, the problem solving and logical thinking skills used by computer scientists and programmers to solve complex problems, which can also be applied to real world issues in many other subjects and disciplines. Writing programs allows you to put these skills to the test and to develop your ability to work through problems and find solutions.

While you may not pursue a career as a programmer, you will almost certainly use a variety of software applications in your everyday lives. Learning how to use software correctly and adeptly – to produce effective presentations, documents or spreadsheets to convey information – is an important skill for many careers. Alongside this comes the ability to develop and edit audio and visual media.

Understanding the development of computing, how computers and the internet work, how to evaluate digital content and the ethical issues surrounding the use of computers help us put the technology into context. Whatever technology we use, it is important we know how to use it safely and respectfully so that we can make the most of opportunities in our future lives.

About the book

Progress in Computing is a complete Key Stage 3 course. It has been designed around a progression framework, to help you to track your progress throughout Key Stage 3, and has been mapped to Key Stage 2 and Key Stage 3 Computing National Curriculums. The progression framework and National Curriculum map can be downloaded at www.hoddereducation.co.uk/ProgressinComputing.

The Student Book is made up of 16 chapters, or modules, and each of these chapters includes six lessons or double-page spreads. The Student Book finishes with three extended six-week-long projects, both to showcase the computing skills you have acquired at Key Stage 3 and to prepare you for one of the many Key Stage 4 options on offer, including GCSEs, Cambridge Nationals and BTECs.

Features

Each chapter begins by introducing you to the topic, explaining why it is relevant.

Before you can use a computer system, you need to know how to access it correctly and this chapter will help you set yourself up on your school computer system and think about what you should use it for. You will learn how to save and organise files and the key principles of internet research and digital wellbeing. You will also learn basic image editing skills.

Reading the text and looking at the images will help you grasp the theory. Key words, which you can look up in the glossary at the back of the book, are in blue bold.

Cloud computing

Cloud computing is where data is stored online and software is used via an internet browser, rather than being stored locally on a computer's hard drive. The data and software files are saved on a **server**. Server farms are located all around the world so you do not know where your data is physically

Working through the activities provides you with an opportunity to check your understanding and apply the theory you have learnt.

Picking up the tabs

Write a program to output the following information about people and their pets:

```
John      Cat
Liz       Dog
Mariya    Hamster
```

You should store the three names in three variables. The three pets will also need to be stored in three different variables, so you will need six variables in total. Your program should then print out the values of these variables using the correct escape characters to format them as shown above.

Occasionally, you will see this icon in an activity box. It means you need to download an additional resource in order to complete the activity. These resources can be downloaded at www.hoddereducation.co.uk/ProgressinComputing.

Checking in questions appear throughout the book. These are short-answer questions designed to test your knowledge and understanding of what you have just learnt. Answers to these questions can be found at the back of the book.

Checking in

1. Why do we need to log into a computer system?
2. What is an acceptable use policy?
3. Explain what is meant by a strong password.

Before you can use a computer system, you need to know how to access it correctly and this chapter will help you set yourself up on your school computer system and think about what you should use it for. You will learn how to save and organise files and the key principles of internet research and digital wellbeing. You will also learn basic image editing skills.

➡ 1 Logging in

Your school computer network

A **computer network** is a collection of computers and other digital devices that are connected together. Your school's computer network probably includes desktop computers, laptops, tablets, printers, scanners and servers.

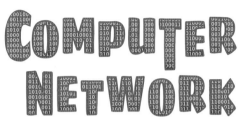

Finding out about your school network

Find out:

- ▶ where the rooms containing computers you can use are located in your school
- ▶ when you can use school computers outside of lesson time
- ▶ where the printers are located
- ▶ what you need to do to gain access to the network
- ▶ if there are any restrictions on where and when you can use your own digital devices in school.

Using computer equipment safely

When you are using school computers, you must remember these rules for ensuring computer equipment is used safely.

- ▶ Do not eat or drink near computers.
- ▶ Keep bags out of the way of computers.
- ▶ Do not unplug or swap any equipment, including keyboards and mice.
- ▶ Sit sensibly, with your monitor, keyboard and mouse directly in front of you.
- ▶ Turn off monitors and keep hands away from keyboards and mice when asked.

You must also follow your school's **acceptable use policy**. These are the rules that govern how a network should be used. Here is an example of a school's acceptable use policy.

- ▶ Systems must only be used for educational use.
- ▶ Usernames and passwords must not be disclosed to anyone else.
- ▶ You must not use another person's username and password.
- ▶ You must not access, copy or delete anyone else's files.
- ▶ Users may not attempt to install programs of any type.

- All communications will be monitored.
- Personal email addresses must not be used to correspond on school matters.
- Any illegal, inappropriate or harmful material must be reported immediately.
- Any damage or faults involving hardware or software must be reported immediately.

Logging in to the school network

Almost all computer systems require the user to enter their **username** and **password** in order to **log in**. Logging in proves the identity of the user so that they can be given access to their own files and programs. Some devices and systems use biometrics, such as fingerprints or facial recognition, to enable a user to prove their identity.

Choosing a strong password

When you first log in you will need to choose a new password. You should always choose a strong password. There are three elements that help to increase the strength of a password:

- length: longer passwords of at least eight characters are more secure
- range of characters used: a password containing a mixture of upper- and lower-case letters, numbers and symbols is more secure
- randomness: passwords that do not contain words people can guess are more secure.

You should also make sure you choose a password that you will remember!

Logging in to the school network

Log in to the school network.

Email

It is important to be polite when you **email** someone and the following rules should be followed when emailing your teachers.

- Always fill in the subject line.
- Greet the person you are writing to appropriately, for example, 'Dear Sir' or 'Hello Mrs Jones'.
- Be polite. If you are requesting something, use the word 'please'.
- Use grammatically correct English. Do not use acronyms or text speak.
- Provide enough detail, so that the recipient does not need to write back and ask for more information.
- Sign off with your full name and form. It is also usual to have a closing salutation, such as 'Kind regards' or 'Yours sincerely'.

Logging in to your email account

Log in to your school email account.

Virtual Learning Environments (VLEs)

A **VLE** is an online system that stores learning resources such as documents, presentations, and video and audio files. VLEs can be used to set, hand in and mark assignments and homework. Some VLEs also include discussion threads, polls, quizzes and surveys, as well as a place where students and teachers can message each other. VLEs can be accessed from home by logging in.

Logging in to the VLE

Log in to your school VLE.

Checking in

1. Why do we need to log into a computer system?
2. What is an acceptable use policy?
3. Explain what is meant by a strong password.

➡ 2 File management, cloud computing and VLEs

Files and folders

All data stored on a computer is saved to a **file**.

A file that contains text is often referred to as a **document**. This is because it is like a piece of paper that has been written on.

A selection of files can be stored in a **folder**. A folder can also contain other folders, which are technically then called sub-folders.

It is important to organise files so that you can find them quickly. It is good practice to use:

▶ relevant file names

▶ relevant folder names

▶ a sensible folder and sub-folder structure.

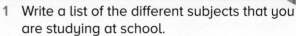
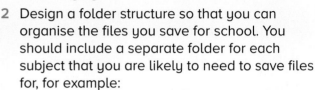

School file management

1 Write a list of the different subjects that you are studying at school.

2 Design a folder structure so that you can organise the files you save for school. You should include a separate folder for each subject that you are likely to need to save files for, for example:

> Science
> > Biology
> > Chemistry
> > Physics

3 Find out where to save files on your school network and create the folder structure you have designed.

Click here to open your 'Documents' folder. Files are normally saved here.

A folder inside the 'Documents' folder.

A file inside the 'Documents' folder.

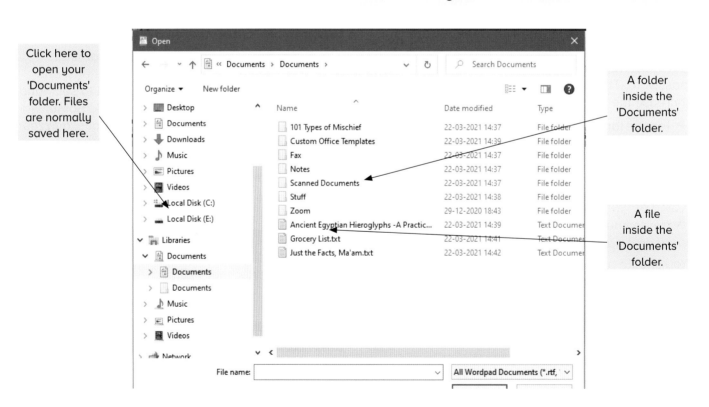

File extensions

When we save a file, we give it a name, for example: 'History_Project'. The software then adds a **file extension** that tells the computer what type of file it is. The file extension is usually three or four characters long. Some common file extensions are:

Extension	File type
.doc / .docx / .pdf	Document
.xls / .xlsx	Spreadsheet
.png / .jpg	Image
.mp3 / .wav	Audio
.mp4 / .mov	Video

The file extension enables the computer to use the correct software to open the file when you double click on it. File extensions can also be used to search for files of a particular type if they have not been saved correctly.

Name	Type	Size
Jupiter_picture.png	PNG File	143 KB
Periodic_table.docx	Microsoft Word Document	53 KB
Periodic_table.xlsx	Microsoft Excel Worksheet	16 KB
Planet_assignment.docx	Microsoft Word Document	53 KB
Planets.jpg	JPG File	98 KB
Planets_image.bmp	BMP File	1,312 KB
Science_experiment.docx	Microsoft Word Document	53 KB
Science_homework.xlsx	Microsoft Excel Worksheet	16 KB
Science_poster.docx	Microsoft Word Document	53 KB
Science_powerpoint.pptx	Microsoft PowerPoint Present...	37 KB
Science_spreadsheet.xlsx	Microsoft Excel Worksheet	16 KB

Saving work

The first time you save a piece of work, make sure you give it a suitable name and save it to the correct folder. You can then save changes to the original file quickly and easily using shortcut keys:

▷ CTRL + S in Windows

▷ CMD + S in MacOS.

If you do not want to overwrite the original file, choose 'Save As' from the 'File' menu to save a copy of your work. Give the new file a suitable name and save it to the correct folder.

Cloud computing

Cloud computing is where data is stored online and software is used via an internet browser, rather than being stored locally on a computer's hard drive. The data and software files are saved on a **server**. Server farms are located all around the world so you do not know where your data is physically

being saved when you store it in the cloud.

Examples of cloud storage are Google Drive, Microsoft OneDrive®, Dropbox™ and your school VLE. Examples of internet-based software are Microsoft 365® and Google Docs.

Advantages of cloud computing

▷ Data is backed up automatically.

▷ Documents and files can be used on any computer with an internet connection.

▷ The software is updated online so you are always using the latest version.

▷ Documents and files can be shared easily with other users.

Disadvantages of cloud computing

▷ The data and software can only be accessed if you have an internet connection.

▷ Cloud-based software does not usually have as many features as downloadable software.

▷ Free storage is limited.

▷ Ongoing subscriptions can become costly over time.

▷ Users can lose legal rights to their material if it is stored online.

▷ Some believe that data may be more vulnerable to being stolen if it is stored online.

Checking in

1 What is data saved as on a computer?

2 What does a folder contain?

3 What is a file extension?

➡ 3 The internet and digital wellbeing

The internet

The **internet** is a global network that connects computers across the world so that they can communicate with one another. These computers include servers hosting software, music and video, and the internet is somewhere to find information, watch videos, play games and connect with friends.

At school, you should be using the internet to access and hand in work via the VLE, carry out research and email your teachers. You should not be using the internet to play games, message your friends or watch videos or listen to music (unless this is something you have been asked to do as part of a lesson).

Using the internet to carry out research

There is a great deal of fantastic stuff on the internet and it is a really useful place to gather information about all sorts of subjects. However, alongside all the accurate information there is a lot of unreliable and even incorrect and misleading information.

Some websites are written by non-specialists who present their own thoughts and ideas on a subject as facts. Other websites are written by very knowledgeable people, but are biased because they present just one side of the story.

In order to work out if information on the internet is trustworthy, look out for:

▶ accuracy: are there facts and figures to back up opinions?

▶ currency: when was the article written? Has it been updated recently?

▶ author: is the author named? Are they qualified to comment on the subject they are writing about?

▶ hosting website: is the organisation hosting the website well known and generally considered to be trustworthy?

▶ balanced presentation: are both sides of an argument covered in equal measure?

▶ professional tone: is the article well written? It should avoid text speak, informal language and inappropriately emotional language.

You will usually begin your research by typing search terms into a search engine. Use keywords rather than long phrases; for example, type 'computer history' to find out how computers have developed over time. Choose words that are likely to be used on the websites you want to visit. Don't worry about small spelling mistakes or capitalisation, because the spell checker that is built into a search engine will automatically use the most common spelling. Use the category options, such as images, video or news, to limit your search. And, finally, remember that you can type 'define' and then a word to find out the word's dictionary definition.

When you are carrying out research on the internet, try to get your information from more than one unrelated source and see what issues the sources agree on to identify the most accurate information. Always rewrite the information in your own words, unless you are quoting something, and include a list of the URLs of the sources you have used so that anyone reading your research knows where you have gathered the information from.

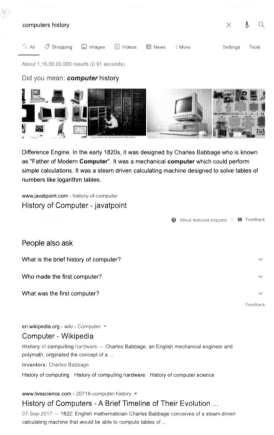

➡ **Google is the most popular search engine in the world**

Researching how to use the internet safely and responsibly

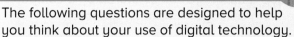

Use the internet to research the things that you should and should not do when using the internet. Consider:

- use of personal information
- use of photos
- use of web cams
- login details and passwords
- what you post.

Copy and paste the URL of each website you visit and then list the things the website advises you should or should not do in a table. For example:

URL: https://www.childnet.com/blog/online-etiquette-or-netiquette-the-dos-and-donts-of-online-communication-	
Do	**Don't**
Be respectful	Be sarcastic

Digital wellbeing

Digital wellbeing is about having a healthy relationship with technology.

Research suggests that 11-year-olds spend up to six hours online every day. Whether or not this is too much depends on the quality of the content you are looking at and the activities you are doing online. However, too much time spent online can affect your friendships, your health and your performance at school.

The effects of spending too much time online include headaches and eye-strain, disturbed sleep, falling out with friends and family, becoming isolated, constantly talking about online activities such as gaming, prioritising your online activities over other things that you should be doing and a decline in the quality of your school work.

Digital wellbeing

The following questions are designed to help you think about your use of digital technology.

- Roughly how much time do you spend online each day?
- What do you spend this time doing?
- Does it add value to your life?
- What would you do if you were not online so much?
- Do you sometimes get tired and grumpy when you are using digital technology?
- Is there anything you would like to change about your use of digital technology?

Tips for managing your use of digital technology

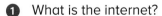

- Before picking up your device, ask yourself what you intend to achieve.
- Make use of tools that tell you exactly how much time you spend on each app.
- Set a time limit for your tech usage each day and try to stick to it.
- Try to make small changes, such as switching off some notifications.
- Put your device into 'Do not disturb' mode before going to bed, or when you have other work to do.

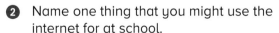

Checking in

1. What is the internet?
2. Name one thing that you might use the internet for at school.
3. Name one thing that you should not use the internet for at school.
4. Explain what we mean by 'digital wellbeing'.

➡ 4 Vector graphics

Data about an image can be stored by a computer as vector graphics or as bitmap graphics.

Vector graphics are stored as a list of **attributes**.

Larger pictures are made up of shapes called **objects** and the attributes for each object are stored separately. The attributes include information such as the object's:

- ▶ height
- ▶ width
- ▶ x and y coordinates for the points
- ▶ outline colour
- ▶ line width
- ▶ fill colour.

The shape of the object is stored as a set of points, and these are connected together by lines. So, for example, the coordinates of the three corners of a triangle are stored.

Each object and its attributes can be edited independently. Objects can be resized by clicking and dragging on the points. The colour and line

width can be changed using formatting options. It is also possible to **layer** objects to create a sense of depth or more complex shapes. Vector graphics are **scalable**, which means that they can be enlarged without any loss in quality as shown here.

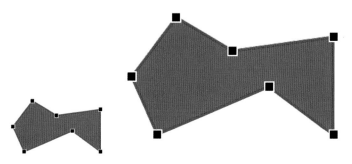

Even if an object in a vector graphic is quite large, it only uses a small amount of memory because the image is recreated from the attributes. Therefore, the file size of a vector graphic is often quite small. Common vector graphic formats are .eps (Encapsulated PostScript File) and .svg (Scalable Vector Graphics File).

➡ **A vector graphic**

Vector graphic picture

Open a new Microsoft Word document and save it with a suitable file name. Then create a vector graphic image of a house and garden. Use the instructions below to help you.

To create an object:

▶ Click on 'Insert' and 'Shapes' and select a shape.

▶ Click and drag the shape to the required size using the handles.

▶ Double-click on the shape and click 'Edit shape' and 'Edit points' to select individual points and drag them to adjust the shape.

▶ Double-click on the shape and click 'Shape Fill' to choose an appropriate colour for the shape, and click on 'No Outline' to remove the coloured outline.

To layer one shape behind another:

▶ Right-click on the object you want to layer behind and choose 'Send to Back'.

To group objects together so that the whole image can be resized:

▶ Click on the one object and hold down the 'Shift' key while clicking on other objects to select them.

▶ Right-click in the selected area and select 'Group' and then 'Group'.

You can group one image in several stages.

Checking in

1. What do we call an image that is made up of objects?
2. How is the shape of an object stored?
3. Vector graphics are scalable. What does this mean?
4. Name one type of vector-graphic file.

➡ 5 Bitmap graphics

Does anything seem strange to you about this picture?

```
0 0 1 1 1 1 0 0
0 1 0 0 0 0 1 0
1 0 1 0 0 1 0 1
1 0 0 0 0 0 0 1
1 0 1 0 0 1 0 1
1 0 0 1 1 0 0 1
0 1 0 0 0 0 1 0
0 0 1 1 1 1 0 0
```

➡ This image has **64** pixels and the computer stores the colour of each pixel, as well as information about the width and height of the image, so that it can be recreated by a computer. White is represented by **0** and black is represented by **1**

It is common practice for the photographs we see in magazines and on posters to be retouched to remove blemishes and make models appear thinner. It raises many ethical issues. If the changes are minor, such as removing an unwanted shadow, it may be considered acceptable. However, it can result in 'impossible' pictures. Often it isn't as easy to spot a fake image as it is to spot that the picture of a person running on the Moon is fake. This can lead to incorrect stories about people circulating on social media and gives people unreal expectations about their appearance.

Bitmap graphics

Bitmap graphics, also called **raster graphics**, store an image as a matrix of dots.

Each dot is called a **pixel**, short for 'picture element'. The colour of every pixel is stored, and every different colour in the picture has its own unique binary code. It is possible to edit the colour of each individual pixel separately to manipulate an image.

The quality of a bitmap image depends on its **resolution**. This is the number of pixels in the image. The higher the resolution, the better quality and more realistic the image. A resolution of 300 dpi (dots per inch) is likely to produce a good quality image. However, when a bitmap graphic is enlarged it loses quality and it is sometimes possible to see the individual pixels.

The size of a bitmap graphic file depends on the resolution of the image, the size of the image and how many unique colours it contains. Bigger images contain more pixels and images that contain a lot of different colours require more bits to store each colour. Bitmap graphic files are generally much larger than vector graphic files because of the amount of information the computer needs to store to recreate the image.

Common bitmap graphic formats are:

▶ .tif: Tagged Image File Format (very high quality but large file size)

▶ .bmp: Bitmap Image File (very high quality but large file size; developed for Microsoft® Windows)

▶ .jpg: Joint Photographic Experts Groups (good for email and presentations)

▶ .gif: Graphics Interchange Format (good for web images with up to 256 colours)

▶ .png: Portable Network Graphics (good for web images with up to 16 million colours).

It is not practical to draw images by defining each pixel separately. At a resolution of 300 dpi, an A4 image will contain 8,640,000 pixels. However, it is possible to save any image in a bitmap file format and then edit the image using **image editing software**.

Isolating an image

Download GIMP (GNU Image Manipulation Program), which is free and open-source image editing software. Then follow the instructions below to begin creating your own 'impossible' photograph.

1 Download and save an image of a real person. Make sure it includes their whole body, not just their head.

2 Open GIMP.

3 Click on 'File' and 'Open' and select your image.

4 Right-click on the layer on the right-hand side of the screen and click 'Add Alpha Channel'.

5 Choose the 'Fuzzy Select Tool' and click on an area of the background that you wish to remove. If necessary, adjust the 'Threshold' to ensure that only unwanted areas of the image are selected. Then press CTRL + X (CMD + X if you're using a Mac) to remove the selected area.

6 Repeat Step 5 to remove as much of the background as possible. If you make an error, remember that you can use CTRL + Z to undo your most recent changes.

7 Next, choose the 'Free Select Tool' to hand draw around the remaining areas of background and use CTRL + X to remove them.

8 Zoom, in using the + key and use the 'Free Select Tool' to remove any background areas with a significant colour difference close to the outline of the person.

9 Once you are happy that all the background has been removed, choose the 'Fuzzy Select Tool' and ensure that 'Feather edges' is selected. Adjust the radius to about 25 to blur the edges of the picture and smooth the colours.

10 Select the background area and then click on 'Select' and 'Invert' to select the part of the image required. Copy the image using CTRL + C or 'Edit' and 'Copy'. Then, create a new layer using the new layer icon at the bottom right of the screen. Make sure that the 'Fill with' field contains 'Transparency'. Then paste your image into the new layer using CTRL + V or 'Edit' and 'Paste'. Finally, click on the anchor symbol to lock your image to the new layer.

11 Hide the original image by clicking on the eye symbol to the left of the first layer, so that only the new layer is selected.

12 Save your image as a GIMP file using 'File' and 'Save', remembering to give it a new name. Then use 'File' and 'Export' to save it as a .png file. Make sure that your image is saved to your documents area.

Checking in

1 How are bitmap graphics saved?

2 What determines the quality of a bitmap image?

3 What happens to the quality of bitmap images when you zoom in?

4 Name one type of bitmap graphic file.

➡ 6 Impossible photographs

You now know how to isolate an image. Now you are going to learn how to insert your cut-out into a new background layer.

Inserting a cut-out into a new background

Follow the instructions below to layer your cut-out of a person into a new background to create an 'impossible' photograph.

1 Make sure that you have finished editing your picture of a person and have exported it as a .png file.

2 Download and save the image that you wish to use for the background.

3 Open GIMP.

4 Click on 'File' and 'New' and set the width to 1920 and the height to 1080. Click on 'Advanced Options' and ensure that the 'Fill with' field is set to 'Transparency' and press 'OK'.

5 Click on 'File' and 'Open' and select your background image.

6 You need to resize your image so that it is the same size as the dotted yellow outline of the canvas. Select the 'Scale Tool' 🖫 and adjust the 'Opacity' on the right-hand side of the screen to 50%. Then use the handles to drag and resize the background picture so that it fills the canvas. Click on 'Scale' and then reset the 'Opacity' to 100%.

7 Click on 'File' and 'Open' and select your edited image of a person.

8 Click on your person image and copy it using CTRL + C (CMD + C if you're using a Mac) or 'Edit' and 'Copy'. Then select the background image from the thumbnail at the top of the screen so that it appears in the centre of the screen.

9 Create a new layer using the new layer icon at the bottom right of the screen: 🗋. Make sure that the 'Fill with' field contains 'Transparency'. Then paste your image into the new layer using CTRL + V or 'Edit' and 'Paste'. Finally click on the anchor symbol ⚓ to lock the cut-out to the new layer.

10 You should now see your image of a person over the top of your background picture. The next task is to resize and reposition it to create your final image. Make sure that the cut-out layer is selected on the right-hand side of the screen and then select the 'Scale Tool'. Resize the image by dragging on the handles. Reposition it by clicking and dragging on the box in the centre of the image. Once you are happy with the result, click on 'Scale'.

11 Finally, you need to save your finished picture. Save your image as a GIMP file using 'File' and 'Save', remembering to give it a new name. Then use 'File' and 'Export' to save it as a .png file. Make sure that your image is saved to your documents area.

Impossible creature

Your final challenge is to use your image editing skills to create an impossible creature, just like the one in this photograph.

Open GIMP and use the instructions on pages 15–16 to help you. You will need to use the:

▶ 'Rectangle Select Tool' to select part of each animal

▶ 'Scale Tool' to match the parts of the two animals together.

Checking in

1. How can different images be combined using graphics software?
2. What does the background need to be set to for this to work?
3. What helps to make the new image look realistic?

Spreadsheets are incredibly useful and powerful tools. They are used every day by people in all sorts of ways, from storing information about products and stock levels to managing multi-million-pound budgets. They can be used to store data, perform complex calculations and to create graphs and charts. They are often used to model what might happen in different situations. This chapter is focused on using spreadsheets efficiently and effectively to perform a range of activities.

➡ 1 Formulae, replication and referencing

A spreadsheet is a type of electronic document used to store data and information. The data can be used to perform calculations, analyse trends, model different scenarios and produce graphs and charts.

The main elements of a spreadsheet

A **spreadsheet** consists of a grid of cells.

A cell is a box on a spreadsheet into which you can place numbers, text or calculations. A spreadsheet is divided into **rows** and **columns** and these are used to provide each cell with a unique **cell reference**.

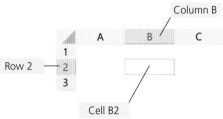

For example, the unique cell reference for cell B2 tells us the cell is in column B and row 2.

Writing formulae using cell references

Spreadsheets are often used to perform calculations. This is done by writing a **formula**. Most formulae use cell references. This means that you can change a value in a cell and the formula automatically recalculates the answer.

Formulae must always start with an equals sign, for example: **=A1+B2**.

The following operators are used to write formulae:

plus sign	+	for addition
minus sign	–	for subtraction
asterisk	*	for multiplication
forward slash	/	for division

Basic formulae

Look at this spreadsheet and write formulae for column D to work out the sums. The first one has been done for you.

	A	B	C	D
5	**Number 1**	**Type**	**Number 2**	**Answer**
6	5	add	3	=A6+C6
8	28	subtract	15	
10	3	multiply by	8	
12	18	divide by	3	
14	356	add	80	

Replicating data and data series

Replication is where you copy information from one cell to another using the **fill handle**. This is a great time-saving feature of spreadsheets.

Click on the cell you want to replicate and move the cursor down to the bottom right of the cell. The cursor should change from a white cross to

a black cross; this is the fill handle. Now click, hold and drag down over the cells you want to fill.

The fill handle can also be used to extend and complete a series of numbers, dates or formulae if you enter the first couple of items in a series:

	A	B	C
1	1	2	Monday
2	2	4	Tuesday
3	3	6	Wednesday
4	4	8	Thursday
5	5	10	Friday
6	6	12	Saturday
7	7	14	Sunday

Relative and absolute cell references

When you replicate cells with formulae in, you have two options. You can use relative cell references or absolute cell references.

Relative cell references are used when you want the formula to change to match the row or column it applies to, across several columns or rows of data; for example: **=A1+B1**.

An **absolute cell reference** is used when you do not want a cell reference to change when replicating cells. An absolute reference is created by adding a dollar sign ($) in front of the column reference, the row reference, or both; for example: **=$A$1+$B$1**.

Any times table

Look at the following spreadsheet.

1 Write a formula with absolute cell references to copy the multiplier in cell G9 to cells C7 to C11.

2 Write formulae with relative cell references for column E.

3 Think about what happens to the values in column E when the multiplier changes.

	A	B	C	D	E	F	G
7	1	times		is			
8	2	times		is			Multiplier
9	3	times		is			5
10	4	times		is			
11	5	times		is			

Cell references

The table below gives the cost of different coloured pencils.

1 Write formulae for column D to calculate the cost of the coloured pencils.

2 Write formulae for column E using an absolute cell reference, to calculate the cost of the coloured pencils plus delivery.

3 Write a formula for cell E22 to calculate the total cost of all the pencils, plus one delivery charge.

	A	B	C	D	E
13	Pencil	Cost	Quantity	Cost	Cost+Delivery
14	Red	£0.30	3		
15	Green	£0.40	8		
16	Blue	£0.20	5		
17	Yellow	£0.40	2		
18	Gold	£0.99	4		
19					
20	Delivery	£0.75			
21					
22	Cost of all pencils plus ONE delivery				

Checking in

1 What is replication? Describe how you would use replication to extend and complete a series of numbers.

2 Explain what is meant by a relative cell reference.

3 Explain what is meant by an absolute cell reference.

➡ 2 Functions using SUM, AVERAGE, MAX and MIN

Functions

Functions are pre-programmed into spreadsheets. They allow us to perform longer or more complex calculations with ease. The following formulae both perform the same calculation, but the second formula, which makes use of a function, is shorter and mistakes are less likely when typing it.

`=A3+B3+C3+D3+E3+F3+G3`
`=SUM(A3:G3)`

All functions start with an equals sign followed by the **function name**.

The data to be used by the function is referenced using individual cell references or a **cell range** enclosed within **parentheses** `( )`; for example:

`=SUM(A3:G3)`.

Function name — Cell range

The SUM function

The **SUM** function adds up the values in a range of cells.

To add up the total score for the group use the formula `=SUM(B4:B7)`.

	A	B
1	Computing Grades	
2		
3	**Name**	**Score/100**
4	Peter	70
5	Vaneet	69
6	Mary	84
7	Zak	32
8		
9	**TOTAL**	=SUM(B4:B7)

The AVERAGE function

The **AVERAGE** function works in much the same way as the **SUM** function.

To work out the average mark use the formula `=AVERAGE(B4:B7)`.

	A	B
1	Computing Grades	
2		
3	**Name**	**Score/100**
4	Peter	70
5	Vaneet	69
6	Mary	84
7	Zak	32
8		
9	**TOTAL**	=AVERAGE(B4:B7)

The MAX and MIN functions

To find the largest value in a range, use the **MAX** function. To find the smallest value in a range, use the **MIN** function.

The highest exam mark is found using the formula `=MAX(B4:B7)`. The lowest exam mark is found using the formula `=MIN(B4:B7)`.

	A	B
1	Computing Grades	
2		
3	**Name**	**Score/100**
4	Peter	70
5	Vaneet	69
6	Mary	84
7	Zak	32
8		
9	**HIGHEST MARK**	=MAX(B4:B7)
10	**LOWEST MARK**	=MIN(B4:B7)

Cinema tickets

	A	B	C	D	E	F	G	H	I
9					Ticket sales				Total weekly
10	Film	Friday	Saturday	Sunday	Monday	Tuesday	Wednesday	Thursday	ticket sales (£)
11	Harry Bond	£800.00	£2,700.00	£2,100.00	£400.00	£350.00	£200.00	£250.00	
12	James Potter	£500.00	£2,000.00	£1,500.00	£200.00	£250.00	£100.00	£150.00	
13	The Happy Princess	£100.00	£250.00	£200.00	£75.00	£300.00	£50.00	£50.00	
14	Starship Wars	£500.00	£1,500.00	£1,400.00	£300.00	£200.00	£100.00	£200.00	
15	Toy Tales	£750.00	£1,000.00	£850.00	£450.00	£150.00	£75.00	£100.00	
16	Mission Possible	£950.00	£900.00	£850.00	£400.00	£350.00	£250.00	£400.00	
17	Mr Pea	£650.00	£1,100.00	£650.00	£325.00	£250.00	£25.00	£250.00	
18	Average ticket sales (£)								
21									
22	What was the smallest amount of money taken by a film on any day?								
23									
24	What was the largest amount of money taken by a film on any day?								

Look at this spreadsheet. It shows the weekly ticket sales for various films at a cinema.

1 Write functions for column I to calculate the total weekly sales for each film.

2 Write functions for row 18 to calculate the average ticket sales each day.

3 Write formulae for the shaded cells in column F to work out the answers to the questions.

Checking in

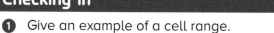
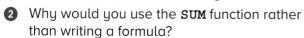

1 Give an example of a cell range.
2 Why would you use the **SUM** function rather than writing a formula?
3 Which function would you use to find the largest value in a set of data?

→ 3 Boolean operators and the IF and COUNT functions

The IF function

The IF function is used to make choices. It has the following structure:

```
=IF( Question, Do this if True,
Do this if False ).
```

There are three elements that need to be included inside the parentheses and they are separated by commas.

1 A question: this is a logical test or logical expression to which the answer can be either True or False.

2 What is to happen or be displayed if the outcome of the logical test, or 'condition', is True.

3 What is to happen or be displayed if the outcome of the logical test, or 'condition', is False.

The logical test in an IF function uses **Boolean operators**:

>	greater than
<	less than
=	equal to
>=	greater than or equal to
<=	less than or equal to
<>	not equal to

Here is an example of an IF function that tells you if a student has passed or failed a test with a pass mark of 60.

The COUNTIF function

The COUNTIF function counts the number of cells in a selected range that meet a specific criterion. It has the following structure:

```
=COUNTIF( Range, Criterion ).
```

The range selects the cells to be checked and the **criterion** is the condition that determines which cells will be counted. It can be a number, a mathematical expression or text that needs to be matched.

Here is an example of a COUNTIF function that counts how many students got a B-:

	A	B
1	**Name**	**Maths**
2	Alison	B+
3	Bob	B-
4	Charlie	A-
5	Deepak	B-
6		
7	**Number of students**	=COUNTIF(B2:B5, "B-")

Test marks

Look at the following spreadsheet. It gives the marks achieved by students in three tests.

1 Write formulae for column E to calculate the total of the three test marks.

2 Write IF functions for column F to decide whether each student has passed or failed. Use absolute cell references.

3 Write functions in the green cells to count the number of students who have passed and failed.

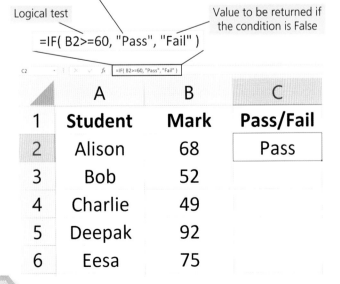

Value to be returned if the condition is True

Logical test

Value to be returned if the condition is False

=IF(B2>=60, "Pass", "Fail")

	A	B	C
1	**Student**	**Mark**	**Pass/Fail**
2	Alison	68	Pass
3	Bob	52	
4	Charlie	49	
5	Deepak	92	
6	Eesa	75	

	A	B	C	D	E	F
11	Name	Test mark 1	Test mark 2	Test mark 3	Total	Pass/Fail
12	Rishi	79	68	88		
13	Bradley	99	63	16		
14	Christopher	26	96	15		
15	Clare	71	44	32		
16	Nuriye	83	25	62		
17	William	8	71	4		
18	Jeevan	34	34	65		
19	Sophie	86	94	28		
20	Freddie	63	76	35		
21	Maya	13	33	64		
22						
23	**Pass mark**	170				

The COUNT and COUNTA functions

The **COUNT** function counts the number of cells in a selected range that contain a number.

Here is an example of a **COUNT** function. The answer is 4, because cells B2 to B5 all contain numbers.

	A	B
1	**Name**	**Score/100**
2	Peter	70
3	Vaneet	69
4	Mary	84
5	Zak	32
6		
7	**Number of results**	=COUNT(B2:B5)

The **COUNTA** function counts the number of cells in a selected range that contain a value (text or a number).

Here is an example of a **COUNTA** function. The answer is 3 because cells B2, B4 and B5 contain a value.

	A	B
1	**Name**	**Maths**
2	Alison	Yes
3	Bob	
4	Charlie	Yes
5	Deepak	Yes
6		
7	**Number of students**	=COUNTA(B2:B5)

Ifcity Zoo

Open the Ifcity Zoo spreadsheet. It lists the different species of animal found at Ifcity Zoo.

1 Write a function in column D to calculate the total number of each type of animal.

2 Write an **IF** function in column H to work out each animal's popularity. If they have more than 30 visitors per hour they are 'Popular'. Otherwise, they are 'Standard'.

3 Write **COUNTIF** functions in cells B36 to B39 to calculate the number of different species for each type of habitat.

4 Write **COUNTIF** functions in cells B42 to B44 to calculate the number of different species for each conservation status.

5 Write a **COUNTA** function in cell G35 to calculate the number of different species at the zoo and a **COUNT** function in cell G36 to calculate the number of different species at the zoo with young.

	A	B	C	D	E	F	G	H
15	**Species**	**Number of adults**	**Number of young**	**Total animals**	**Habitat**	**Conservation status**	**Visitors per hour**	**Popularity**
16	Giraffe	2	3		Savannah	Vulnerable	51	
17	Rhinocerous	2	1		Savannah	Critically endangered	55	
18	Zebra	4	4		Savannah	Vulnerable	22	
19	Emu	4	7		Savannah		12	
20	Owl	1			Forest		15	
21	Gorilla	2	1		Forest	Critically endangered	38	
22	Camel	3			Savannah	Critically endangered	30	
23	Crocodile	2			Swamp		24	
24	Orang-Utan	4	3		Forest	Critically endangered	41	
25	Cheetah	2			Savannah	Vulnerable	40	
26	Egret	6	4		Wetland		19	
27	Python	1			Swamp	Vulnerable	25	
28	Flamingo	6	6		Wetland		21	
29	Pelican	5	3		Wetland		37	
30	Lion	2	2		Forest	Endangered	48	
31	Tiger	2	1		Forest	Critically endangered	45	
32	Kangaroo	2	2		Savannah		39	
33								
34								
35	**Habitat**	**Number of species**				**Number of different species**		
36	Forest					**Number of species with young**		
37	Savannah							
38	Swamp					**Number of 'Popular' species**		
39	Wetland					**Number of 'Standard' species**		
40								
41	**Conservation status**	**Number of species**				**Most visitors per hour**		
42	Vulnerable					**Least visitors per hour**		
43	Endangered							
44	Critically endangered							

6 Write **COUNTIF** functions in cells G38 and G39 to calculate the number of 'Popular' species and the number of 'Standard' species.

7 Write functions in cells G41 and G42 to determine the most visitors per hour and the least visitors per hour for any species.

Checking in

1 What are the three elements needed to write an **IF** function?

2 What does the **COUNT** function tell you?

3 Which function would you use to find out how many cells in a range contain a specific value?

➡ 4 Formatting, graphs and charts

Formatting cells

Formatting cells helps to make a spreadsheet easier to read. You can change the:

▶ font, text size and text colour

▶ fill colour

▶ number format

▶ text alignment

▶ border.

You can format cells using the tools in the ribbon on the Home tab.

Formatting practice

Recreate this spreadsheet, with all the formatting shown. Can you make your spreadsheet look exactly like the screenshot?

Title	Type	Cost
The Dark Sun	Science Fiction	£16.90
Goblins and Other Creatures	Fantasy	£9.99
The Battle of the Dragons	Fantasy	£11.49
My Secret Diary	Comedy	£7.95
Murder at the Bridge	Crime	£8.99

Conditional formatting

Conditional formatting allows you to alter the appearance of a cell depending on the value it contains. This enables you to quickly identify patterns in your data. For example, in the below spreadsheet, conditional formatting has been applied to column C so that any cell containing a number greater than 10 has a green fill and any cell containing a number less than 8 has a red fill.

	A	B	C
1	Title	Type	Cost
2	The Dark Sun	Science Fiction	£16.90
3	Goblins and Other Creatures	Fantasy	£9.99
4	The Battle of the Dragons	Fantasy	£11.49
5	My Secret Diary	Comedy	£7.95
6	Murder at the Bridge	Crime	£8.99

You can apply conditional formatting by selecting 'Conditional Formatting' and 'Highlight Cells Rules' from the 'Home' tab.

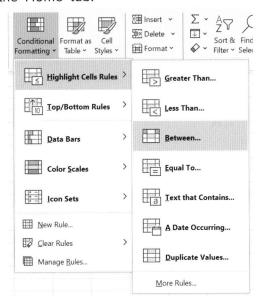

Picture

Create the following spreadsheet and add conditional formatting to reveal a picture. The key tells you the fill colours to use for different cell values.

Remember to select all of the cells in the grid before applying each conditional formatting rule.

	A	B	C	D	E	F	G	H	I	J	K	L	M	N	O
7	1	1	1	2	2	2	1	1	1						
8	1	1	1	2	2	2	1	1	1						
9	2	1	3	3	2	3	3	1	2				Equal to 1		
10	1	3	3	3	2	3	3	3	1						
11	1	3	2	3	2	3	2	3	1				Equal to 2		
12	2	3	3	3	2	3	3	3	2						
13	1	3	2	3	2	3	2	3	1				Equal to 3		
14	1	3	3	3	2	3	3	3	1						
15	2	1	3	3	2	3	3	1	2						
16	1	1	1	1	2	1	1	1	1						

Graphs and charts

Graphs and charts give a visual representation of data and presenting data in graphs or charts can make data easier to understand or interpret.

There are several different types of graph and chart and each is designed to display different types of data.

▶ **Bar charts** and **column charts** allow you to compare categories of data that are not directly related to identify similarities and differences.

▶ A **pie chart** shows the individual parts that make up a whole. They are useful to show percentages.

▶ **Line graphs** are used when you want to show how something has changed over time. They are useful for plotting the results of experiments.

To create a graph or chart, select the data on the spreadsheet, go to the 'Insert' tab and then choose the type of chart you require from the 'Recommended Charts' drop-down list.

Temperature

Copy the data in the table below into a spreadsheet and use the data to insert a clustered column chart to show the temperature across the year. Make sure your chart includes a suitable title and labels for each axis.

Month	Temperature (°C)
Jan	6
Feb	8
Mar	12
Apr	13
May	17
Jun	21
Jul	25
Aug	22
Sep	15
Oct	10
Nov	6
Dec	1

Height

Copy the data in the table below into a spreadsheet and use the data to insert a line graph to show a person's height compared to their age. Make sure your chart includes a suitable title and labels for each axis.

Age (years)	Height (cm)
0	45
1	68
2	85
3	94
4	101
5	108
6	115
7	121
8	127
9	133
10	138
11	144
12	151
13	157
14	160
15	162
16	163

Checking in

❶ Identify three ways in which the appearance of a cell could be formatted.

❷ When might we use conditional formatting?

❸ What chart should we use to show the percentage of students in the class who own a pet?

→ 5 Modelling

Using spreadsheets for modelling

Modelling allows us to predict what is likely to happen when something changes. It is used for many different purpose, for example, for weather forecasting, to predict what the weather will be like in the future.

Modelling is also used in financial decision making to work out, for example, how much profit will be made if prices change. It is also used by engineers designing roller coasters to work out, for example, how variations in the design will affect the speed of the roller coaster.

Spreadsheets are excellent for modelling because it is easy to set them up and perform calculations on data. It is also possible to try out lots of different scenarios to find the best result.

Goal Seek

Goal Seek is a spreadsheet tool that allows you to see how changing one value in a formula affects another. It enables you to ask 'what-if' questions to achieve a specific goal. For example, you can use it to find out the price you need to sell an item for to make a certain amount of profit.

To use Goal Seek, go to the 'Data' tab, click on 'What-If Analysis' and select 'Goal Seek …'.

Sweet shop

This spreadsheet allows us to set a budget (in this case, £5) and then model how we can best spend the money to buy a wide range of different sweets.

Look at the spreadsheet.

1 Think about how to format cells D13 to D21, cell D23 and cell D25 as currency.

2 Write formulae for column D to calculate the cost of whatever quantities of sweets are entered into column C.

3 Write a function for cell D21 to calculate the total cost of all the sweets selected.

4 Write a formula for cell D23 to calculate the budget remaining, by subtracting the total cost from the budget amount.

5 Think about how to add conditional formatting to cell D21 so that the background colour is green if the total is less than or equal to the budget amount and red if the total is more than the budget amount.

	A	B	C	D
12	**Item**	**Cost per 100g**	**Quantity (g)**	**Cost**
13	Humbugs	0.38		
14	Chocolate buttons	1.23		
15	Jelly snakes	0.63		
16	Pear drops	0.37		
17	Fizzy cola bottles	0.47		
18	Wine gums	0.53		
19	Jelly babies	0.53		
20	Liquorice allsorts	0.53		
21			Total	
22				
23			Budget remaining	
24				
25			Budget	

6 Think about how you would use Goal Seek to work out how many grams of Jelly Snakes you can buy for your budget. In Microsoft Excel, you need to open the Goal Seek dialogue box, enter **D21** in the 'Set cell' box, **0** in the 'To value' box because you want your budget to end up at zero, and **C15** in the 'By changing cell' box.

Cupcake challenge

You have decided to hold a charity cake sale. You are going to use the cake and icing recipes below to make 12 cupcakes.

Open the Cupcake challenge spreadsheet and then follow the instructions below.

1   Enter a formula in cell E14 to calculate the cost of 1 g of butter. Replicate this down to cell E20 to calculate the unit cost of the other ingredients. Make sure the cells are all formatted as currency. Note that the cell value will show £0.00 if the cost of 1 g or 1 ml of the ingredient is less than 1p.

2   Enter a formula in cell E24 to calculate the cost of the butter needed for the cake recipe, making sure the cell is formatted as currency. Then enter similar formulae in cells E25 to E28 to calculate the cost of the other ingredients needed for the cake recipe, again making sure the cells are formatted as currency.

3   Enter similar formulae in cells E32 to E35 to calculate the cost of the ingredients needed for the icing recipe. Make sure the cells are formatted as currency.

4   Enter a function in cell C37 to calculate the total cost of the ingredients needed to make 12 iced cupcakes.

5   Enter a formula in cell C39 to calculate the total cost of the ingredients needed to make one iced cupcake.

You now want to work out how much profit you will make if you sell each cupcake for 50p.

6   Enter the number of cupcakes sold (12) into cell C49 and the selling price (50p) into cell C51.

7   Enter a formula in cell C53 to calculate the profit/loss per cupcake. You will need to subtract the cost price per cupcake from the selling price.

8   Enter a formula in cell C55 to calculate the total profit/loss for the number of cupcakes sold. Add conditional formatting to cell C55 so that the fill colour is light green if there is a profit, and pale red if there is a loss.

9   Use Goal Seek to work out how many cupcakes you will need to sell if you want to make £25 profit for charity. Enter the number of cupcakes in cell D59.

	A	B	C	D	E
12	**Cost of ingredients**				
13	**Ingredient**	**Cost**	**Quantity**	**Unit**	**Cost per unit**
14	Butter	£1.50	250	g	
15	Caster sugar	£0.90	500	g	
16	Self-raising flour	£0.90	500	g	
17	Icing sugar	£1.10	500	g	
18	Eggs	£1.20	6	egg	
19	Vanilla extract	£2.00	40	ml	
20	Milk	£0.40	500	ml	
21					
22	**Cake recipe**				
23	**Ingredient**		**Quantity needed**	**Unit**	**Cost**
24	Butter		110	g	
25	Caster sugar		110	g	
26	Eggs		2	egg	
27	Self-raising flour		110	g	
28	Vanilla extract		5	ml	
29					
30	**Icing recipe**				
31	**Ingredient**		**Quantity needed**	**Unit**	**Cost**
32	Butter		150	g	
33	Icing sugar		300	g	
34	Vanilla extract		5	ml	
35	Milk		20	ml	
36					
37	**Cost price for 12 cupcakes**				
38					
39	**Cost price per cupcake**				
40					
49	**Number of cupcakes sold**				
50					
51	**Selling price**				
52					
53	**Profit / Loss per cupcake**				
54					
55	**Total Profit / Loss**				
58					
59	**Number of cupcakes to make £25 profit**				

Checking in

1   What is meant by modelling?

2   Why are spreadsheets good to use for modelling?

3   What does Goal Seek enable you to do?

6 Theme park challenges

Theme park challenge 1

You have been engaged by a local theme park to help them calculate their costs and ticket prices. The theme park is open 365 days per year, for 8 hours per day.

Open the Theme park challenge spreadsheet, which contains data about the rides that you will need to complete the activity.

1 Enter a formula in cell C31 to calculate how many minutes the park is open each day.

2 Enter a formula in column E to calculate the number of times each ride runs per day. Each run takes the length of the ride plus 2 minutes for changeover. Use absolute cell references to link to the park opening time per day and the time between each ride in your formula.

3 Enter a formula in column F to calculate the total number of guests who can go on each ride in a day.

4 Enter a formula in column G to calculate the cost of operating each ride for one day. This is the total number of guests multiplied by the thrill factor multiplied by the cost per ride (50p). Make sure that the cells are correctly formatted as currency.

5 Enter a function to work out the total cost of operating all the rides for one day.

6 Format the table so that the column headings are bold, use a font size of 14pt and have a light grey fill colour.

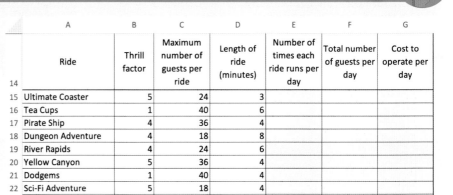

	A	B	C	D	E	F	G
	Ride	Thrill factor	Maximum number of guests per ride	Length of ride (minutes)	Number of times each ride runs per day	Total number of guests per day	Cost to operate per day
15	Ultimate Coaster	5	24	3			
16	Tea Cups	1	40	6			
17	Pirate Ship	4	36	4			
18	Dungeon Adventure	4	18	8			
19	River Rapids	4	24	6			
20	Yellow Canyon	5	36	4			
21	Dodgems	1	40	4			
22	Sci-Fi Adventure	5	18	4			
23	Drop Tower	5	12	2			
24	Chair Swing	2	32	8			
25	Log Flume	3	20	6			
26	Ferris Wheel	2	50	13			
27	Haunted House	2	24	10			
28	Runaway Mine Train	4	46	3			
29						Total	

31	Park opening time per day (minutes)	
33	Time between each ride (minutes)	
35	Cost per ride	
46	Number of guests per day	
48	Ticket price per day	
50	Income from food/drink per guest	
52	Total income	
54	Staffing costs per day	
56	Total expenditure	
58	Profit/Loss	
62	Ideal ticket price	

	Thrill factor	Number of rides
69	1	
70	2	
71	3	
72	4	
73	5	

The Theme Park usually has 5000 guests per day and the entrance ticket costs £15. As well as the cost of the entrance ticket, each guest spends an additional £5 on food and drink.

7 Format cells C48, C50, C52, C54, C56, C58 and C62 as currency.

8 Enter a formula in cell C52 to work out the total income each day.

9 As well as the cost of running the rides, the theme park has staffing costs each day (£7500). Enter a formula in cell C56 to work out the total expenditure each day.

10 Enter a formula in cell C58 to work out how much profit the park will make each day. This is the total income minus the total expenditure.

11 Add conditional formatting to cell C58 so that the background fill is light red if the profit is less than £50,000 and light green if it is higher than £50,000.

12 Work out the ideal ticket price the theme park should charge if it wants to make £75,000 profit per day. Enter the figure in cell C62.

The theme park is creating some new publicity materials. It would like to include a chart to show what percentage of rides have each thrill factor.

13 Use functions to count how many rides there are for each thrill factor (cells B69 to B73).

14 Insert a suitable chart to show the percentage of rides for each thrill factor. Make sure that the chart has a suitable heading and shows the percentage of rides for each thrill factor.

Theme park challenge 2

Now that you have completed the main theme park challenge, use your knowledge and skills to model some new situations and answer the following questions.

1 The number of guests per day increases to 6,000. If the ticket price is £15, how much profit will the park make each day?

The cost per ride increases to 75p.

2 If the ticket price is £15 and there are 6,000 guests, how much profit will the park make each day?

3 If the income from food/drink per guest decreases to £4.25, how much profit will the park now make each day?

4 What should the park change the ticket price to in order to make £65,000 profit each day?

5 A new queueing system allows the time between each ride to decrease to 90 seconds. If the cost per ride is 55p, how much will it cost to operate all the rides for one day?

Checking in

1 Name three things you now know how to do on a spreadsheet.

2 Describe the three things you now know how to do on a spreadsheet.

Without knowledge of the history of computers and computer science, it is impossible to predict how things might change in the future. It is only by looking back, realising how far we have come and appreciating the exponential increase in the processing power of our digital devices that we are able to project this trend into the future and make an educated guess about the changes information technologies may bring.

This chapter serves a dual purpose, helping you develop your word processing and presentation skills at the same time as giving you an appreciation of the rapidly changing technologies that have brought the computer to where it is today.

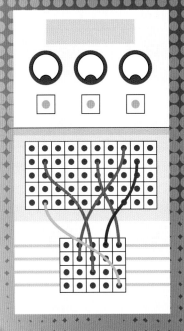

➡ 1 The history of word processing

Before word-processing applications, most people wrote documents by hand.

From the mid-nineteenth century, people who wrote a lot were able to make use of a mechanical device known as a typewriter to format their text. A typewriter prints text directly onto sheets of paper and there is only one font and one font size.

It is impossible to assess the full impact that the invention of word processing has had on the world since the first commercial **word-processing software**, WordStar, was published in 1978. The combination of word-processing applications, spreadsheets and affordable personal computers triggered an explosion in the market for computers, both for office and home use.

➡ A typewriter is a mechanical text-printing machine

Using word-processing software to create a mind map

A mind map is diagram that organises information around a central concept or topic. Pieces of information are linked together, with more important information closer to the centre.

You can create a mind map in a Microsoft Word document using 'Shapes' on the 'Insert tab' and typing text into the shapes. You can create a mind map in Google Docs using the 'Drawing' tools on the 'Insert' tab and typing text into text boxes.

You can format the colour of the text and the fill colour and outline colour of the objects, and you can link your objects together using lines. When you have finished your mind map, you should group the objects to create one block that can be moved and resized.

Creating a mind map

Use word-processing software to create a mind map about the 'Features of word-processing software'. Include features you already know about, explore the tools to find features you are not yet familiar with and group similar features together.

Use experimentation, 'Help' or 'Tell me' features and online tutorials to discover for yourself how to use the tools in Microsoft Word or Google Docs to create the mind map.

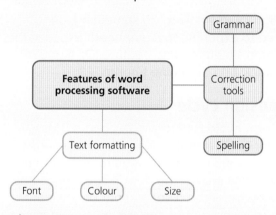

⇨ **A part-completed mind map**

Finished but not complete?

It is very common for people to think they have finished a piece of work when it is very far from complete. When you think you have finished work on a document, remember to:

▶ **Review:** Have you done everything you set out to do? Is the content presented clearly?

▶ **Reflect:** What could you do to make it better?

▶ **Edit:** Make the changes.

Completing your mind map

Use the following questions to help you review, reflect on and edit the mind map you created.

▶ Can you use different colours to emphasise the connection between similar features?

▶ Can you resize and/or reposition shapes or text boxes to make better use of space and make the mind map easier to read?

▶ Can you add screenshots to make your mind map more useful?

▶ Have you corrected all grammatical errors and spelling mistakes?

Templates

A **template** is a blank document with a pre-set format. Templates can make word processing standard documents much quicker.

How did word processors change the world?

Use the internet to carry out research to answer the question above. Use the mind map template on Worksheet 1.4 to keep notes as you carry out your research. The template is designed to get you started and you may have to add or remove, or change the shape of, shapes or text boxes as you work.

Remember the following key principles when carrying out research on the internet.

▶ Do not plagiarise! Never pretend you wrote words that were originally written by someone else.

▶ If you want to use someone else's words, quote them. Use quotation marks around the text you are copying and cite your source (give the name of the author and the URL of the website you copied the quote from).

▶ Do not use copy and paste unless you have read, understood and are quoting the text you are pasting.

▶ Assess the trustworthiness of each source. Look back at page 10 for tips on how to do this.

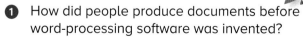

Checking in

❶ How did people produce documents before word-processing software was invented?

❷ What is a mind map?

❸ What should you do to ensure a piece of work is completed to a high standard?

➡ 2 Designing a leaflet

Word-processing applications today

Compared with WordStar, modern word-processing applications are incredibly feature rich. Yet, in spite of all these new features, these word-processing applications perform much the same functions as the very first word processor: you enter and format text and save and retrieve electronic documents.

➡ Microsoft Word and Google Docs are the most popular word-processing software applications in the world

Here are some of the most commonly used word-processing commands:

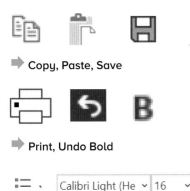

➡ Copy, Paste, Save

➡ Print, Undo Bold

➡ Bullet points, Font and Font size

Exploring word-processing software

The **user interfaces (UI)** of word-processing applications have been designed so that they are intuitive, that is, so that they are easy to use and understand.

The ribbon across the top of the application gives you access to a vast array of features, so the first thing you need to do is investigate what the application has to offer. Place your mouse over the icons on the toolbars for more information.

➡ The Home tab in Microsoft Word

If you don't know how to do something, be prepared to experiment. If you need help, use the application's built in 'Help' feature. Or, if you're really stuck, find an online tutorial.

The design cycle

The **design cycle** is iterative; it repeats. This allows for the fact that a design is rarely perfect first-time around and it will need to be tested and improvements made. The design cycle does not need to be repeated a set number of times but, each time it is repeated, the design should improve until, eventually, it is fit for purpose and no more improvements are required.

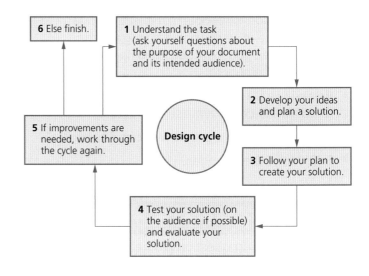

6 Else finish.

1 Understand the task (ask yourself questions about the purpose of your document and its intended audience).

2 Develop your ideas and plan a solution.

5 If improvements are needed, work through the cycle again.

Design cycle

3 Follow your plan to create your solution.

4 Test your solution (on the audience if possible) and evaluate your solution.

Planning and creating a leaflet

Design a flyer to publicise a cause or event of your choice. To make the flyer as cheap as possible to print, your A4 document must contain two identical copies of the leaflet side by side, like this:

Job Expo

10 a.m. to 3 p.m.
14.12.2021

JOB OPPORTUNITIES AVAILABLE!

We invite all employment and career resource centres, community centres, public service organisations and educational facilities from the City.

www.yourwebsite.co.uk

Job Expo

10 a.m. to 3 p.m.
14.12.2021

JOB OPPORTUNITIES AVAILABLE!

We invite all employment and career resource centres, community centres, public service organisations and educational facilities from the City.

www.yourwebsite.co.uk

Use the questions below to help complete stage 1 of the design cycle, then move on to stages 2 and 3.

▶ **Purpose:** What does the leaflet need to do? What information does it need to give to the person reading it? What should the person reading it do?

▶ **Audience**: Who is the leaflet for? What will the intended audience find attractive and enticing?

Tips for creating a flyer

▶ Set the page to landscape and make the margins narrow to make room for two flyers on one A4 page.

▶ The main heading should be large and clear, to grab the attention of your intended audience.

Use sub-headings to break up large chunks of text.

▶ Images should add meaning to the text and you could consider including image captions.

▶ Use all the available space, but don't be afraid of empty white space.

▶ Limit the number of fonts, font sizes and font colours; too many can be confusing.

▶ Remember to save your work regularly.

Commenting on your partner's leaflet

Swap computers or share your work with a partner and use the comments tool to give feedback on the design of your partner's flyer. In Microsoft Word, highlight the word or phrase you want to comment on, then click on 'Review' and 'New comment'; in Google Docs, click on the + sign in the right margin to add a comment. Remember to save your partner's document when you have finished adding your comments.

This is part of stage 4 of the design cycle.

Finishing your leaflet

Evaluate the feedback you received on your leaflet and, if necessary, make improvements. Remember to 'Save as' before you begin making improvements, so you always have your partner's comments to refer back to.

This is the rest of stage 4 of the design cycle. It is also stage 5 and stage 6.

Checking in

1. How can you find out how to do something using word-processing software that you don't know how to do?

2. What happens if you highlight text I and then click on this button?

3. True or false? When you have worked through the design cycle once, your design is complete.

→ 3 Moore's Law

The incredible shrinking computer

The 1940s: valve computers

The early computers were enormous. They filled a large room. The switches used to process data were **valves** the size of a thumb.

ENIAC, the first electronic general-purpose digital computer, contained nearly 18,000 valves within its circuits. That might sound like a lot but ENAIC's processing power was miniscule; less than a small electronic calculator today.

→ ENIAC

1947: the invention of the transistor

The first big reduction in the size of electronic computers came when valves were replaced by much smaller **transistors**.

→ An early transistor

1959: the invention of the microchip

The next big reduction in the size of electronic computers came when the **microchip** was invented. Many tiny transistors can be etched into a single silicon microchip and, with each transistor added, the processing power of a device increases.

All our digital devices today contain microchips.

Moore's observation

Moore's Law is named after Gordon Moore. In 1965, Moore founded Intel Corporation with Robert Noyce. Intel was to become the world's largest producer of computer microchips.

As a chip developer, Moore had observed the gradual miniaturisation of the transistor and the increase in the number of transistors that could be etched onto a microchip. He pointed out that the number of transistors on a single microchip was doubling about every two years. In the mid-1960s, Moore predicted that this exponential trend would continue into the future and this is Moore's Law.

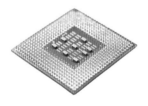

→ Over time, more and more transistors have been etched onto a microchip. The one on the left contains 137 transistors, the one on the right has about 42 million

Moore's Law graph

If we draw a line on a graph to represent Moore's Law and plot the development of the number of transistors on a microchip, we can see that Moore accurately predicted the development of the microprocessors at the heart of our digital devices many decades into the future.

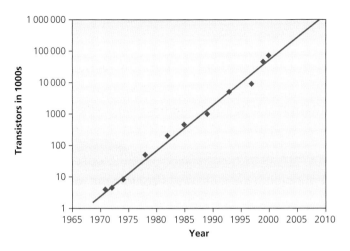

- ▶ Images add meaning to the text and are accompanied by captions. Text could flow around images.
- ▶ The number of fonts, font sizes and font colours is limited; too many can be confusing.
- ▶ The information is logically ordered so that the narrative flows from one point to the next.
- ▶ Data, in the form of tables or graphs, is used to support the text if appropriate.
- ▶ All sources of information are cited.

A report on Moore's Law

Use the text and images provided in Worksheet 3.1 to design a two-page report on Moore's law. The report must explain Moore's Law to students of your own age.

You do not need to include all the text and images provided. You can select whatever you think is most relevant and interesting. You can also edit the content and may even carry out your own research.

Use the questions below to help you complete stage 1 of the design cycle, then move on to stages 2 and 3.

- ▶ **Purpose:** What does the report need to do? What information does it need to give to the person reading it and how should the information be presented to make it accessible to the audience?
- ▶ **Audience:** Who is the report for? What will the intended audience find attractive and enticing?

The qualities of a well-designed report

- ▶ The report has a title. It could also have a sub-title.
- ▶ Headings and sub-headings are used to break up large chunks of text.
- ▶ Line spacing and margins ensure the content is easy to read and doesn't feel cramped.

Commenting on your partner's report

Swap computers or share your work with a partner and use the comments tool to give feedback on the design of your partner's report. Remember to save your partner's document when you have finished adding your comments.

This is part of stage 4 of the design cycle.

Finishing your report

Evaluate the feedback you received on your report and make improvements. Remember to 'Save as' before you begin making improvements, so that you always have your partner's comments to refer back to.

This is the rest of stage 4 of the design cycle. It is also stage 5 and stage 6.

Checking in

1. Whose was the law that predicted that the number of transistors that could be etched onto a microchip would continue to double every two years named after?
2. Which of the following did the first general-purpose digital computer, ENIAC, contain: transistors, valves, or microchips?
3. Which of the following do all our digital devices today contain: transistors, valves, or microchips?

➡ 4 The history of computing

Presenting the history of computing

The history of computing is longer than the history of modern computer technology and includes early methods and devices for carrying out calculations.

Examples of good or bad design?

Here are four slides from a presentation about the history of computing. For each slide, identify examples of good and bad presentation design.

---

al-Khwarizmi (780–850 AD)

Known as the father of algebra, al-Khwarizmi was an outstanding Persian mathematician and one of the first Directors of the House of Wisdom in Baghdad in the early ninth Century.

He oversaw the translation of important Greek and Indian books about mathematics and astronomy into Arabic.

The word 'algorithm' is derived from his name.

A stamp bearing the image of al-Khwarizmi.

© Hodder & Stoughton Limited 2021

© Roman Vukolov/stock.adobe.com · © Kaitlyn McLachlan/stock.adobe.com · © Daniel Berkmann/stock.adobe.com

© Hodder & Stoughton Limited 2021

Alan Turing

In 1936, the mathematician, Alan Turing, wrote a mathematics paper, 'On Computable Numbers, with an Application to the Entscheidungs problem', which came to be seen as a theoretical basis for today's computers. In his paper, Turing imagined a single machine that could compute any problem, effectively uniting all human or problem-specific 'computers' into one universal device.

When Turing was moved to Bletchley Park during the Second World War to join a team of code breakers put together to crack Nazi military codes, he got a chance to put some of the theories into practice. Working with Flowers and Newman, they built Colossus, the first model of a general-purpose computer. After the war, Turing went on to build the Pilot ACE, one of Britain's earliest stored program computers and the world's first general-purpose electronic computer in Britain.

By the mid-1950s, the computers imagined by Turing started to be built in real life and were becoming common in large institutions, companies and university departments. Such early machines, like the Pilot ACE and EDVAC were so enormous that they filled large rooms and they required a team of people to operate them.

Alan Turing is now celebrated as the inventor of the modern electronic computer and is considered to be the single most important figure in the history of computing.

Quantum computing

Computer scientists are investigating completely new methods of computation, such as **quantum computing**.

The computer shown uses the spin property of electrons so that individual electrons are processing and storing date.

This means that a single atom can store many pieces of data, opening the door for infinite parallel processing.

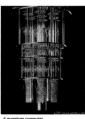

A quantum computer

© Hodder & Stoughton Limited 2021

Design your own presentation

Use the text and images provided in Worksheet 4.3 to design a four-slide presentation for your classmates on one aspect of the history of computing. The presentation should take no longer than two minutes to deliver next lesson.

You do not need to include all the text and images provided. You can select whatever you think is most relevant and interesting. You can also edit the content and may even carry out your own research.

Use the questions below to help you complete stage 1 of the design cycle, then move on to stages 2 and 3.

▶ **Purpose:** What does the presentation need to do? What information does it need to give to the person reading it and how should the information be presented to make it accessible to the audience?

▶ **Audience:** Who is the presentation for? What will the intended audience find attractive and enticing?

The qualities of a well-designed presentation

▶ The presentation has a title and most slides have headings.

▶ The same approach to design is used throughout the presentation.

▶ The number of fonts, font sizes and font colours is limited; too many can be confusing.

▶ Use of animations should add to the audience's understanding not detract from it.

▶ There is a strong contrast between the background colour(s) and the font colour(s).

▶ There is a good balance between text and images and the slides are not overcrowded.

▶ Images relate to the text, can be seen clearly and have credits.

▶ Audio and video clips should be embedded into the presentation; avoid linking to clips in another software application.

Commenting on another presentation

Look at someone else's presentation and use the comments tool to give feedback on the design of your partner's report. In Microsoft PowerPoint, click on 'Review' and 'New comment'. In Google Slides, click on the 'Add comment' icon in the toolbar. Remember to save your partner's document when you have finished adding your comments.

This is part of stage 4 of the design cycle.

Finishing your presentation

Evaluate the feedback you received on your presentation and make improvements. Remember to 'Save as' before you begin making improvements, so you always have your partner's comments to refer back to.

This is the rest of stage 4 of the design cycle. It is also stage 5 and stage 6.

Checking in

❶ What do you consider to be the most important quality of a well-designed presentation?

❷ True or false? The history of computing begins with the first digital device.

❸ Who invented the World Wide Web?

➡ A brief history of computing

In simple terms, a computer is any person or device that carries out mathematical calculations. People have been inventing devices to help them to compute numbers for hundreds of years. Early computing devices were mechanical and it is only very recently that we have come to associate the word computer with the electronic devices that we use today.

Here are some of the milestones that make up the history of computing.

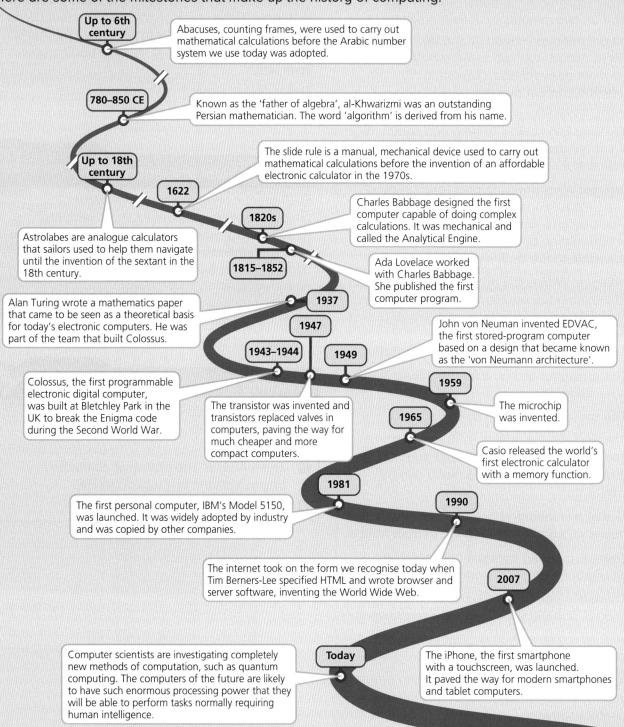

Up to 6th century
Abacuses, counting frames, were used to carry out mathematical calculations before the Arabic number system we use today was adopted.

780–850 CE
Known as the 'father of algebra', al-Khwarizmi was an outstanding Persian mathematician. The word 'algorithm' is derived from his name.

Up to 18th century
Astrolabes are analogue calculators that sailors used to help them navigate until the invention of the sextant in the 18th century.

1622
The slide rule is a manual, mechanical device used to carry out mathematical calculations before the invention of an affordable electronic calculator in the 1970s.

1820s
Charles Babbage designed the first computer capable of doing complex calculations. It was mechanical and called the Analytical Engine.

1815–1852
Ada Lovelace worked with Charles Babbage. She published the first computer program.

1937
Alan Turing wrote a mathematics paper that came to be seen as a theoretical basis for today's electronic computers. He was part of the team that built Colossus.

1943–1944
Colossus, the first programmable electronic digital computer, was built at Bletchley Park in the UK to break the Enigma code during the Second World War.

1947
The transistor was invented and transistors replaced valves in computers, paving the way for much cheaper and more compact computers.

1949
John von Neuman invented EDVAC, the first stored-program computer based on a design that became known as the 'von Neumann architecture'.

1959
The microchip was invented.

1965
Casio released the world's first electronic calculator with a memory function.

1981
The first personal computer, IBM's Model 5150, was launched. It was widely adopted by industry and was copied by other companies.

1990
The internet took on the form we recognise today when Tim Berners-Lee specified HTML and wrote browser and server software, inventing the World Wide Web.

2007
The iPhone, the first smartphone with a touchscreen, was launched. It paved the way for modern smartphones and tablet computers.

Today
Computer scientists are investigating completely new methods of computation, such as quantum computing. The computers of the future are likely to have such enormous processing power that they will be able to perform tasks normally requiring human intelligence.

➡ 5 Learning to present

The dos and don'ts of good presentations

DO

- ▶ Look at the audience.
- ▶ Talk about the information on the slides.
- ▶ Speak loudly and clearly.
- ▶ Give the audience time to fully absorb the information on each slide before moving on.
- ▶ Keep to the time limit you've been given.

DON'T

- ▶ Stand in front of the screen.
- ▶ Stand with your back to the audience.
- ▶ Read the text on the slides.
- ▶ Talk too quickly, mumble or gesticulate too much.
- ▶ Move through the slides too quickly.
- ▶ Overrun the time limit you've been given.

Rehearsing your presentation

Rehearse your two-minute presentation on the history of computing. If you are working in pairs or groups, decide which slide or slides each of you will be presenting. Work out what you want to say and practise giving the presentation as many times as you can. Practice, as they say, makes perfect.

Delivering the presentations

When you have watched each presentation, write down your observations about the design of the presentation *and* the delivery of the presentation in a copy of the table below.

Presenter/s	What I particularly liked	Suggestion for improvement

Checking in

1. What is your greatest strength when giving a presentation?
2. What do you need to work on when giving a presentation?

➡ 6 The future of computing

Will we be using these technologies in the future?

➡ Will robot dogs provide companionship?

➡ Will we be able to select an item in a shop and walk straight out with it, paying without queuing or interacting with a cashier?

➡ Will drones deliver small packages to our homes?

➡ Will your fridge be able to tell you when food inside it is about to go off?

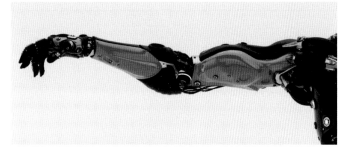

➡ Will we have brain chips implanted that will be able to control computers, including our mobile phones and artificial limbs, with no physical interaction?

Predicting the future isn't as easy as it might seem. Here are some of the predictions made about the computer.

> 'I think there is a world market for maybe five computers.'
>
> — Thomas Watson, President of IBM, 1943
>
> 'There is no reason anyone would want a computer in their home.'
>
> — Ken Olsen, founder of Digital Equipment Corporation, 1977

➡ Thomas Watson and Ken Olsen's predictions were wildly inaccurate!

Where might computing take us next?

Produce a one-page report or a three-slide presentation titled, 'Where might computing take us next?' It is up to you how you interpret the word 'next'. You might want to think about the *next* few years, the *next* 30 years or a time in the more distant future.

The audience for your work is anyone who has no specialist knowledge of computer science and the purpose is to stimulate their thinking about how computing may impact their lives in the future. The content can be factual and based on data and statistics or be completely imaginative. If it is completely imaginative, it must be rooted in computer science and be realistic.

Before you begin your report or presentation, look back at the qualities of a well-designed report on page 35 and the qualities of a well-designed presentation on page 37.

Checking in

Is it possible to guess how computers might impact our lives in the future?

All computer programs are designed with three key **programming constructs** in mind: sequence, selection and iteration.

This chapter introduces you to these constructs using Scratch and a range of block-based programming activities. Understanding them will make you a better problem-solver, both in everyday life and as a computer programmer.

→ 1 Introduction to the Scratch environment and sequencing

Sequencing

Sequencing is when a set of instructions is carried out in order. Sequencing is important because, if your instructions are in the wrong order, what you want to happen won't happen! This is because a computer cannot interpret instructions and work out what they mean, like a human can. A computer does exactly what it is told to do, in the order it is told to do it.

Look at this sequence of instructions to find the average of three numbers. There are some problems with it.

Total = number 1 + number 2 + number 3
Enter number 1
Enter number 3
Enter number 2
Mean = Total / 3
Display Mean

The total cannot be calculated before the numbers are entered.

The numbers can be entered in any order because the program is calculating their average.

What is Scratch?

Scratch is a program that allows you to piece blocks of code together to solve problems. It is called a block-based programming language because you do not need to type any code.

Your first Scratch program

Follow these instructions to complete your first Scratch program.

1 Go to https://scratch.mit.edu/.

2 Select 'Create'.

3 Find the following blocks to make the cat say 'Hello [your name]' for 5 seconds. Here is an example:

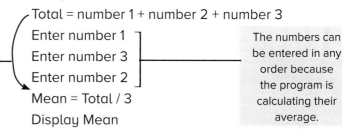

4 Press the flag icon to test your program. It should do something like this:

5 Now it's time to save your first Scratch program to your computer. Select 'File' and choose 'Save to your computer'.

6 Let's practise loading a Scratch program from your computer. Select 'File' and choose 'Load from your computer'. Select the Scratch program that has been saved and click on 'Open'.

Using the pen to draw shapes

Use the pen extension to get the cat to draw different shapes.

1 Create a new Scratch program.
2 Select the 'Add Extensions' icon.

3 Select the 'Pen' extension.

4 Locate the blocks and create the following program:

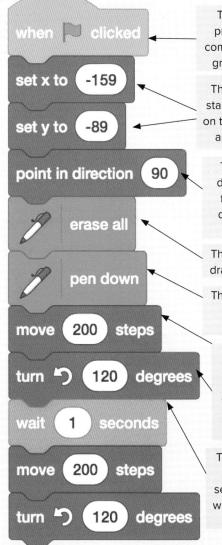

This block tells the program to do what comes after it when the green flag is clicked.

These blocks set the start location of the cat on the horizontal axis (x) and vertical axis (y).

This block sets the direction the cat will face, in degrees. 0 degrees is north on a compass.

This block deletes any drawings on the stage.

This block puts the pen on the stage ready to draw.

These blocks move the cat 200 steps in the direction it is facing and then turn the cat 120 degrees to the left.

This block makes the program wait for 1 second before it does what the blocks below tell it to do.

Drawing a square

1 Use the skills you have just learnt to draw a square. This is what you should see on the stage when your program finishes running:

2 Improve your program so that the cat draws the following shape:

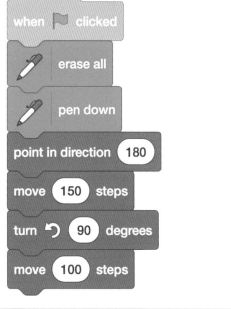

Checking in

1 What is sequencing?
2 What would the following blocks output?

➡ 2 Sequencing

It is important to practise breaking down a complex problem into a sequence of instructions that the computer can carry out.

Remember, if the instructions are incorrectly sequenced, the computer will not do what you want it to do.

Drawing a hexagon

1   Use these blocks to program the cat to draw a hexagon. You will need to adjust the values in some of the blocks.

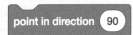

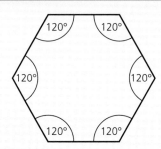

➡ **The internal angles of a hexagon are 120 degrees**

2   Use the 'repeat' block to reduce the number of blocks in your program.

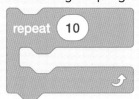

3   Refine your code further so that the cat draws two hexagons like this:

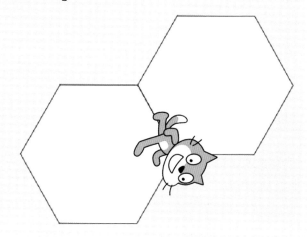

➡ Using the 'erase all' block clears the stage of all the lines the cat previously drew. Using the 'set x to' block and the 'set y to' block sets the coordinates of the cat's starting point

Creating a picture

Now you have learnt how to sequence blocks to create a shape, it is time to make a drawing made up of more than one shape. Use sequencing to program the cat to draw this house:

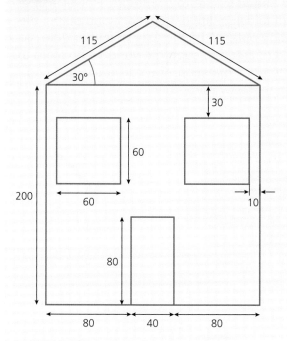

The only new block you will need in addition to those you have already used is this one, the 'pen up' block:

Think about:

▶ the shapes you need to create

▶ the dimensions and angles of each shape

▶ the order in which you are going to create each shape.

Checking in

What would this code do?

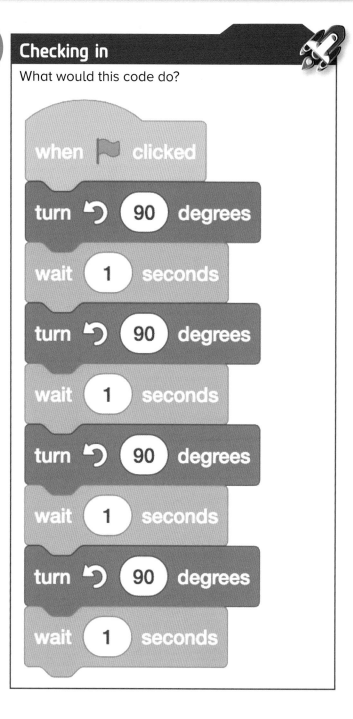

➡ 3 Using variables

Variables

A **variable** is a container that temporarily holds a **value** (a number or a piece of text). The value can be retrieved within the program using its variable name. This is very similar to cell references in spreadsheets, where you refer to the cell reference instead of the value in the cell.

Using variables means that if the value changes, you do not have to rewrite your code because it will update automatically.

The content of a variable can change as the program runs, so it might not always stay the same.

New blocks

Here are some of the new blocks that you will need to use to work with variables in Scratch.

The 'join' block is used to join text together with variables. This is called **concatenation**.

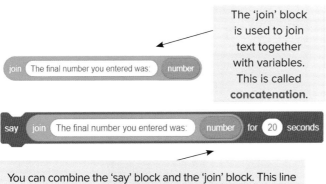

You can combine the 'say' block and the 'join' block. This line of code would **output The final number you entered was:** and then the value that is stored in the **number** variable.

The 'ask' block displays a message and you can customise what it says in the white area. This block requires a response from the user. The user has to type something in; enter an **input**.

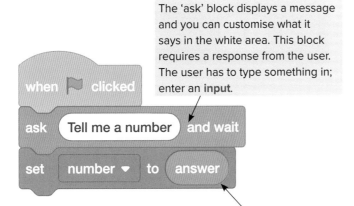

The 'set' block sets your chosen variable to something. You have to create your variable first, in the 'Variables' category of the palette. In this example, the variable **number** is set to the value entered by the user when answering the question in the previous block.

When the 'ask' block is used, it automatically creates a variable called 'answer' that stores whatever is entered by the user. This means that, if you want to output the answer straight away, you don't need to create a variable. However, if you want to ask multiple questions and output the information entered by the user at a later date, you will need to create a separate variable fto store the answer to each question. You can see why if you compare these two programs:

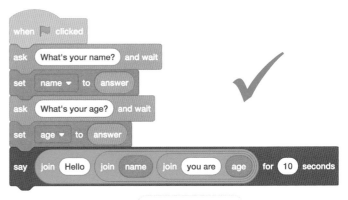

Hello Peter you are 24

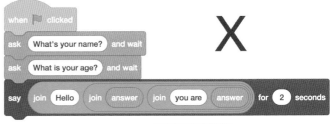

Hello 24 you are 24

Asking your name

1 Program the cat to ask the user their name and then output **Hello**, followed by the user's name, followed by **, nice to meet you!**. Here are the blocks you need to create the program.

2 Extend your program so that the cat asks a second question and gives an appropriate response.

Shopping list

Here is the start of a program that should ask for five items to be added to a shopping list. At the moment it asks for just the first item.

Create these blocks and then add to the program so that it asks for five items, one at a time, and then displays a message that lists all the items entered.

HINT: You will need to create five variables, one to store the answer to each of the five questions.

Chatbot aka 'Cat Bot'

A chatbot is a program that asks a question and then uses the answer to the question in its next question. Create a chatbot that asks five questions; the questions it asks are up to you, but start with **What is your name?** The chatbot *must* use the response from each question to make a comment or feed into the next question. At the end of the five questions, the chatbot needs to say **Thank you for talking to me**, followed by the user's name.

HINT: You will need to make use of a variable to store the user's name when it is entered in response to the first question.

Checking in

1 What is a variable?

2 How many variables are there in this code? What are the names of the variables?

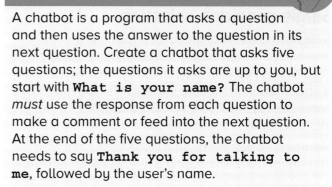

➡ 4 Selection

Single condition selection

Selection is used to check a condition and then do one thing if the condition is True and one thing if the condition is False. In programming, this is done using **if statements** and **if-else statements**. You may have come across the IF function in spreadsheets, if-else statements work in exactly same way.

Here is an example of an if statement. An if statement does something if the condition is True.

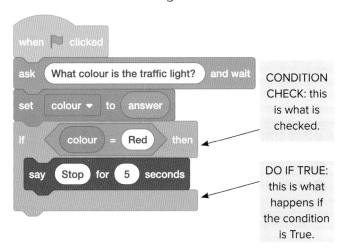

CONDITION CHECK: this is what is checked.

DO IF TRUE: this is what happens if the condition is True.

Here is an example of an if-else statement. An if-else statement performs one **action** if the condition is True and another if it is False; it will not perform both actions.

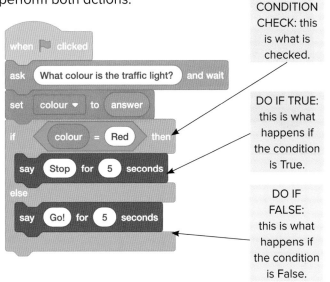

CONDITION CHECK: this is what is checked.

DO IF TRUE: this is what happens if the condition is True.

DO IF FALSE: this is what happens if the condition is False.

Social media sign up

Create a program that tells the user whether or not they are old enough to use social media.

You need to be 13 or older to use social media. If the user is 13 or older, the cat should say **You are old enough to sign up to social media**. If the user is not 13 or older, the cat should say **You are not old enough to sign up to social media**.

Multiple condition selection

We have seen how you can use selection to check one condition. But what if you need to check more than one condition? You can nest if-else statements inside if-else statements, so that multiple conditions can be checked.

Below is an example of how you can check multiple conditions. If the first condition is True, the second condition check *will not* take place.

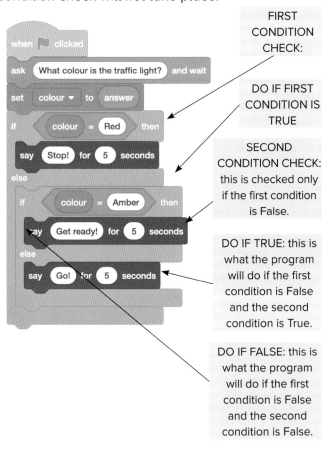

FIRST CONDITION CHECK:

DO IF FIRST CONDITION IS TRUE

SECOND CONDITION CHECK: this is checked only if the first condition is False.

DO IF TRUE: this is what the program will do if the first condition is False and the second condition is True.

DO IF FALSE: this is what the program will do if the first condition is False and the second condition is False.

Computer game level up

1 Program a computer game where you collect gemstones. Each gemstone is worth 50 experience points (XPs). The program should:

- ask the user how many experience points (XPs) they started with
- ask the user how many gemstones they collected
- calculate how many XPs they got from collecting the gemstones
- add the number of XPs they got from collecting the gemstones to the number of XPs they started with
- check to see if the total is more than 1000
- if the total is more than 1000, say **Well done you have levelled up!**
- if the total is not more than 1000, say **You didn't get enough experience points to level up. Sorry!**

2 Improve your program so that, if the user does not have enough points to level up, it tells them how many points they need. You will need to:

- calculate how many points they need. This is done by subtracting the total number of points from 1000
- add the number of points they need into the message that says they didn't get enough points to level up. The message should say: **You didn't get enough experience points to level up. You needed [number of points] more points.**

3 The game has been updated so that you can level up twice. To level up twice, you need to collect a total of more than 2000 XP points and the cat will say **Well done you have levelled up twice!** If you don't get more than 2000 points, you can still level up once with 1000 points.

HINT: You will need to nest an if-else statement inside an if-else statement, so you can check more than one condition.

Checking in

1 What is selection?

2 What would this program output if the age entered was 16?

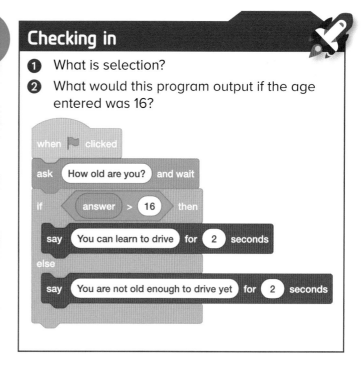

5 Selection and logical operators

Logical operators

Logical operators return a **Boolean value**, a value that can be only True or False. There are three logical operators that can be used in programming to help determine what a program should do: **AND**, **OR** and **NOT**.

The AND operator

The **AND** operator allows for two conditions to be checked. For it to return True, both conditions must be true. Here are some examples:

Statement	Returns	Reason
(10 > 12) AND (15 > 10)	False	Only one condition is true. 10 is not more than 12.
(A = A) AND (C = C)	True	Both conditions are true.
(5.5 < 3) AND (G = F)	False	Both conditions are false.

Here is an example of **AND** being used in Scratch. If **120** is entered, the program would say **FALSE** because 120 is more than 50 but it is not less than 100 so both conditions are not met. If **67** is entered, the program would say **TRUE** because 67 is more than 50 and less than 100 so both conditions are met.

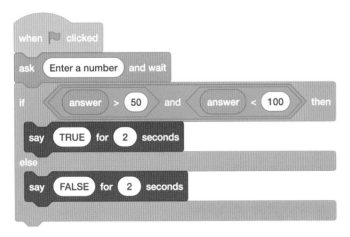

Using logical operators makes programs simpler and easier to follow. Here is the same program without a logical operator. You can see that it is more complicated, with more than one if-else statement.

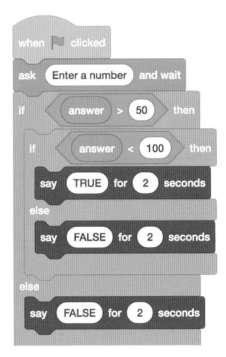

The OR operator

The **OR** operator allows for two conditions to be checked. For it to return True, at least one condition must be true. Here are some examples:

Statement	Returns	Reason
(10 > 12) OR (15 > 10)	True	At least one condition is met. 15 is more than 10.
(A = A) OR (C = C)	True	Both conditions are true.
(5.5 < 3) OR (G = F)	False	Both conditions are false.

Here is an example of **OR** being used in Scratch. If **120** is entered, the program would say **TRUE** because 120 is more than 50 and it doesn't matter if it isn't less than 100 because only one condition needs to be met. If **67** is entered, the program would say **TRUE** because 67 is more than 50 and less than 100 and at least one condition needs to be met.

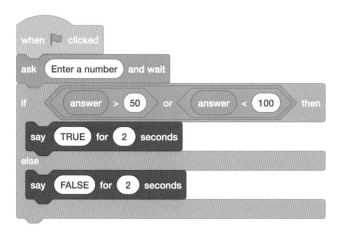

The NOT operator

The **NOT** operator allows for one condition to be checked. For it to return True, the value has to be anything but the value being asked for. Here are some examples:

Statement	Returns	Reason
C = NOT(B)	True	The letter C is NOT the letter B.
15 = NOT(14)	True	The number 15 is NOT the number 14.
14 = NOT(14)	False	The number 14 is the number 14.

Here is an example of **NOT** being used in Scratch. If **14** was entered, the program would say **TRUE** because the number entered is NOT 15. If **15** is entered, the program would say **FALSE** because the number entered IS 15.

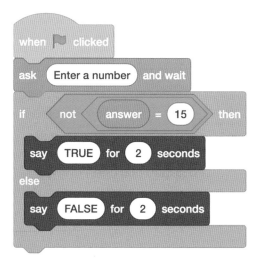

What is the weather like?

1 Create a program that uses selection and a logical operator (**AND**, **OR** or **NOT**). The program should:

- ask the user if it is raining
- ask the user the temperature
- check if it is raining *and* the temperature is more than 18 degrees
- if it is raining and the temperature is more than 18 degrees, say `Don't forget to take your umbrella`
- otherwise say `Better take your raincoat!`

2 Improve your program so that it outputs an appropriate message according to the inputs entered by the user. This table shows the different combinations that your program needs to respond to:

Rain	Temperature	Output
Y	>18	Don't forget to take your umbrella
Y	<19	Better take your raincoat and an umbrella
N	>18	What a lovely warm day
N	<19	Better take your coat, it's chilly!

Checking in

1 How many conditions need to be true for the **AND** operator to return True?

2 How many conditions need to be true for the **OR** operator to return True?

3 What is the problem with the **AND** operator in this program?

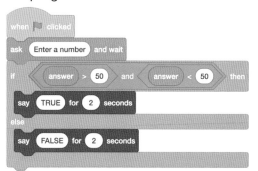

6 Iteration

Iteration is when a set of instructions is repeated. It is used when a program needs to complete the same process multiple times to make programs shorter and easier to code. Iteration can also be referred to as using a **loop**.

The most common form of iteration in Scratch is the 'repeat' block. You set how many times you want something to repeat, or ask it to repeat until a condition is met.

Here are two programs that ask the user to enter three scores. They add the scores and display the total. Both programs do exactly the same thing, but the second one makes use of iteration. The repeated blocks are placed inside the 'repeat' block (inside the loop) to reduce the amount of code needed.

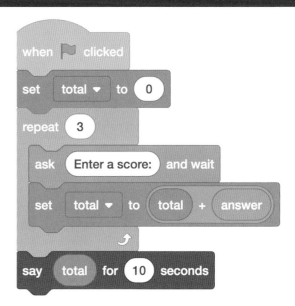

➡ Uses iteration: six blocks required

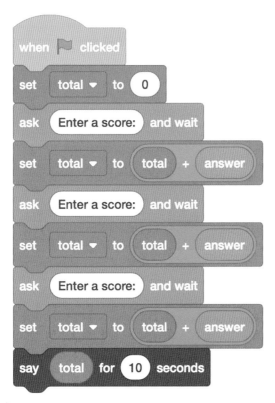

➡ Doesn't use iteration: nine blocks required

Octagon

1 You have been given a program – Programming in Scratch Scratch 6.1.sb3 – that draws an octagon. The program contains a lot of blocks. Identify the pattern (repeated blocks) and then use iteration to reduce the number of blocks in the program.

2 Amend your program to create a program that draws the shapes below using iteration. You should be able to do this by adding only three blocks!

HINTS:

▶ You will need a variable to store the size of the shape. Set it to 100 at the start and change it to 50 after the first octagon has been drawn.

▶ You will need to put your original loop inside another loop that repeats twice.

▶ You will need to change **move X steps** to **move variable steps**.

Nested iteration and variables

Nesting can be used with iteration to make programs even shorter.

The program below draws the shape to the right:

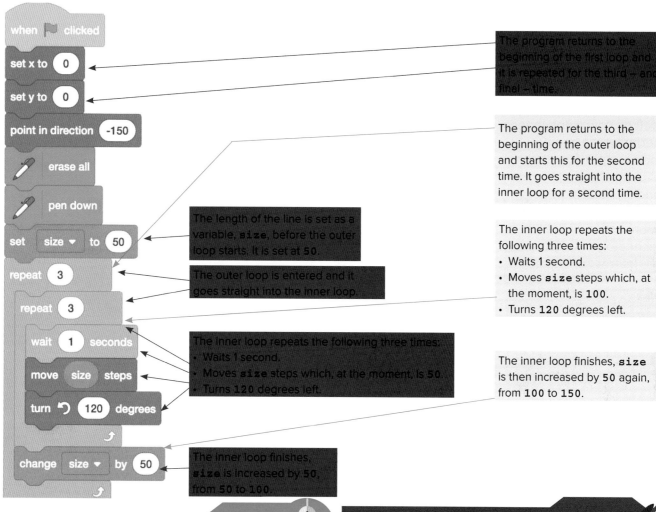

```
when 🏳 clicked
set x to 0
set y to 0
point in direction -150
erase all
pen down
set size ▼ to 50
repeat 3
  repeat 3
    wait 1 seconds
    move size steps
    turn ↺ 120 degrees
  change size ▼ by 50
```

The program returns to the beginning of the first loop and it is repeated for the third – and final – time.

The program returns to the beginning of the outer loop and starts this for the second time. It goes straight into the inner loop for a second time.

The length of the line is set as a variable, **size**, before the outer loop starts. It is set at **50**.

The outer loop is entered and it goes straight into the inner loop.

The inner loop repeats the following three times:
- Waits 1 second.
- Moves **size** steps which, at the moment, is **100**.
- Turns 120 degrees left.

The inner loop repeats the following three times:
- Waits 1 second.
- Moves **size** steps which, at the moment, is **50**.
- Turns 120 degrees left.

The inner loop finishes, **size** is then increased by **50** again, from **100** to **150**.

The inner loop finishes, **size** is increased by **50**, from **50** to **100**.

Spirograph

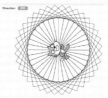

Create a program that uses iteration to drawing the following image. It is made up of 36 squares. Each square is drawn at an angle 10° degrees different from the angle of the previous square.

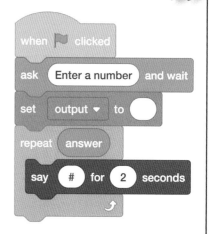

HINTS:

▶ Use iteration to get the cat to draw a single square.

▶ Create a variable that changes the direction of the square by 10 each time it is drawn.

▶ Use the 'repeat' block to repeat this process 36 times.

Checking in

❶ What is iteration?

❷ How many times will the following program say # if the user enters 4?

```
when 🏳 clicked
ask Enter a number and wait
set output ▼ to ( )
repeat answer
  say # for 2 seconds
```

Knowing about the core components that make up digital devices is essential if you want to understand what you are using, make good decisions when you choose new tech and fix problems.

This chapter explores what is inside a computer as well as how a computer's performance can be measured. It also looks at computer peripherals and types of storage, and culminates in an examination of the latest technology available with the Internet of Things.

➡ 1 Computer hardware

Hardware, software and peripherals

Hardware is the name given to the physical parts of the computer that you can touch. Different hardware components are connected to the motherboard of a computer via dedicated sockets.

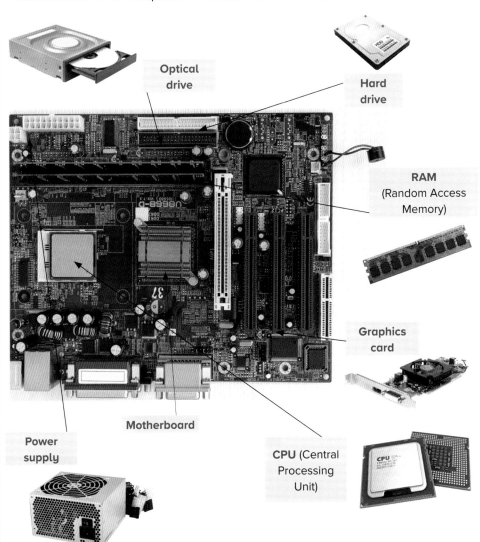

Optical drive

Hard drive

RAM (Random Access Memory)

Graphics card

Motherboard

Power supply

CPU (Central Processing Unit)

Software is the name given to the programs that use the computer hardware to run. Examples of software include:

▶ word-processing software such as Microsoft Word or Google Docs

▶ web browsers, such as Chrome and Firefox

▶ operating systems such as Microsoft Windows and MacOS.

There is often lots of additional equipment that comes with a computer, such as a monitor, a keyboard and a mouse. These devices can be classed as hardware, but they have another name as well: **peripherals**.

Infographics

An infographic is a visual representation of information. It can include images, text, data and colours. Here are some examples of infographics.

➡ The images are clear, the text is easy to read and there is space for explanations of the statements

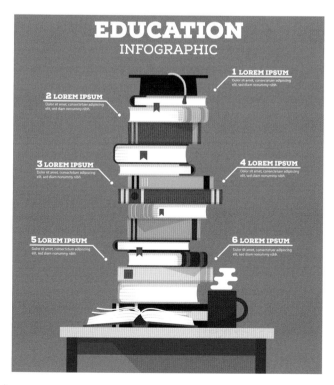

➡ The layout is clearly structured, the text stands out from the background and the images are not intrusive

Computer hardware infographic

Create an infographic about computer hardware. Your infographic should:

▶ include the seven main hardware components:
- CPU
- RAM
- motherboard
- graphics card
- power supply
- hard drive
- optical drive

▶ include, for each hardware component:
- name
- image
- role

▶ have an appropriate title

▶ use appropriate fonts and colours.

See the 'Computing components catalogue 1.1' for information to help you create your infographic.

Checking in

1. I am the smart part of the computer. I complete all the processing. What am I?

2. Everything connects to me. Without me, none of the other hardware could work together. What am I?

3. I store large amounts of data permanently, even when the power is off. What am I?

➡ 2 Measuring computer performance

Hardware components do different things and so their performance is measured in different ways using different units.

▶ CPU performance is measured by its **clock speed** (**hertz**). This is how many fetch–decode–execute cycles the CPU can process per second and is often referred to as just 'speed'.

▶ RAM performance is measured by its speed (hertz) and how much it can store (**bytes**).

▶ Hard drive performance is measured by how much it can store (bytes).

You can convert different units of storage so you can compare the performance of different hardware.

You can also convert different units of speed so you can compare the performance of different hardware.

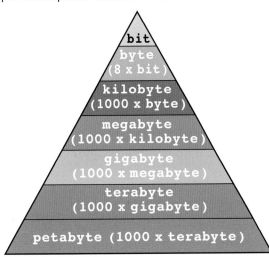

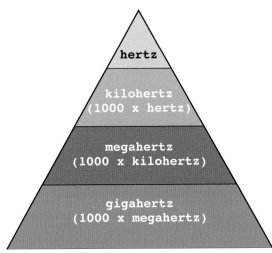

➡ 1 terabyte = 1,000 gigabytes = 1,000,000 megabytes (1000 × 1000)
2 terabytes = 2,000 gigabytes = 2,000,000 megabytes (2 × 1000 × 1000)
1,000,000 kilobytes = 1,000 megabytes = 1 gigabyte
4,000,000 kilobytes = 4,000 megabytes = 4 gigabytes

➡ 1 megahertz = 1,000 kilohertz = 1,000,000 hertz (1000 × 1000)
5 megahertz = 5,000 kilohertz = 5,000,000 hertz (5 × 1000 × 1000)
1,000,000,000 hertz = 1,000,000 kilohertz = 1,000 megahertz = 1 gigahertz
6,000,000,000 hertz = 6,000,000 kilohertz = 6,000 megahertz = 6 gigahertz

Measuring performance (Part 1)

1 Order the following units of storage in order, from 1 (the smallest) to 7 (the largest):

- byte
- petabyte (PB)
- megabyte (MB)
- bit
- gigabyte (GB)
- kilobyte (KB)
- terabyte (TB)

2 Order the following units of speed in order, from 1 (the slowest) to 4 (the fastest):

- megahertz (MHz)
- hertz (Hz)
- kilohertz (KHz)
- gigahertz (GHz)

Computer performance

1 Which computer has the fastest CPU?
2 Which computer has the largest amount of permanent storage?

Computer A		Computer B	
CPU	2.8 GHz	CPU	750 MHz
RAM	8 GB	RAM	2 GB
Hard drive	750 GB	Hard drive	256 GB

Computer C		Computer D	
CPU	1.6 GHz	CPU	3.4 GHz
RAM	512 MB	RAM	128 MB
Hard drive	1 TB	Hard drive	128 GB

Measuring performance (Part 2)

1 How many bytes in 2 kilobytes?
2 How many terabytes in 1000 gigabytes?
3 How many megabytes in 5 gigabytes?
4 How many kilobytes in 2 gigabytes?
5 How many bytes in 3 megabytes?
6 How many hertz in 4 kilohertz?
7 How many kilohertz in 6 gigahertz?

Why does hardware performance matter?

Hardware performance matters because you want your computer to do exactly what you need it to do, but different people have different requirements. A gamer wants a fast CPU so that their computer plays the latest games smoothly. They also want a powerful graphics card and lots of RAM. A teacher does not need a particularly powerful computer, so CPU speed is less important, but wants lots of storage space to store all the resources for their lessons.

Choosing the right device

Imagine you are employed by a company called HodTech and your manager has asked you to source computers for the following employees.

▶ A receptionist who works in one location sending emails, using word-processing software and printing documents. Budget: £400.

▶ A software developer who works in one location developing websites, using social media and collaborating with colleagues. Budget: £800.

▶ A marketing manager who works in multiple locations sending emails, creating images and videos for marketing and hosting video meetings. Budget: £1000.

▶ A games developer who works in one location collaborating to design games, rendering graphics and testing games. Budget: £1500.

Identify the best computer for each employee and justify your decision. Use the 'Computing components catalogue 1.1' to see the selection of computers you have to choose from.

Checking in

1 Is a kilobyte larger than a megabyte?
2 Which is faster, 1.5 gigahertz or 1600 megahertz?
3 Why might a professional photographer require a large amount of storage space on their computer?

➡ 3 Computer peripherals

A peripheral is a device that allows information to be entered into or retrieved from a computer. Peripherals are normally split into different three types:

▶ **input devices**: devices that allow the user to enter data into a computer

▶ **output devices**: devices that allow the user to display the results after processing

▶ **external storage devices**: an external device that stores data.

Categorising peripherals

Categorise each of the following peripherals as an input device, an output device or an external storage device.

➡ Headphones

➡ Keyboard

➡ Monitor

➡ Mouse

➡ Laptop trackpad

➡ Scanner

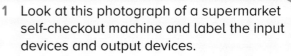
➡ Microphone   ➡ Printer

Input and output

1 Look at this photograph of a supermarket self-checkout machine and label the input devices and output devices.

2 Explain what each device is used for.

Data input

There are a large number of input devices. Each one enables data to be entered into a computer so that it can be processed by the computer. Data can be input in different ways, including as:

▶ text typed

▶ images scanned

▶ voices recorded.

Text typed using a keyboard is the most common form of input:

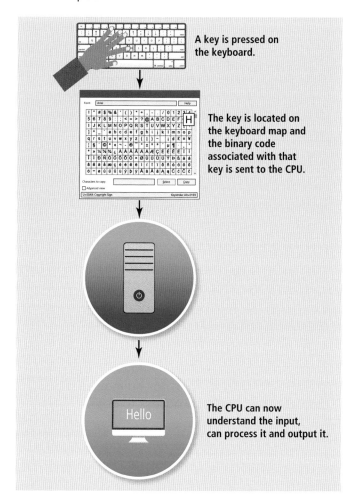

A key is pressed on the keyboard.

The key is located on the keyboard map and the binary code associated with that key is sent to the CPU.

The CPU can now understand the input, can process it and output it.

Processing input

Binary	Character	Binary	Character
01000001	A	01100001	a
01000010	B	01100010	b
01000011	C	01100011	c
01000100	D	01100100	d
01000101	E	01100101	e
0100110	F	01100110	f
01000111	G	01100111	g
01001000	H	01101000	h
01001001	I	01101001	i
01001010	J	01101010	j
01001011	K	01101011	k

Binary	Character	Binary	Character
01001100	L	01101100	l
01001101	M	01101101	m
01001110	N	01101110	n
01001111	O	01101111	o
01010000	P	01110000	p
01010001	Q	01110001	q
01010010	R	01110010	r
01010011	S	01110011	s
01010100	T	01110100	t
01010101	U	01110101	u
01010110	V	01110110	v
01010111	W	01110111	w
01011000	X	01111000	x
01011001	Y	01111001	y
01011010	Z	01111010	z
00100000	[space]	00111111	?
00101110	.	00100001	!
00101100	,	00111010	:

1 Look at the binary code below and use the table to process it, turning it from binary code into meaningful text.

a 01000011 01101111 01101101 01110000 01110101 01110100 01101001 01101110 01100111

b 01001001 01101110 01110000 01110101 01110100 00100000 01000100 01100101 01110110 01101001 01100011 01100101

c 01000001 01100100 01100001 00100000 01001100 01101111 01110110 01100101 01101100 01100001 01100011 01100101

2 Now create your own binary code and challenge a partner to process it and turn it into meaningful text.

Checking in

1 Name one input device that a receptionist might use.

2 Name one output device that a DJ might use.

3 Explain the peripherals that a teacher might use and what they would use them for.

➡ 4 Storage devices and media

A **storage device** is the hardware or computer peripheral that stores data or saves data to a storage medium. Magnetic hard drives, USB flash drive and Solid State Drives store data directly, while CD drives, DVD drives, Blu-ray Disc™ drives and tape drives save data to a storage medium.

A **storage medium** is the thing that stores the data for a storage device that cannot store it itself. Examples of storage media include CDs, DVDs and Blu-ray Discs. Note that the plural of 'medium' is 'media', so one CD is an example of a storage medium and five CDs are an example of storage media.

Capacity of storage devices and media

Different storage devices/storage media have different capacities; they can hold different amounts of data.

Capacity of storage devices and media

1 Copy and complete this table using spreadsheet software, such as Microsoft Excel or Google Sheets, and convert the storage capacity of each storage device/storage medium to megabytes. CD drive/CD has been done for you.

2 Create a chart to show the storage devices/ storage media and their storage capacity in megabytes.

Storage device/storage medium	Storage capacity	Storage capacity (MB)
CD drive/CD	0.7 GB	700
DVD drive/DVD	4.7 GB	
Blu-ray Disc drive/Blu-ray Disc	25 GB	
Magnetic hard drive	2 TB	
USB flash drive	32 GB	
Solid State Drive	256 GB	
Tape drive/data tape	1 TB	

Primary and secondary storage

Computers use two types of storage.

▶ **Primary storage** is accessed directly by the CPU and is normally the fastest memory in a computer. RAM is an example. Most of the time, primary storage will lose all the data it contains when the power is switched off.

▶ **Secondary storage** is not accessed constantly by the computer. It includes a computer's hard disc and external storage. Secondary storage will retain all the data it contains even when the device is switched off.

There are three types of secondary storage.

▶ **Optical storage** uses a laser to write data to and read data from a disc.

▶ **Magnetic storage** uses magnetic platters and a write/read head to write to and read from the disc.

▶ **Solid State storage** uses miniature electronic switches to store data. It has no moving parts and provides very fast access to data.

Cloud storage is where the data is stored online. It is a form of secondary external storage but, unlike the types of secondary storage you will be learning about, it is not physically attached to the computer.

Types of secondary storage device and medium

Categorise each of the following types of secondary storage device/medium as magnetic, optical or Solid State.

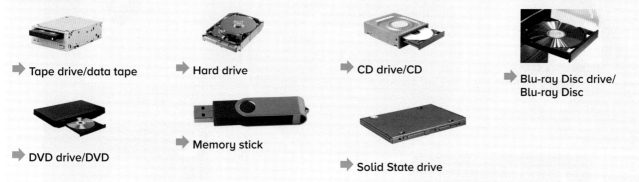

➡ Tape drive/data tape   ➡ Hard drive   ➡ CD drive/CD   ➡ Blu-ray Disc drive/Blu-ray Disc

➡ DVD drive/DVD   ➡ Memory stick   ➡ Solid State drive

Comparing secondary storage devices and media

Eight secondary storage devices/media have been ranked on a scale of 1 to 5 according to their capacity (how much data they can hold). Use the table below to rank each secondary storage device/medium on a scale of 1 to 5 according to its:

1 speed (how fast it can write and read data)

2 portability (how easily it can be moved around)

3 cost (how expensive it is).

1 = very good and 5 = very bad, and devices/media can share the same ranking.

You will need to use the Storage section in the 'Computing components catalogue 1.1' to find out about the secondary storage devices/media.

Storage device/medium	Capacity	Speed	Portability	Cost
CD drive/CD	5			
DVD drive/DVD	4			
Blu-ray Disc drive/Blu-ray Disc	3			
Tape drive/data tape	1			
Hard drive	1			
Memory stick	3			
Memory card	3			
Solid State Drive	2			

Checking in

❶ Name one type of primary storage.

❷ Name one type of secondary storage.

→ 5 The Internet of Things

An **Internet of Things (IoT)** device is a device that connects to the internet so that it can 'talk' to other devices. An IoT device collects data, analyses it and, if appropriate, automates a process by talking to another IoT device. IoT devices in the home are often referred to as 'smart' devices, but IoT devices are used in factories and other industries too.

Above is an example of how IoT devices work together to automate processes.

For or against?

IoT devices have benefits and drawbacks. Construct an argument FOR or AGAINST the use of IoT devices. Remember, regardless of whether you are arguing FOR or AGAINST IoT devices, you need to consider the benefits and drawbacks to create an effective argument.

The IoT decision-making process

There are three parts to the IoT decision-making process:

▶ Trigger(s): the data collected by input device.

▶ Condition(s): what the data has to be for the action to be performed.

▶ Action(s): what happens if the condition is met.

The data that enables IoT devices to make decisions and automate processes is collected by input devices.

▶ **Keyboards** collect data when text or numbers are input.

▶ **Microphones** collect data when speech or other sounds are detected.

▶ **Temperature sensors** collect data on how warm or cold an area is.

▶ **Light sensors** collect data on how much light there is in an area.

▶ **Motion sensors** collect data on movements in an area.

▶ **Pressure sensors** collect data on the force being applied to a device.

▶ **GPS** collects data on the location of a device.

Once data that has been collected, the IoT device uses it to make a decision.

You can compare the decision-making process of an IoT device with an IF statement in spreadsheets or computer programs: IF this data is captured, do this.

Automation

Think of three processes performed in the home that could be automated by IoT devices. For each automation, identify:

▶ the trigger(s) (the data collected by input device)

▶ the condition(s) (what the data has to be for the action to be performed)

▶ the action(s) (the output if the condition is met).

Here is an example:

Description of automation	The main light in a room is turned on when the TV is on and it is dark, to prevent eye strain while watching TV.
Device providing trigger(s)	TV Light sensor
Condition(s)	The TV is turned on. The light sensor detects low levels of light.
Action(s)	The main light in the room is turned on.

Automating a home

Imagine you have been asked to design a home automation system by a property developer.

Look at the floor plan of a home and:

▶ identify at least one automation for each different type of room

▶ identify the trigger(s), condition(s) and action(s) for each automation

▶ explain how each automation will help the people living in the home

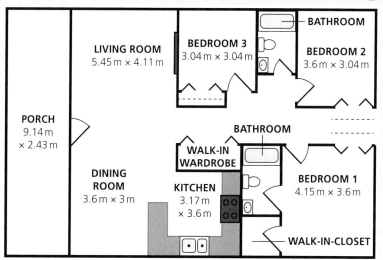

IoT devices and the environment

In pairs or small groups, discuss the following question: How could the automation you designed for your smart home help the environment?

Checking in

1 What is an IoT device?

2 What does an IoT device do?

3 What are the three parts to an IoT device's decision-making process?

➡ 6 What do you know?

What do you know?

1 What piece of computer hardware is this?

2 What piece of computer hardware is this?

3 What piece of computer hardware is this?

4 What is the role of the optical drive?

5 What is the role of the hard drive?

6 What is the role of the RAM?

7 Order the following units of storage capacity from largest to smallest.

bit   byte   gigabyte   kilobyte
megabyte   petabyte   terabyte

8 Which of the following CPU speeds is fastest?

A 400 MHz

B 9000 KHz

C 2.6 GHz

D 3300 MHz

9 Which of the following CPU speeds is slowest?

A 400 MHz

B 9000 KHz

C 2.6 GHz

D 3300 MHz

10 Sort the computer peripherals into input devices and output devices.
speakers   graphics tablet   projector
webcam   joystick   barcode scanner

11 I want to take a hand-drawn image and send it to someone over email. Which peripheral do I need to do this?

A Webcam

B Scanner

C Printer

D Microphone

12 I want to show pictures of a school trip to the whole school, on a big screen in the hall. Which peripheral do I need to do this?

A Monitor

B Printer

C Projector

D Speakers

13 What type of storage device is a DVD drive?

  A Magnetic

  B Optical

  C Solid State

14 What type of storage device is a hard drive?

  A Magnetic

  B Optical

  C Solid State

15 What type of storage device is a memory stick?

  A Magnetic

  B Optical

  C Solid State

16 True or false? The IoT is a device that connects to the internet and interacts with other devices.

17 True or false? IoT devices are often referred to as Smart Hubs.

18 Which of the following are benefits of IoT devices?

  A People living in the same house can personalise their routines.

  B Not all devices are compatible with each other.

  C They can save people time.

  D Private data can be exploited.

  E The devices can cost a lot of money.

  F They can help the environment.

19 Which of the following are drawbacks of IoT devices?

  A People living in the same house can personalise their routines.

  B Not all devices are compatible with each other.

  C They can save people time.

  D Private data can be exploited.

  E The devices can cost a lot of money.

  F They can help the environment.

20 When automating processes using IoT devices, what is a trigger?

  A The data collected by input device.

  B What the data has to be for the action to be performed.

  C What the output is if the condition is met.

21 When automating processes using IoT devices, what is a condition?

  A The data collected by input device.

  B What the data has to be for the action to be performed.

  C What the output is if the condition is met.

22 When automating processes using IoT devices, what is an action?

  A The data collected by input device.

  B What the data has to be for the action to be performed.

  C What the output is if the condition is met.

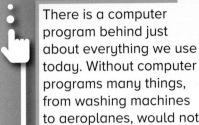

There is a computer program behind just about everything we use today. Without computer programs many things, from washing machines to aeroplanes, would not have the technological capabilities we have come to rely on.

Python is one of the most popular programming languages in the world and this chapter will teach you how to write basic programs in Python. All the activities require you to code in Python. The key programming construct underpinning all the work in this chapter is sequencing.

➡ 1 Computer programs

Computer programs are everywhere

We are surrounded by devices that require **computer programs** to work. We rely on computer programs to:

▶ bring us entertainment

▶ cook our food

▶ access our bank accounts online and shop online

▶ move from one place to another

Smart devices and programming

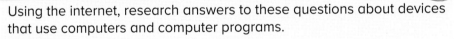

Using the internet, research answers to these questions about devices that use computers and computer programs.

1 How many computers are there in a car?
2 Which programming language is used for a car computer?
3 What does an internet-connected refrigerator do?
4 What features does a smart doorbell provide to a householder?
5 Which programming language is used to program a washing machine?
6 Which programming languages does the Amazon Echo™ (Alexa) use?

Programming languages

A computer program is a set of instructions that a computer follows precisely. This means that a computer program must accurately describe what the computer has to do if it is to work as we expect it to. The instructions must also be correctly sequenced because the computer will carry out each instruction in turn. There is often more than one way to write most computer programs; what is important is that the program is precise, accurate and correctly sequenced.

Programmers use many different programming languages to write computer programs, and each programming language was designed for a specific purpose, for example:

▶ **Java** is used to code video games, mobile apps, as well as Google Docs applications.

▶ **Ruby** is used to code web apps.

▶ **JavaScript** is used to add interactive elements to websites.

▶ **SQL** is used to access data in a database.

▶ **Low-level and assembly languages** are used to create programs that directly control hardware, such as printers and washing machines.

▶ **Python** is used to code web apps and in game development, artificial intelligence and a lot more.

With simple syntax and English-like commands, Python is easy to read and one of the easiest programming languages to learn. According to www.techrepublic.com, 'Python developer' was one of the top 10 in-demand tech jobs in 2019.

Printing things on screen

A computer must be able to communicate with its user if it is going to be useful, and a computer needs **data** to communicate. The simplest form of communication is for the computer to print messages.

Hello World

The following program will output the message **Hello World**. It is outputting the data **Hello World**.

```
1 print('Hello World')
```

1 Copy the program and run it. Make sure you copy the program accurately. If the program doesn't work, check you have included both the opening and closing brackets and the opening and closing quotation marks.

2 Now modify the program so that it prints:

Hello World

Pleased to meet you

Variables

It is not very useful having to include the data we want the computer to output in every print line. This is why we store data in variables and ask the computer to print the content of the variables. Variables are storage locations in the computer, similar to a set of small drawers used to keep objects in.

Names

The following program outputs **John**.

```
1 name = 'John'
2 print(name)
```

1 Copy the program and run it. If it doesn't work, check that you have included both the opening and closing brackets and the opening and closing quotation marks.

2 We have created a variable called **name** and assigned the value **John** to it, but we could assign a different value to the variable. Try modifying the program and changing the data assigned to **name** to something different. Your new program might look something like this:

```
1 name = 'elephant'
2 print(name)
```

3 Now modify the program so that it prints: **banana**

When naming a variable, it is important to choose a name that is instantly recognisable. The name:

▶ must start with a letter (it cannot start with a number)

▶ may contain letters, numbers and the underscore symbol (_)

▶ is case sensitive (**name**, **Name** and **NAME** are all different variables).

Checking in

❶ What is a variable?

❷ Explain why it is a bad idea to name a variable that will store the name of a car **xyz**.

❸ Explain why the variable name **2ndname** is not allowed in Python.

➡ 2 Getting data from the user

Computers function on the basic model of:

A program will be more useful if it can ask its user to input data. This data can then be stored in a variable and used when needed by the program. We use a **prompt** to tell the user what data to input.

Enter your first name

To prompt the user to enter their first name, we can use the following program:

```
1  name = input('Enter your first
   name: ')
2  print('Hello')
3  print(name)
4  print('Pleased to meet you.')
```

The program will output **Enter your name**. It will wait until a name is typed in and the return key is pressed and then it will print a greeting to the person whose first name has been entered.

Copy and run the program. If it does not work, check that you have included both the opening and closing brackets and that the opening and closing quotation marks are there and match.

We can ask for more than one input by using as many variables and input prompts as we need.

Say my name

Write a program that asks the user to input their first name and then their second name. You will need to have two variables, one for the first name and one for the second name.

If the user inputs **Lily** and **Jackson**, the program should output the following message:

```
Hello
Lily
Jackson
Nice to meet you
```

Concatenation

So far, we have used multiple inputs and multiple print lines when we want the program to use more than one piece of data. However, it is possible to combine multiple inputs in one print line using the '+' sign. This is called concatenation. Here is an example:

```
1  name = 'John'
2  print('Hello ' + name +
   ' pleased to meet you')
```

Notice the spaces included within the quotation marks, which will be included in the finished sentence to separate what's contained within the variable name from the other parts of the output.

Concatenate my name

Write a program that asks the user to input their first name and their second name, and then outputs the following greeting on one line:

Hello [first name] [second name] pleased to meet you.

If the inputs **John** and **Smith** are used, the program should output: **Hello John Smith pleased to meet you.**

Remember to include a space after **Hello**, between **John** and **Smith** and before **pleased**.

Escape characters

If we want to print the phrase, **It's his 'BIG' dog**, we will have a problem printing the quotation marks because both single and double quotation marks are used in Python code to identify the beginning and end of the text to be printed. This means we can't write the code **print ('It's his 'BIG' dog')** because the Python interpreter will get confused about where the quoted text ends. Does it end after **it**? Does it end after **his**? Does it end after **BIG**? Or does it end after **dog**?

To overcome this problem, Python has a set of **escape characters** that we can use to add punctuation and formatting to print lines. Some examples include:

Escape character	Output
\"	"
\'	'
\n	new line
\t	tab
\\	\

Look at this code:

```
1  name = 'John'
2  pet = 'Cat'
3  print(name+'\'s pet is a \t' +
   pet )
```

It outputs: **John's pet is a   Cat**

Picking up the tabs

Write a program to output the following information about people and their pets:

John	**Cat**
Liz	**Dog**
Mariya	**Hamster**

You should store the three names in three variables. The three pets will also need to be stored in three different variables, so you will need six variables in total. Your program should then print out the values of these variables using the correct escape characters to format them as shown above.

Favourite fruit

Write a program that asks the user for three first names and the favourite fruit of each named person and outputs the data entered by the user.

When your program runs, it should look like this. The circled words are entered by the user.

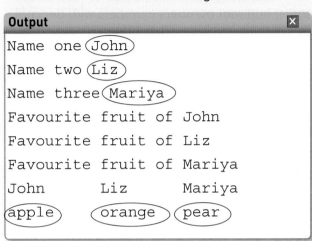

Checking in

❶ What is wrong with this line of Python code?

```
input('What is your name?')
```

❷ What will this code output? Why will it output what it does?

```
name = 'John'
print('name')
```

→ 3 Data types

Data types and variables

So far, we have used **strings** of characters as data, but computer programs need to be able to deal with different types of data, including numbers. On these pages, we will be working with two different types of numbers: **integers** (whole numbers, such as 2, 3 and 4) and **real numbers** (numbers with decimal points in them, such as 2.3, 5.44 and 10.9). Real numbers are also known as **floating point numbers**.

When we set up variables, Python chooses the most appropriate data type for the data:

▶ Entering **pi = 3.14** will set the variable **pi** to a floating point number.

▶ Entering **radius = 6** will set the variable **radius** to an integer.

▶ Entering **name = 'John'** will set the variable **name** to a string.

Data types and input prompts

We have been using input prompts to get data from the user, for example:

```
1 first_name = input('Enter first
  name ')
```

Python assumes data entered after an input prompt is a string unless we tell it otherwise. Telling the computer what type of data to expect is called typecasting or **casting**.

To tell the computer that an integer will be entered, we use **int**. The following command will create a location labelled **number** and the computer will expect the user to enter a whole number.

```
1 number = int(input('Enter a
  number '))
```

To tell the computer that the number that will be entered will be a floating point number, we use **float**. The following command will create a location labelled **decimal** and the computer will expect the user to enter a number with a decimal point.

```
1 decimal = float(input ('Enter a
  number '))
```

Adding integers

If you add two or more integers, the result will also be an integer. This means we can create a new integer variable by adding together two integer variables, for example:

```
1 first_number = 5
2 second_number = 7
3 sum=first_number+second_number
4 print(sum)
```

Asking the user to input the **first_number** and the **second_number** will create a calculator program that adds any two integers provided by the user. To do this, you will need to change the first and second lines of the program. The first line of the calculator program will look like this:

```
1 first_number = int(input
  ('Enter the first number '))
```

It is always a good idea to explain what the output is to the user. In this case, it is the sum of the two numbers inputted by the user, and so we need to use **+** to create a concatenated string output containing the words, **'The sum of the numbers is'**, followed by the value of the sum. To do this, we must cast the value of the sum as a string using **str**. The output line then becomes:

```
1 print('The sum of the numbers
  is ' + str(sum))
```

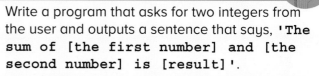

Adding and concatenating

Write a program that asks for two integers from the user and outputs a sentence that says, **'The sum of [the first number] and [the second number] is [result]'**.

In other words, if the user inputs 5 and 7, the output will be: **The sum of 5 and 7 is 12**.

Adding and concatenating floats

Write a program that asks for two floating point numbers from the user and outputs a sentence that says, **'The sum of [the first number] and [the second number] is [result]'**.

In other words, if the user inputs 3.3 and 5.4, the output will be: **The sum of 3.3 and 5.4 is 8.7**.

Constants

Sometimes we use the same value more than once in a program. We can avoid having to type the value each time by specifying it as a **constant**. This can be very beneficial if we want to change the constant once the program has been written; changing the value of a constant modifies the value throughout the program.

In Python, we simply state the value of the constant at the very beginning of the program and then call on it when it is needed. Here are some common constants and how they are set up:

▶ pi, which, to five decimal places, is 3.14159 is set up like this: **pi = 3.14159**.

▶ A discount, such as a 10% discount on the cost of a purchase, is set up like this: **discount = 0.9** (100% − 10% = 90%, expressed as a decimal value).

▶ VAT (Value Added Tax), which is a UK tax of 20% added to the cost of a purchase, would be set up like this: **vat = 1.2** (100% + 20% = 120%, expressed as a decimal value).

You can multiply a number by pi, or apply a discount or VAT to a number, by multiplying the number by the constant using *****.

Discounted prices

This is what a program to apply a 10% discount to the cost of a purchase looks like in a block programming language:

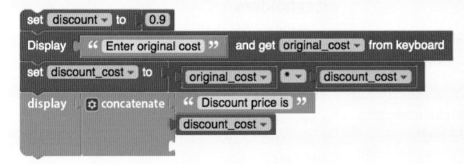

Write a program in Python that asks the user for the original cost of a purchase, applies a 10% discount and prints the discounted price.

When you have written the program, try running it with a cost of purchase of £20, remembering not to type in the '£' sign. The output should look like this: **Discount price is 18.0**.

Checking in

1. What data type is **'013314567'**?
2. What data type is **123456**?
3. What data type is **-3.15**?
4. How do we tell Python that the data is a string?
5. How do we tell Python to expect an integer?
6. How do we tell Python to expect a real number?

➡ 4 Placeholders and lists

Data and information

Here is the output from a program: **May, 23, 7, 24**. It shows that, by itself, data is often quite meaningless.

Data needs context to give it meaning: data + context = information. If the output from the program is formatted to give it context it has meaning: **The average weather for May in Birmingham is a temperature of 23 degrees, 7 hours of sunshine and 24 cm of rain.**

Formatting output using placeholders

In the previous section, we used **+** to concatenate more than one piece of data into a single print statement. The messages we are outputting are simply strings of characters and we have been using spaces before and after these strings to format the output properly, for example:

```
1 first_name = input('Enter first
  name ')
2 second_name = input('Enter
  second name ')
3 print('Hello ' + first_name + '
  ' + second_name + ' pleased to
  meet you')
```

However, there is also another option for formatting print statements: we can use **placeholders**.

Counting from '0', we can number the variables and use the numbers as placeholders for the variables in the print line. We put the placeholders inside curly brackets **{}** and then add the spaces as you would if you were typing the print line, for example:

```
1 first_name = input('Enter first
  name ')
2 second_name = input('Enter
  second name ')
3 print('Hello {0} {1} pleased to
  meet you' .format(first_name,
  second_name))
```

{0} refers to the first input listed in the brackets after **.format** and **{1}** refers to the second input listed in the brackets after **.format**.

Formatting output

Write a program that outputs the following conversation between the computer and its user (note that the circled words are entered by the user). Use the **format** command to output the final response.

```
Output                               ☒
Hello, what's your name? (Jane)
What's your second name? (Doe)
How are you today? (Fine)
That's good, Jane Doe, I'm glad
you are fine.
```

Formatting input prompts using placeholders

Placeholders can also be used with the input prompt, for example:

```
1 first_name = input('Enter first
  name ')
2 second_name = input('Enter
  second name {0} ' .format(first_
  name))
3 print('Hello {0} {1} pleased to
  meet you' .format(first_name,
  second_name))
```

Lists

As you know, variables are storage locations in the computer, similar to a set of small drawers used to keep objects in.

It is much easier to remember what is in each drawer if we label the drawers with meaningful names. Similarly, when we set up variables in our programs, we should always try to give each variable a name that indicates what is stored in that variable. So, for example, if we have a variable that contains the score of a match, we should call it **score** and not **number** or **s**.

Sometimes we need several variables that have the same basic description. For example, if we have three variables, all types of fruit, we might call them **fruit1**, **fruit2** and **fruit3**. However, there is a simpler way to organise variables of the same type. We can create a **list**.

▶ A list uses a single identifier such as **fruit** to create a container for a set of variables.

▶ Each variable refers to an **element** in the list. The list stores the elements one after another separated by a comma.

▶ A list can be modified by adding, deleting or changing elements.

▶ The elements in a list are identified by an **index value**. The first element in a list has the index value **0**.

For example, a list called **names** can be created by the following command:

```
names = ['John' , 'Jayne' , 'Ali',
'Li', 'Anwar']
```

This list, called **names**, contains five elements, which a program can use by calling them by their index value. **John** has the index value **[0]** (because the first element in a list is always numbered **0**) and is, therefore, called with **names[0]**. **Anwar** has the index value **[4]** and is, therefore, called with **names[4]**. Notice the square brackets used around the index value.

This means that a program to print **John** and **Anwar** from the list would look like this:

```
1 names = ['John', 'Jayne', 'Ali',
  'Li', 'Anwar']
2 print(names[0])
3 print(names[4])
```

Changing the values stored in the elements of a list

We can change an element stored in a list by assigning a different value to it. For example, the following program will set the element in the list

with the index value **[3]** to 'Sally'. Also notice how we can print the whole list by asking the program to **print(names)**.

```
1 names = ['John', 'Jayne', 'Ali',
  'Li','Anwar']
2 names[3] = 'Sally'
3 print(names)
```

Changing list elements

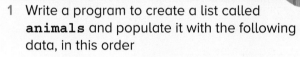

1 Write a program to create a list called **animals** and populate it with the following data, in this order

Monkey	Chicken	Dog
Cat	Cow	Horse

2 Once the list has been created, print out the third and fifth elements from the list.

3 Next, change **Chicken** to **Rabbit**.

4 Finally, print the whole list.

Adding elements to lists

If we want to add another element to a list, we can add it at the end of the list using **.append()**. For example, **animals. append('Hamster')** adds **Hamster** to the end of the list and the output is: **['Monkey', 'Chicken', 'Dog', 'Cat', 'Cow', 'Horse', 'Hamster']**

```
1 animals = ['Monkey','Chicken',
  'Dog', 'Cat', 'Cow', 'Horse']
2 animals.append('Hamster')
3 print(animals)
```

Checking in

Look at this list: **veg = ['carrot', 'onion', 'cabbage', 'potato', 'leek', 'parsnip', 'kale']**

❶ Which vegetable would be retrieved with **veg[1]**?

❷ How would you retrieve the element from the list that contains the word **kale**?

➡ 5 Working with lists

User input to select an item

We can ask the user to input a value and tell the computer to output the element stored at the location corresponding to that value using the **input()** command:

```
1  names = ['Harry','Jane',
   'Ahmed', 'Syed', 'Anne', 'Mary']
2  index = int(input('Which
   element from the list would
   you like to see?'))
3  print(names[index])
```

The value input by the user is stored as an integer in the variable called **index** and the print statement tells the computer to output the element stored at the position identified by the variable **index**.

Printing a whole list

We can print the whole list by referring to the list identifier in the print statement, for example:

```
1  names = ['Harry', 'Jane',
   'Ahmed', 'Syed', 'Anne', 'Mary']
2  print(names)
```

Printing the number of elements in a list

We can instruct the computer to print the number of elements in the list using the **len()** function, for example:

```
1  names = ['Harry', 'Jane',
   'Ahmed', 'Syed', 'Anne', 'Mary']
2  print(len(names))
```

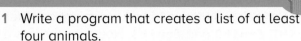

Wild animals

1 Write a program that creates a list of at least four animals.

2 Once the list has been created, print out the complete list.

3 Next, ask the user to select an item from the list by its index value and print that value.

4 Finally, print the number of elements in the list.

Adding an element to the end of a list

The **.append()** command is used to add a new element to the end of a list:

```
1  fruits = ['apple', 'pear',
   'banana', 'orange']
2  fruits.append('raspberry')
```

We can ask the user to input data to be added to the list, appending the data contained within the variable to the list instead of adding a string of characters to the list:

```
1  fruits = ['apple', 'pear',
   'banana', 'orange']
2  new_fruit = input('Enter a new
   fruit to add to the list: ')
3  fruits.append(new_fruit)
```

In the kitchen

1 Write a program that creates a list of four objects you may find in a kitchen: kettle, oven, sink and fridge.

2 Once the list has been created, print the length of the list and the list.

3 Next, ask the user to input a new object and add to the list.

4 Finally, print the length of the list and the list again.

Adding an element to a specified location in a list

We may want to add a new element at a specific point in the list rather than at the end, and we can use the `.insert()` command to do this. For example, the following program inserts 'pineapple' into the list at the location with index value **2**.

```
1 fruits.insert(2, 'pineapple')
```

Wilder animals

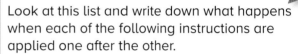

This table represents a list in Python called **animals** created with the following code:
`animals = ['monkey', 'lion', 'tiger', 'zebra', 'deer', rabbit'].`

0	1	2	3	4	5
monkey	lion	tiger	zebra	deer	rabbit

Use the table to answer these questions.

1 How many elements are there in the list?

2 The command **animals.append('duck')** will create a new element. Is the new element correctly referred to as **animals[5]** or **animals[6]**?

3 The command **animals.insert(3, 'elephant')** will create a new element. How should the new element be correctly referred to?

4 After the commands **animals. append('duck')** and **animals.insert(3, 'elephant')** have added two new elements to the list, which of the following animals will be referred to as **animals[4]**: tiger, zebra or deer?

In the bathroom

Write a program to create a list of bathroom items: bath, toilet, shower, basin.

1 Print the full list.

2 Print the length of the list.

3 Add 'towel' to the end of the list.

4 Insert 'shampoo' at the location with index value **2**.

5 Insert 'soap' at the location with index value **5**.

6 Print the new list and the length of the new list.

Checking in

Look at this list and write down what happens when each of the following instructions are applied one after the other.

`clothing = ['hat', 'coat', 'shoes', 'gloves']`

❶ `print(clothing[1])`

❷ `clothing.append('socks')`

❸ `clothing.insert(2, 'scarf')`

❹ `print(len(clothing))`

❺ `newvalue = input('Enter a new value: ')`

`clothing.insert(3, newvalue)`

And the user enters **tie**.

➡ 6 Working with strings

As you know, a string is a sequence of characters that can include any combination of letters, numbers, spaces and punctuation. For example, the string **'Hello World!'** includes uppercase letters, lowercase letters, spaces and punctuation. A string must be inside quotation marks, otherwise Python thinks it is a variable.

It is possible to manipulate strings in various ways, including adding and taking away characters, and viewing or changing individual characters.

Indexing strings

You already know that each item, or 'element', in a list can be referred to using its index value. Each individual character in a string can be indexed in the same way. The first character has the index value **0**.

The following example uses the string **'Great work'**, which has been stored in the variable **myString**.

```
1  myString = 'Great work'
```

The table below shows how each character is mapped to its index value:

Character	G	r	e	a	t		w	o	r	k
Index value	0	1	2	3	4	5	6	7	8	9

We can access a single character from a string using its index value in square brackets. So, for example, **myString[0]** would return **G** and **myString[2]** would return **e**.

Indexing strings

1 What will be printed to the screen when the following program is run?

```
1  myString = 'Hello World!'
2  print(myString[6])
```

2 What line of code do you need to add to this program to output **u** from the string?

```
1  colour = 'purple'
```

Characters

Write a program that stores the word **computer** in a variable and then prints out the fourth character.

Slicing strings

It is possible to return a **substring** from a longer string using 'slicing'. A substring is a string contained within a string. For example, the words **cat** and **log** are substrings of **catalogue**.

To slice a string, we need to specify the starting index value and the ending index value, separated by a colon. The starting index value represents the first character of the substring and the ending index value represents the character after the last character in the substring. Look at these tables to help you visualise this:

myString = 'catalogue'

0	1	2	3	4	5	6	7	8
c	a	t	a	l	o	g	u	e

myString[0:3]

0	1	2	3	4	5	6	7	8
c	a	t	a	l	o	g	u	e

Slicing up the catalogue

1 Which code will isolate the substring **log** from **myString = 'catalogue'**?

2 What will be printed to the screen when the following program is run?

```
1  myString = 'String slicing'
2  print(myString[3:9])
```

Upper-case string

Write a program that:

1 asks the user to enter a sentence of their choice.

2 converts the sentence entered to upper case.

3 prints a five-character substring that starts with the third character in the sentence.

Joining together characters from a string

It is possible to join together, or concatenate, characters from a string to produce a single output. To do this we use **+**.

In the example below, four characters from the original string are concatenated when they are output to form a new word. What will be printed?

```
1  myString = 'Hello World!'
2  print(myString[0] + myString[1]
   + myString[8] + myString[4])
```

It is important to note that using a comma (**,**) rather than a plus sign (**+**) will add spaces between the characters in the output. Sometimes it might be desirable to include spaces in your print statement, but here we want the characters to appear next to each other to form a word, and so **+** must be used.

Upper and lower case

Python includes a number of built-in functions that we can use with strings. For example, it is possible to convert a string to upper-case letters using **.upper()** and to lower-case letters using **.lower()**.

Look at this program:

```
1  myString = 'I am good at
   Computing'
2  print('Here is the original
   string: ', myString)
3  print('Here it is in upper case:
   ', myString.upper())
4  print('And here it is in lower
   case: ', myString.lower())
```

Notice that the original string has not been changed; the program has simply returned new versions of the string. However, if we did want to save the changed string, we could assign it to a new variable, for example:

```
1  lowercaseString = myString.
   lower()
```

Name change

Create a program that asks the user to input their first name and then their last name. The program should then print out the second and third letters of their first name in upper case followed by the first and second letters of their last name in lower case. To do this you will need to change the case of each name and assign the changed names to new variables. Then you will need to print out the correct letters from the strings contained in the new variables.

You can use string slicing to complete this challenge, but we would like you to use concatenation.

Checking in

Look at this program:

```
1  text = 'Phone app'
```

❶ What would be output if **print(len(text))** was added to the program and the program was run?

❷ What would be output if **print(text. upper())** was added to the program and the program was run?

❷ What would be output if **print(text[7] + text[4] + text[3])** was added to the program and the program was run?

❹ What would be output if **print(text[1:4])** was added to the program and the program was run?

As you know, spreadsheets are incredibly useful and powerful tools. They are used every day by people in all sorts of ways, from storing information about products and stock levels to managing multi-million-pound budgets.

Following on from *Introducing spreadsheets*, this chapter focuses on more advanced features of spreadsheets, including new functions, form controls and macros to develop more bespoke and user-friendly spreadsheets.

➡ 1 Drop-down lists, VLOOKUP and sorting data

Drop-down lists

A **drop-down list** is a type of **validation**. It limits the values that can be entered into a cell to help keep the data in the spreadsheet consistent and accurate, reducing errors and making the spreadsheet more useful.

To create a drop-down list, you type the words you want to use in your drop-down list into a column in an area of the spreadsheet that will not normally be seen, but which can still be accessed easily. It is best practice to type them alphabetically. Then you click on the cell in which you want the drop-down list to appear, select 'Data' and 'Data Validation', choose 'Allow List' and select the cells containing the data you want to appear in the drop-down list.

The VLOOKUP function

The **VLOOKUP** function takes the value in a cell, searches for it in a table of data elsewhere on the spreadsheet and returns the value in an adjacent cell.

In this example, the **VLOOKUP** function is comparing Ali's mark in cell B2 to the scores in column F to find out his grade. A score of 68 is a grade C and so **C** is returned to cell C2.

C2   *fx* =VLOOKUP(B2,F2:G6,2)

	A	B	C	D	E	F	G
1	**Student**	**Mark**	**Grade**	**Pass/Fail**		**Score**	**Grade**
2	Ali	68	C			0	U
3	Bob	52				50	D
4	Carol	49				60	C
5	Devanshi	92				75	B
6	Eesa	75				85	A

The **VLOOKUP** function has the following structure:

```
=VLOOKUP( lookup value, range, column number )
```

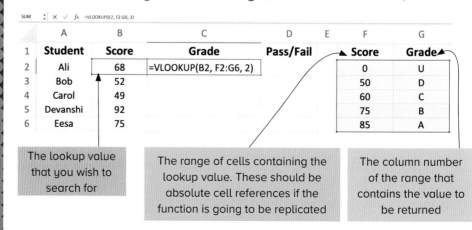

SUM   × ✓ *fx* =VLOOKUP(B2, F2:G6, 2)

	A	B	C	D	E	F	G
1	**Student**	**Score**	**Grade**	**Pass/Fail**		**Score**	**Grade**
2	Ali	68	=VLOOKUP(B2, F2:G6, 2)			0	U
3	Bob	52				50	D
4	Carol	49				60	C
5	Devanshi	92				75	B
6	Eesa	75				85	A

The lookup value that you wish to search for

The range of cells containing the lookup value. These should be absolute cell references if the function is going to be replicated

The column number of the range that contains the value to be returned

Sorting data

Data in the first column of the table used in a **VLOOKUP** needs to be in alphabetical (A–Z) or numerical (0–100) order. It is easy to **sort** the data into order using the sort facility, and you can sort the whole spreadsheet or just a selected range of cells.

Select the range of cells that you need to sort, then choose 'Sort' from the 'Data' tab. You can then specify which columns to sort the data by and whether you want it in ascending (A–Z, smallest to largest) or descending (Z–A, largest to smallest) order.

Stationery shop

Look at the following spreadsheet. It shows a pricing system for a stationery shop.

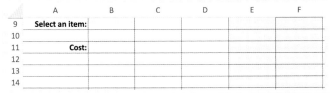

	A	B	C	D	E	F
9	Select an item:					
10						
11	Cost:					
12						
13						
14						

1 Type a list of stationery items into cells E9 to E14 of a spreadsheet.

2 Sort the list into alphabetical order.

3 Create a drop-down list in cell B9 so that the user can select an item of stationery.

4 Type a price for each item in your list into cells F9 to F14 and format the cells as currency.

5 Write a **VLOOKUP** function in cell B11 to display the correct price for whichever item of stationery is selected in cell B9.

Cars

Open 'Advanced spreadsheets Microsoft Excel workbook 1.4'. The main table shows the basic list price for a range of cars. The actual purchase price includes a fuel tax, which is derived from the purchase price and the car's economy rating.

1 Format cells B16 to B24 and F16 to G24 as currency.

2 Write a function in column D to look up the fuel economy for each car based on the code in column C.

3 Write a function in column E to look up the fuel economy tax rate for each car based on the fuel economy shown in column D.

4 Write a formula in column F to work out the fuel tax for each car by multiplying the list price by the fuel economy tax rate.

5 Write a formula in column G to calculate the purchase price, by adding together the list price and the cost of the fuel tax.

Checking in

1 How can we limit the values that a user can enter in a cell on a spreadsheet?

2 Why do we use validation in programs and on spreadsheets?

3 What does the **VLOOKUP** function enable you to do?

➡ 2 Check boxes

Drop-down lists enable the user to select one item from a list. **Check boxes** (or **tick boxes**) allow the user to select one or more items from a range of options. They can, for example, allow the user to select the countries they have visited from a range of countries.

Check boxes are a type of **form control**. Form controls are objects that can be placed onto a spreadsheet to help the user interact with the data and select items from lists.

Check boxes in Microsoft Excel

To add check boxes in Microsoft Excel, the 'Developer' tab must be visible. You can then click on 'Insert', click on the check box icon and drag the check box to where you want it on your spreadsheet. Once you have added a check box to your spreadsheet, you can link it to a cell where you would like its current state to be stored by right clicking on it and selecting 'Format Control'.

When a check box is ticked, the **linked cell** returns **TRUE** and when it is not selected, it returns **FALSE**. **TRUE** and **FALSE** are Boolean values.

It is possible to refer to the Boolean value in the linked cell in functions in Microsoft Excel. For example, the spreadsheet below contains the options **France** and **Spain**, which are linked to cells D1 and D2 respectively.

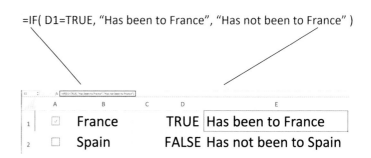

An **IF** function in cell E1 is linked to the value in D1: `=IF( D1=TRUE, "Has been to France", "Has not been to France" )`. It says **Has been to France** if the value in D1 is TRUE and **Has not been to France** if the value in D1 is FALSE.

Pizza orders

You are going to create a system to help customers select and calculate the cost of a pizza order. Your system will include:

▶ a range of toppings to choose from

▶ a range of pizza sizes to choose from

▶ the option to choose between collection or delivery

▶ formulae and functions to calculate the total cost for the chosen options.

There is an example of what your pizza ordering system could look like on the next page.

Part one

1 Type a list of at least five pizza toppings into cells in column C. Leave an empty row between each topping.

2 Insert a check box in column B alongside each topping.

3 Link each check box to a cell in the same row in column M.

Part two

4 Copy the list of toppings to column I and enter the cost of each topping in column J. Make sure that the cells in column J are formatted as currency.

5 In column E, write an **IF** function for each topping that displays the price if the topping has been selected. For example, if M9 is **TRUE** then the value in J9 should be shown in E9.

6 Use a **SUM** function to add together the cost of all the toppings that have been selected. Change the colour of the answer and format it as bold so that it stands out.

7 In column I, enter a range of pizza sizes, such as small, medium and large, and add the cost of each size in the adjacent cell in column J.

8 Make sure that the pizza sizes are in alphabetical order and then create a drop-down list to enable the user to select the pizza size they want.

9 Write a **VLOOKUP** function to display the correct price for the pizza size that has been chosen. Change the colour of the answer and format it as bold so that it stands out.

10 In column I, enter the options 'Collect' and 'Deliver'.

11 Create a drop-down list to enable the user to choose 'Collect' or 'Deliver'.

12 Write a function to show the price for delivery if 'Deliver' has been selected. Change the colour of the answer and format it as bold so that it stands out.

13 Write a formula to calculate the total cost of the pizza. This should include the cost of the toppings, the cost of the size of pizza chosen and any cost for delivery.

14 Save your spreadsheet. You'll be adding to it later.

	A	B	C	D	E	F	G	H	I	J	K	L	M
9	Toppings	✓	Cheese		£0.50				Cheese	£0.50			TRUE
10													
11		☐	Pineapple						Pineapple	£0.85			FALSE
12													
13		☐	Ham						Ham	£0.75			FALSE
14													
15		✓	Tomato		£0.40				Tomato	£0.40			TRUE
16													
17		☐	Pepper						Pepper	£0.60			FALSE
18													
19			Cost of toppings		£0.90								
20													
21													
22	Pizza size	Large	Cost of pizza base		£10.95				Large	£10.95			
23									Medium	£8.25			
24									Small	£6.00			
25													
26	Collect/Deliver	Deliver	Delivery charge		£2.00				Collect				
27									Deliver	£2.00			
28			Total cost		£13.85								

Checking in

1 How many values can be selected from a drop-down list?

2 What form control do we use if we want the user to be able to select one or more options?

3 What value does a check box return if it has been selected?

4 Where is this value stored?

→ 3 Macros

Macros are small programs that record your mouse clicks and key strokes as you complete a task. They automate routine tasks, just like a robot. They speed tasks up, make sure they are completed accurately, and relieve a human from the boredom of doing the same thing over and over again.

Macros in Microsoft Excel

In Excel, the actions are saved as **Visual Basic** code that can be viewed and edited if necessary.

Recording a macro

Before recording a macro, resave your spreadsheet as a macro-enabled spreadsheet. Then select 'Record Macro' on the 'Developer' tab and give your macro a name.
As soon as you click 'OK' the macro will begin recording every key press and mouse click you make until you press on the 'Stop Recording' button in the ribbon. When you have finished recording your macro, it will automatically save to the spreadsheet.

```
Sub ClearSheet()
' ClearSheet Macro
    Range("M8").Select
    Selection.ClearContents
    Range("M10").Select
    Selection.ClearContents
    Range("M12").Select
    Selection.ClearContents
    Range("M14").Select
    Selection.ClearContents
    Range("M16").Select
    Selection.ClearContents
    Range("B21").Select
    Selection.ClearContents
    Range("B25").Select
    Selection.ClearContents
End Sub
```

Once a macro has been recorded it can be assigned to a **button**. A button is inserted from the 'Form Control' menu, in the same way you insert a check box. The macro is assigned by right-clicking on the button and selecting the macro required.

When the macro is run it will repeat the mouse clicks and key strokes you recorded.

7	**Toppings**	✓ Cheese	£0.50
8			
9		☐ Pineapple	
10			
11		✓ Ham	£0.75
12			
13		✓ Tomato	£0.40
14			
15		☐ Pepper	
16			
17		Cost of toppings	£1.65
18			
19			
20	**Pizza size**	Small Cost of pizza base	£6.00
21			
22			
23			
24	**Collect/Deliver**	Deliver Delivery charge	£2.00
25			
26		Total cost	£9.65
27			
28			
29		Reset	

Pizza orders

You have created a spreadsheet to calculate the cost of a pizza order, but the values entered need to be cleared before the next order can be input. It is possible to automate this process using a macro.

Part 3:

1 Record a macro to reset the spreadsheet ready for the next order. You will need to clear the contents of the cells in column M linked to the check boxes, and also clear the contents of the two cells in column B containing values selected from drop-down lists. To clear these values, you simply need to right click on each relevant cell and select 'Clear contents'.

2 Insert a button and give it a suitable name.

3 Assign your macro to the button and test it to check that it resets the spreadsheet correctly.

Editing a macro

Once a macro has been recorded in Microsoft Excel, you can edit the Visual Basic code to correct errors or to add extra functionality. Click on 'View Macros' and select 'Edit' to see the code. The code can be edited by typing directly into the code window.

Here are some examples of VB formatting commands:

▸ `Range("A1").Font.Color = vbGreen` changes the text colour of cell A1 to green.

▸ `Range("A1").Interior.Color = vbYellow` sets the cell background colour to yellow.

▸ `Range("A1").Border.Color = vbBlue` sets the cell borders colour to blue.

▸ `Range("A1").Font.Name = "Courier"` changes the font to Courier.

▸ `Range("A1").Font.Size = 16` changes the font size to 16 point.

▸ `Range("A1").Font.Bold = True` sets the font to bold using a Boolean value of True.

Here are the colours available:

vb Color Name	Colour
vbBlack	
vbWhite	
vbMagenta	
vbRed	
vbYellow	
vbGreen	
vbBlue	
vbCyan	

Editing macros

1 Type five sentences, similar to those below, into a spreadsheet.

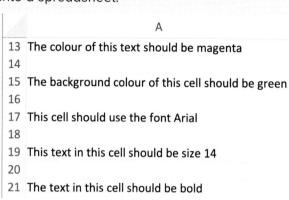

	A
13	The colour of this text should be magenta
14	
15	The background colour of this cell should be green
16	
17	This cell should use the font Arial
18	
19	This text in this cell should be size 14
20	
21	The text in this cell should be bold

2 Record a macro called 'Format' that selects cell A13.

3 Edit the macro to change the text colour of cell A13 to magenta.

4 Edit the macro to add a line of code to change the background colour of cell A15 to green.

5 Edit the macro to add a line of code to change the font of cell A17 to Arial.

6 Edit the macro to add a line of code to change the font size of cell A19 to 14 pt.

7 Edit the macro to add a line of code to change the text in cell A21 to bold.

8 Assign your finished macro to a button labelled 'Format'.

9 Record a macro called 'Unformat', which removes all the formatting set by the 'Format' macro. Start by recording a new macro that selects cell A13 and then edit the code to make the necessary changes.

10 Assign your finished macro to a button labelled 'Reset Formatting'.

Checking in

❶ Why would you use a macro in a spreadsheet?

❷ What programming language does an Microsoft Excel spreadsheet use to record and save macros?

❸ How do you run a macro?

4 Logical operators and the `REPT` function

Using `AND` in an `IF` function

So far, we have used `IF` functions to check if a single condition has been met, for example:
`=IF( B2>60, "Pass", "Fail" )`.

	A	B	C
			fx =IF(B2>=60, "Pass", "Fail")
1	Student	Mark	Pass/Fail
2	Alison	68	Pass
3	Bob	52	
4	Charlie	49	
5	Deepak	92	
6	Eesa	75	

We can include the logical operator **AND** in an `IF` function to check that more than one condition is True, for example: `=IF( AND( B2>60, C2>60 ), "Pass", "Fail" )`.

	A	B	C	D
			fx =IF(AND(B2>60, C2>60), "Pass", "Fail")	
1	Student	Score1	Score2	Pass/Fail
2	Andy	68	70	Pass
3	Bob	52	56	
4	Chris	49	61	
5	Dhriv	92	87	
6	Eesa	75	62	

This `IF` function requires both the value in cell B2 *and* the value in cell C2 to be greater than 60 for the student to achieve a pass.

Competition 1

Look at this spreadsheet. Students have taken part in the first two rounds of a competition. To qualify for the final, they need to have scored more than 75 in both of the first two rounds.

Write functions for column D to work out if each student has qualified for the final. It should say "Yes" if they have qualified and "No" if they have not qualified.

	A	B	C	D
8	Name	Round 1	Round 2	Qualified?
9	Adam	71	74	
10	Bhuvan	63	76	
11	Chloe	73	75	
12	Devanshi	82	77	
13	Eashan	78	81	

Using `OR` in an `IF` function

If we want one or more conditions to be met, we can use the **OR** operator in an `IF` function, for example:
`=IF( OR( B2>60, C2>60 ), "Pass", "Fail" )`.

	A	B	C	D
				fx =IF(OR(B2>60, C2>60), "Pass", "Fail")
1	Student	Score1	Score2	Pass/Fail
2	Andy	68	70	Pass
3	Bob	52	56	
4	Chris	49	61	
5	Dhriv	92	87	
6	Eesa	75	62	

This `IF` function requires the value in cell B2 *or* the value in cell C2 to be greater than 60 for the student to achieve a pass.

Competition 2

Look at the following spreadsheet. The rules of the competition have changed. Students now qualify for the final if they have scored more than 75 in at least one of the rounds.

Write functions for column D to work out if each student has qualified for the final. It should say "Yes" if they have qualified and "No" if they have not qualified.

	A	B	C	D
8	Name	Round 1	Round 2	Qualified?
9	Adam	71	74	
10	Bhuvan	63	76	
11	Chloe	73	75	
12	Devanshi	82	77	
13	Eashan	78	81	

The REPT function

The **REPT** function is used to repeat a string of characters a given number of times:
=REPT(text, number of times).

In this example, the text in cell A2 is repeated the number of times specified in cell B2:

C9		fx	=REPT(A9, B9)
	A	B	C
8	**String**	**Number**	
9	:-)	5	:-):-):-):-):-)

You can also use the **REPT** function without cell references:

A1	fx	=REPT(":-)", 3)
	A	
1	:-):-):-)	

Homework

Look at this spreadsheet. It shows whether students handed their homework in on time. 'G' means that it was on time and 'L' means that it was late.

	A	B	C	D	E	F	G	H	I	J
9	**Name**	**Computing**	**English**	**French**	**Maths**	**Geography**	**Science**	**Number handed in late**	**X**	**Detention**
10	Adam	L	L	G	L	G	L			
11	Bhuvan	G	G	G	G	G	L			
12	Chloe	L	L	G	G	L	G			
13	Devanshi	G	G	G	G	G	G			
14	Eashan	G	L	G	L	G	L			

1 Write functions for column H to count how many pieces of homework each student handed in late.

2 Write functions for column I so that each piece of homework each student handed in late is represented by an 'X'.

3 If students have handed in their Maths, English and Science homework late they are given a detention. Write functions for column J to show 'Yes' if each student has a detention.

Checking in

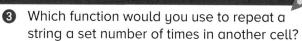

❶ Which logical operator would you use to check that at least one condition is true in an **IF** function?

❷ Which logical operator would you use to check that several conditions are all true?

❸ Which function would you use to repeat a string a set number of times in another cell?

→ 5 and 6 Quiz

Quiz questions

You are going to use your knowledge of spreadsheets to create a five-question self-marking quiz. Your quiz should include four questions that use drop-down lists to allow the user to select their answer and one question that uses check boxes. You will need to record a macro to calculate the score and give bespoke feedback for each answer selected. Finally, you will need to record a macro to reset the spreadsheet ready for the next user.

1 Write the four questions that will use drop-down lists. Each question must have three answers to choose from. Each answer must have bespoke feedback. Here is an example of what the four questions could look like:

Question number	Question	Answers	Feedback
1	In which year was the Battle of Hastings?	1065	That's a bit too early.
		1066	Spot on!
		1067	It was over by then.
2	What is the capital city of Lithuania?	Riga	That's the capital city of Latvia.
		Tallinn	That's the capital of Estonia.
		Vilnius	Excellent!
3	Who wrote The BFG?	Charles Dickens	I don't have great expecatations for your score.
		J.K. Rowling	Expelliarmus!
		Roald Dahl	Of course!
4	What is the square root of 64?	8	Well done!
		16	That's a quarter of 64.
		32	That's half of 64.

2 The fifth and final question needs to allow the user to select their answer using check boxes. The question needs to have five answers to choose from. To be correct the question should require three, and only three, of the boxes to be ticked. You will need to indicate which of the three answers needs to be ticked. Here is an example of what the question could look like:

Question number	Question	Answers	Must be selected?
5	Which of these are types of cheese?	Brie	YES
		Manchego	YES
		Monterey Jill	
		Provolone	YES
		Salami	

Quiz

You are now going to develop your quiz spreadsheet. Look at the example of what the final spreadsheet could look like on the next page.

Part one

1 Type the first four questions into the spreadsheet.

2 Create **look-up tables**, on the right-hand side of the spreadsheet, for questions 1–4, listing the answers in alphabetical/numerical order and the feedback for each answer in an adjacent cell.

3 Use the look-up tables to create drop-down lists to select the answers.

4 Add **VLOOKUP** functions to give the appropriate feedback when each answer is selected.

Part two

5 Type the fifth question and the five possible answers into the spreadsheet. Leave an empty row between each answer.

6 Create check boxes alongside each answer and link them to cells on the right-hand side of the spreadsheet.

7 Write an **IF** function to show "Correct!" if the correct three cells have been selected or "No. That's not correct." if the selection is incorrect in any way. You will need to use **AND** to check the status of the cell linked to every check box to ensure that only the correct three boxes have been selected.

Part three

8 For questions 1–4, write **IF** functions to check whether the selected answer is correct and award 1 mark if it is and no marks if it is not.

9 For question 5, write an **IF** function to see if the feedback says "Correct!" and award 1 mark if it does and no marks if it does not.

10 Write a function to add up the marks for each question to get the total score.

11 Write a function to display the final score as *s, one * per mark.

Part four

12 Resave your spreadsheet as a macro-enabled spreadsheet and record a macro to reset your spreadsheet for the next user. The macro should clear the contents of the cells containing the drop-down lists and the **TRUE/FALSE** values linked to the check boxes.

13 Edit your macro to include code to change the colour of the text in the cells showing the feedback and score to white.

14 Insert a button and assign your macro to it. Edit the button's label to 'Reset'.

Part five

15 Write a macro to show the score and feedback by changing the colour of the text in the cells showing the feedback to blue and the cell showing the score to green.

16 Insert another button and assign your macro to it. Edit the button's label to 'Mark quiz'.

Checking in

❶ On which tab do you find the data validation tools?

❷ Which tools do you use to create a drop-down list?

❸ Which function should you be using to look up the bespoke feedback for whichever answer has been selected?

Informally, the term 'algorithm' has come to refer to any set of rules that precisely define a sequence of operations, such as making a cup of tea or cleaning your teeth. In the world of computing, an algorithm is a set of instructions that can be implemented as code to program a computer.

Computational thinking is a logical, strategic approach to problem-solving involving four cornerstones: decomposition, abstraction, pattern recognition and algorithm design to formulate an efficient and effective algorithm.

→ 1 Using computational thinking to solve problems

Imagine your cousin visits your house and sees a model helicopter you have built with a construction toy. She asks you to send her some instructions to follow so that she can build the same model for herself, using the same construction toy. What are you going to do?

A computer scientist would tackle the problem in a logical way, by applying an approach known as **computational thinking**. Computational thinking allows us to take a complex problem, understand what the problem is and develop possible solutions.

There are a number of distinct stages to computational thinking. The first is called **decomposition**.

Decomposition

To gain a really good understanding of a complex problem, it helps to break it down or decompose it into a number of smaller problems. These problems might, in turn, need to be decomposed further until the true nature of the problem is fully understood.

 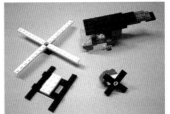 

By decomposing a problem, you gain a much deeper understanding of it.

Each one of the smaller problems is easier to solve than the big problem you started with. And when you have solved the smaller problems, you have also solved the big problem.

Decomposition can be applied to any problem, even a simple daily routine such as brushing your teeth.

Here is a student's first attempt at decomposing the problem of how to brush your teeth.

▶ Place your mobile phone beside you.

▶ Locate a toothbrush.

▶ Choose a blue toothbrush.

▶ Locate the toothpaste.

▶ Locate the sink.

▶ Start brushing your teeth.

▶ Put on some loud music.

▶ Finish brushing your teeth.

It is illogical and unhelpful to include tasks that do not help you solve the problem. The second cornerstone of computational thinking is, therefore, to remove unnecessary and unhelpful detail. This process is known as **abstraction**.

Abstraction

If we carry out abstraction on the student's first attempt at decomposing the problem of how to brush your teeth, we can cross out the things that do not help teeth get clean:

▶ ~~Place your mobile phone beside you.~~

▶ Locate a toothbrush.

▶ ~~Choose a blue toothbrush.~~

▶ Locate the toothpaste.

▶ Locate the sink.

▶ Start brushing your teeth.

▶ ~~Put on some loud music.~~

▶ Finish brushing your teeth.

Lots of steps in the process of brushing your teeth have been left out though, including squeezing toothpaste onto the brush and rubbing the brush backwards and forwards against your teeth. The student has decomposed the teeth brushing problem and we have abstracted it, but the list is not detailed enough. Further decomposition is needed.

Further decomposition

If we further decompose the first item in the list, 'Locate a toothbrush', we might come up with something like this:

▶ What sort of brush do you need?

▶ Is the brush clean?

▶ You need a toothbrush but should it be a manual or an electric toothbrush?

▶ If it is an electric toothbrush, is it charged?

▶ If it needs charging, is there a charging point nearby?

▶ Do you have a brush head that fits an electric toothbrush?

Decomposing a daily routine

Choose a daily activity, such as making a cup of tea or sending a text, and decompose the activity into as many simpler questions about the problem as you can.

Algorithm design

The third cornerstone of computational thinking is **algorithm design**, planning a solution based on your understanding of the problem.

The solution should take the form of a series of simple, logical, step-by-step instructions that must be followed in a strict sequence. To make a good **algorithm**, the instructions must be:

▶ clear

▶ simple

▶ unambiguous

▶ precise

▶ correctly sequenced

▶ sufficiently detailed to complete the task.

Paper aeroplane algorithm

1 Write an algorithm containing a series numbered steps to construct a paper aeroplane.

2 Swap your algorithm with a partner and use their algorithm to build a paper aeroplane.

3 Work with your partner, comparing the aeroplanes you have made and discussing the bugs (errors) in your algorithms. Try to debug (correct the errors in) your algorithms by annotating or editing them.

Checking in

❶ Why must the solution to a problem be written as a series of instructions if a computer is going to implement the solution?

❷ What term does a computer scientist use to describe what happens when unhelpful details are ignored?

❸ What is decomposition?

➡ 2 Pattern recognition

Pattern recognition is the fourth cornerstone of computational thinking.

It is an important part of problem solving because, if you can identify similarities between two different problems, you might be able to apply the same or a slightly modified solution to both problems.

This enables computer programmers to work efficiently, solving problems more quickly and writing less code.

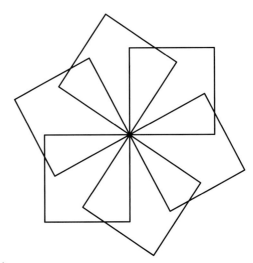

➡ The abstracted flower design

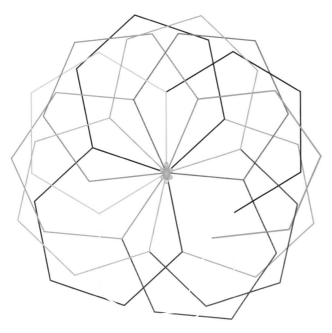

➡ The original flower design

Flower design problem

Look at the original flower design.

1 Identify as many patterns in the flower as you can.

2 Make a list of any elements of the design that could be removed or changed and still leave a flower design that is similar to the original flower design.

Two flowers

Look at the original flower design and at the abstracted flower design.

1 How are the two flowers similar?

2 How are the two flowers different?

When you were thinking about the flower designs, you were carrying out computational thinking.

When you were identifying patterns in the original flower, you were decomposing the flower and carrying out pattern recognition.

When you made a list of elements that could be removed or changed and still leave a recognisable flower design, you were carrying out abstraction.

When you were identifying the similarities and differences between the flowers, you were carrying out pattern recognition.

Computational thinking will help you create an algorithm for drawing the abstracted flower, an algorithm that could then be adapted to draw an infinite number of different flowers.

Flower algorithm

Create an algorithm that could be used to program a computer to draw the abstracted flower design.

Modular programming

Where possible, you should take a modular approach to programming. Modules are small chunks of code that perform a discrete task. In Logo, these chunks of code are called 'procedures'. They are called on by the main program when needed.

Modularity brings a number of important benefits to the programmer:

▶ A module can be used many times within a single program.

▶ A module can be used in more than one program.

▶ A module can easily be changed to do something similar but slightly different.

▶ Code written in modules is easier to read and debug than a single long sequence of code.

▶ Modules are more efficient for the programmer to write because they use fewer lines of code.

Flower program

A Go to www.logointerpreter.com. Do not register; just click on the EDITOR tab at the top of the screen.

B Program your turtle to draw the abstracted flower design. It is made up of squares and the four internal angles of a square are all 90 degrees. Try to make your code as short as possible by making use of a procedure.

Here are some commands in Logo to help you.

Command	Example commands	What result do the example commands produce?
cs	cs	This clears the canvas and moves the turtle to the starting position.
fd	fd 100	This moves your turtle forward by, in this case, 100 steps.
rt	rt 90	This turns your turtle to the right by, in this case, 90 degrees.
setpencolor	setpencolor 0	This sets the colour of the pen that your turtle draws with. 0 is black.
repeat n [ ]	repeat 4 [fd 100 rt 90]	This repeats code. In this case, forward 100 steps and and right turn 90 degrees is repeated 4 times.
setwidth	setwidth 10	This sets the width of the pen to, in this case, 10.
ht	ht	This hides the turtle and is useful when the turtle has finished drawing.
st	st	This shows the turtle so you can continue drawing.
to	to drawsquare repeat 4 [fd 100 rt 90] end	This creates a procedure called drawsquare that draws a square. To run the procedure, you call it by its name in your program.

Checking in

❶ What is the name given to a carefully sequenced series of instructions that can be coded in a computer programming language?

❷ Which cornerstone of computational thinking often relies on numerical data in the form of graphs and charts?

❸ Use your skills of pattern recognition to identify the picture that is most unlike the others.

a   b   c   d   e

➡ 3 Using flow diagrams to solve computational problems

A **flow diagram** is a graphic representation of the flow of something through a system, and flow diagrams are often used to illustrate the sequence of instructions in an algorithm. Flow diagrams use standard symbols.

Imagine a lighthouse needs to be programmed so that the main light beam flashes in a strict sequence to enable shipping to identify it. The sequence is: **ON for 2 seconds and OFF for 3 seconds**.

The programmer needs an algorithm to follow and she likes to work from flow diagrams, so we need to turn this sequence into a flow diagram.

1 The flow diagram should begin with an oval start symbol. The oval symbol can also represent an end point.

2 Arrows represent the direction of flow through the diagram.

3 When data is sent into or out of a system, we use the parallelogram input/output symbol. Text is added to explain what the input/output will do. In this case, it will turn the main light beam on.

4 The sequence is ON for two seconds and OFF for three seconds, so we must keep the light on for two seconds. The processor must pause or wait for two seconds before doing anything else. No data is being sent into or out of the system, so we use the rectangular process symbol to indicate internal processing. Text is added to explain what the processing is.

5 After two seconds, we need another input to turn the light off.

6 The light must stay off for three seconds.

7 The light must continue to flash so we need to repeat the sequence. This is easily done, by adding an arrow to take the flow back to the first output. The lighthouse will now flash forever.

Flow diagram boxes:
- Start
- Turn main light beam on
- Wait two seconds
- Turn main light beam off
- Wait three seconds

But we do not want the lighthouse to flash forever. We only need it to flash when it is dark. A light sensor will be fitted to the lighthouse to detect day and night. The sensor will be on if there is daylight. We now have to send data from a light sensor into the system so we need to add to our flow diagram.

8 Because we now have to send data from a light sensor into the system, we add an input symbol at the beginning of our flow diagram.

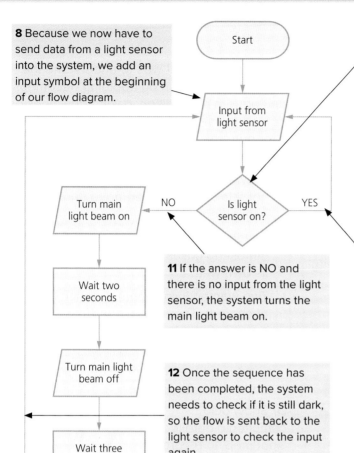

9 The algorithm now needs to make the following decision.
- If there is daylight, the main light beam must be turned off.
- Else, the main light beam must flash.

The input must be followed by a diamond **decision** symbol to take the flow in the correct direction depending on the input from the light sensor. The text in the decision symbol must always be phrased as a question that has a YES or NO answer.

10 If the answer is YES, the system does not turn the main light beam on and feeds the flow back to the sensor to check the input again. This will keep happening until the light sensor is not on (it is dark).

11 If the answer is NO and there is no input from the light sensor, the system turns the main light beam on.

12 Once the sequence has been completed, the system needs to check if it is still dark, so the flow is sent back to the light sensor to check the input again.

Traffic light flow diagrams

The diagram below is a traffic light control algorithm illustrated as a sequence of pictures.

red	red + amber	green	amber	red
10 seconds	2 seconds	14 seconds	3 seconds	start again

1 Draw a flow diagram algorithm, making use of standard flow diagram symbols, for the traffic light control sequence shown above.

2 Now imagine you want to control the traffic lights at a pedestrian crossing. The sequence of the lights is the same but the lights are now controlled by a button.

3 Turn the algorithm below, written in text, into a flow diagram.

The lights must stay green to keep the traffic moving and only change to red if the pedestrian presses the button. When the button is pressed, the lights must change to amber for three seconds and then to red. The light must stay red for 10 seconds, to give the pedestrians plenty of time to cross the road, before changing to red AND amber for two seconds and then back to green.

Checking in

❶ How many different ways to represent an algorithm can you spot in the three first lessons of this module? What are they?

❷ How many decisions are made in the completed lighthouse flow diagram?

❸ How many process symbols are there in the completed lighthouse flow diagram?

➡ 4 Cholera in Soho

Covid-19 has had a big impact on our lives since the start of 2020, but the experience of battling disease is not new and we have overcome serious health crises in the past.

The Soho cholera outbreak of 1854

In 1854, the Soho district of London was being ravaged by cholera. Hundreds of people had already died and more were dying every day. Bacteria had not yet been identified as the cause of cholera. A commonly held view was that it was 'miasma', foul-smelling air, possibly from the highly polluted River Thames, that spread the disease.

PUNCH, OR THE LONDON CHARIVARI.—JULY 3, 1858.

FATHER THAMES INTRODUCING HIS OFFSPRING TO THE FAIR CITY OF LONDON.
(A Design for a Fresco in the New Houses of Parliament.)

➡ Father Thames introduces his offspring to the fair city of London

This was the challenge facing Dr John Snow. He did not accept the miasma theory and set about proving that something else was causing the spread of cholera in Soho. Although the term was not used at the time, Dr Snow applied some of the principles of computational thinking as he set about working out what was killing people.

➡ Dr John Snow

Dr Snow's first goal was to understand the outbreak. He began by applying decomposition and pattern recognition, asking questions and gathering as much data as he could and examining it for patterns. Here are some of the vital clues Dr Snow collected:

▶ Brewery workers rarely caught cholera. They did not drink water, preferring to drink the free beer available to them.

▶ A workhouse near Soho had 535 inmates but almost no cases of cholera. The workhouse had its own well.

▶ Two women living some distance from Soho died of cholera. They had water from the Broad Street pump in Soho brought to them regularly.

▶ Hundreds of people contracted cholera after spending time in schools, restaurants, businesses and pubs near the Broad Street pump.

Dr Snow also compiled a detailed 'spot map' to record the locations where people died of cholera. Without much personal information about each person, Dr Snow was able to recognise patterns in the locations of infected people.

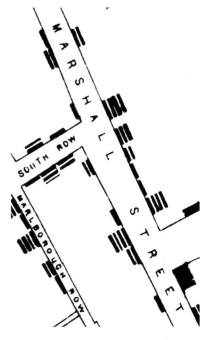

The map is an abstraction of the cholera outbreak. Each bar drawn on the map represents a person who died. Some houses on Marshall Street have no bars; no one died in these houses. Some houses have four bars. If we count all the bars that run parallel to a road, we can see how many people died in each street.

Dr Snow's map also recorded the locations of the drinking water pumps, where people collected water. People did not have taps in their houses.

Dr Snow's cholera map

Study your copy of Dr Snow's map of the cholera outbreak on 'Algorithms Worksheet 4.1' and carry out two important stages of computational thinking.

Decomposition and data collection

1 How many drinking water pumps are there?

2 Where are the pumps located? Mark each pump with a blue circle on your map.

3 Add up the number of cholera deaths in each street and record the number of deaths for each street on your map. Remember, each bar on the map represents a person who died of cholera.

Pattern recognition

4 Colour in the streets where:
- more than 20 people died in red
- between 16 and 19 people died in orange
- between 10 and 15 people died in yellow
- between 3 and 9 people died in blue
- fewer than 3 people died in green.

Once the data has been processed it is easier to see patterns. Look at the data you have processed; look at your annotated map and draw your own conclusions.

5 Explain what you think caused the Soho cholera outbreak.

6 Explain why Dr Snow's map shows no deaths at the brewery and only five deaths at the workhouse even though 535 people lived there.

7 What would you do to put a stop to the cholera outbreak?

The Broad Street pump and 40 Broad Street

Dr John Snow discovered that the Broad Street pump was the cause of the outbreak. A cesspit filled with toilet waste, below 40 Broad Street, was leaking into the well that the Broad Street pump drew water from. A child living at 40 Broad Street died of cholera two days before the outbreak and the child's mother had been disposing of the child's toilet waste into the cesspit. This was the cause of the infected pump water.

Dr Snow and epidemiology

Dr Snow saved many lives in Soho, but his greater contribution to medicine is the algorithm he invented. He is considered to be the 'father of epidemiology'.

Epidemiology is the study of the distribution (who, when and where) and causes of health and disease in defined populations. The computational-thinking approach to tackling disease outbreaks that Dr Snow invented can be seen in epidemiologists' important role in responding to Covid-19.

Dr Snow's algorithm

Reorganise the statements and questions below to create a flow diagram to summarise the algorithm Dr Snow invented.

Test the hypothesis

Is the hypothesis correct?

Look for patterns

Come up with a hypothesis

Collect data

Treat the disease

Dr Snow's algorithm is still relevant today. When a solution to a problem – like Dr Snow's algorithm – is applied to many similar types of problems, this is known as **generalisation** and it is a key technique used in computing. Computer programmers frequently borrow and adapt code written for a different but similar purpose. Generalisation makes coding much more efficient and improves productivity.

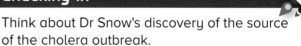

Checking in

Think about Dr Snow's discovery of the source of the cholera outbreak.

1 What role did decomposition play?

2 What role did abstraction play?

3 What role did pattern recognition play?

➡ 5 Malaria in Kitanga

Dr Snow's algorithm can be generalised and applied to a malaria outbreak in the Kitanga District of East Africa. Decomposition, data collection, abstraction and pattern recognition can be carried out to identify the source of the outbreak and decide which swamp or swamps should be sprayed with insecticide to destroy the mosquito in its breeding grounds.

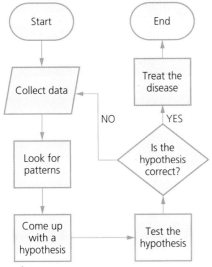

➡ Dr John Snow's algorithm

Decomposition

The purpose of decomposition is to break down a complex and seemingly impossible problem into smaller problems to gain a better understanding of it.

Decomposition

Read the front page of the *East African News* and look at the scale map of Kitanga District and make a note of all the pieces of information that you think might be of use to an epidemiologist working on the malaria outbreak in the area.

East African News

More deaths in Kitanga District

Over 1000 people live in the four villages in Kitanga District in East Africa and recent deaths from malaria are causing concern.

Village A, the largest village with a population of 400, has already lost six people. Villages

B and C have populations of 200 and 340 respectively. So far only one person has died in Village B but three people have died in Village C in the last week. Village D has a smaller population of just 100 and has not yet suffered any deaths.

➡ The *Anopheles mosquito* spreads malaria by biting people

Prompted by the deaths, a Government Health Minister recently visited Kitanga District and called for the immediate spraying of all the possible mosquito breeding grounds with insecticide.

However, an association of village elders does not think mass spraying is the answer. 'Who will pay for the expensive chemicals?' they ask. They have also expressed concern about pollution. 'These are powerful chemicals. What effect will they have on the delicate ecosystem of the swamps which are an important source of fish as well as drinking water for our cattle? If spraying is used it will be vital to identify which swamp the mosquitos are using as their breeding ground.'

Use of mosquito nets, which prevent people from being bitten in the first place, is currently patchy. A survey has shown that 26 people in Village A use nets, 10 in village B and 15 in Village C. Village D has only three net users.

The local Kitanga clinics have just published the infection rates for the four villages in the District. These are shown in the table below.

Village	Number of people infected	Number of clinics
A	20	2
B	139	1
C	35	1
D	88	0

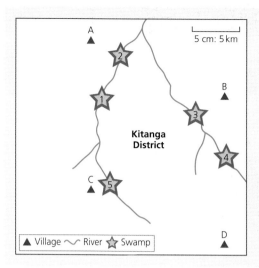

Data collection

A spreadsheet is a good tool for collecting data.

Data collection

Open the 'Algorithms Excel workbook 5.2' and then follow the instructions below.
1 Type in the population of each village in cells B17, C17, D17 and E17.
2 Type in the number of clinics in each village in cells B18, C18, D18 and E18.
3 Type in the number of mosquito net users in each village in cells B19, C19, D19 and E19.
4 Type in the number of people infected in each village in cells B20, C20, D20 and E20.
5 Write a formula in cells B21, C21, D21 and E21 to calculate the infection rate in each village. infection rate = number of people infected / (population - mosquito net users)
6 Type in the number of deaths in each village in B22, C22, D22 and E22.
7 Type the distances between the swamps and the villages into cells B23 to E27.
8 Write a formula in cells B29, C29, D29 and E29 to calculate the infection risk for Swamp 1 for each village. infection risk = infection rate / distance to swamp
9 Replicate the formulas written for Swamp 1 to calculate the infection risk for Swamps 2, 3, 4 and 5 for each village.
10 Use the **AVERAGE** function in cell F29 to calculate the average infection risk for Swamp 1. Replicate this function to cells F30 to F33.

Abstraction

Abstraction is removing unnecessary and unhelpful detail.

Abstraction

Abstract the information from the newspaper article from the *East African News*, the map of Kitanga District and the data you have collected.

List the items of information or data that you think are not relevant to solving the problem of identifying which swamp or swamps are linked to the outbreak of malaria so they can be sprayed with insecticide. Then explain why each item is not relevant.

Pattern recognition

Pattern recognition is about identifying patterns in data.

Pattern recognition

Now that you have collected all the data in a spreadsheet and know what information and data to abstract, you can use the spreadsheet to analyse the data and see if you can spot any patterns.

Charts and graphs are very useful tools for pattern recognition. Use the spreadsheet to create some charts and graphs that will help you spot patterns.

Underneath each chart or graph, write down your conclusion. What do the patterns tell you? Which swamp should be sprayed?

Checking in

1 Give examples of decomposition from this module.
2 Give examples of abstraction from this module.
3 Give examples of pattern recognition from this module.
4 Give examples of algorithm design from this module.

➡ 6 Meet the Potato Heads

Meet the potato heads

A	B	C
D	E	F

1 a Decompose Potato Head B, listing all
      the elements making up the head. (2 marks)

   b Explain the purpose of decomposition
      in computational thinking.   (3 marks)

2 a Describe the pattern that has been used
      to build all the heads.   (2 marks)

   b What do we call this cornerstone of
      computational thinking?   (1 mark)

3 a Which elements in the list below could be
      ignored if we wanted to develop a
      Potato-Head-building algorithm?   (3 marks)

- feet
- colour of items
- size of potato
- hair
- shape of potato
- nose
- eyes
- type of potato
- mouth
- age of potato
- ears

   b What do we call the cornerstone of
      computational thinking involving
      removing unhelpful detail?   (1 mark)

4 a Use standard flow diagram symbols
      to draw a flow diagram for a Potato-Head-
      building algorithm. The algorithm should
      enable you to make any Potato
      Head, with adding feet optional.   (4 marks)

   b Write out a text algorithm for building
      Potato Head D, with adding ears
      optional.   (4 marks)

spock	square	curly	nostril	tight	boots
handle	beady	mohican	ordinary	happy	stilettos
long	lashy	fringe	triangle	square	flippers
floppy	boggle	centre	button	toothy	winkles
small	angry	tuft	carrot	sad	rollers
big	sad	spiky	dot	tiny	flip flops

Programming in Python: selection

An important feature of a computer program is the ability to make decisions and respond to them. This chapter will teach you how to code programs that make decisions in Python. The key programming construct underpinning all the work in this chapter is selection.

➡ 1 Selection

We make decisions all the time by selecting a course of action based on the data we receive. For example, if we look outside and see it is raining, we take an umbrella, but, if we look outside and see it is not raining, we do not take an umbrella.

In a flow diagram, we use a diamond to represent a decision. The course of action selected depends on the answer to the question inside the diamond.

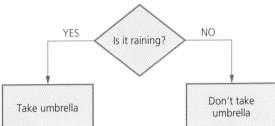

Half price or full price?

Using standard flow diagram symbols, draw a flow diagram (turn to page 92 if you need to remind yourself of the symbols). The algorithm should ask the user to input their age. Then, if the user is under 11, the algorithm should output 'Pay half price'. And, if the user is 11 or over, the algorithm should output 'Pay full price'. The flow diagram should use a decision to decide what to output.

When we want to make a decision in a program, we use selection. Selection involves asking a question to which the answer is either True (yes) or False (no). Depending on the answer, the program will follow certain steps and ignore others.

The most common way of doing this is using an if statement.

The structure of an if statement

The first line of an if statement has three parts to it:

```
if <<condition>>:
```

1 the word **if**
2 the condition, which must be a question that can be answered with True or False. For example, the answer to the question 'Is 5 equal to 7?' is 'False' ('No').
3 a colon **:**.

To create the condition, we must create a **logical test**. A Boolean value is a value that can only be True or False and a logical test involves comparing two Boolean values and obtaining an answer that is either True or False.

There are several Boolean operators that can be used to create a logical test and we can use them to create a condition in an if statement.

Boolean operator	Meaning
>	greater than
>=	greater than or equal to
<	less than
<=	less than or equal to
==	equal to
!=	not equal to

Look at this program:

```
1  sweets = int(input('How many
   sweets have you eaten? '))
2  if sweets > 10:
3      print('That is a lot of
   sweets!')
```

The first line of the program asks the user to input how many sweets they have eaten and stores the data input in a variable called **sweets**. Python assumes data entered after an input prompt is a string unless we tell it otherwise and so here, we tell the computer an integer will be entered using **int**. The second line of the program is the if statement, which checks to see if the number of sweets is greater than 10; this is the condition. The final line of code outputs the message if the answer is True, if the number of sweets input is greater than ten.

Notice that the code telling the computer what to do if the condition is True is indented. It is an example of a programming block. It is usual to indent a block of code like this by four spaces.

When we want to stop the if part of the program, we stop indenting the code. If we add an additional output to the end of our program, we can see what happens when we exit the if block.

```
1  sweets = int(input('How many
   sweets have you eaten? '))
2  if sweets > 10:
3      print('That is a lot of
   sweets!')
4  print('I hope they were tasty.')
```

When the number of sweets is greater than 10, both print statements are output to the screen. When the number of sweets is less than 10, the first print line is skipped because the if condition is False and only the second print statement is output.

Using multiple if statements

By adding another if statement we can make the feedback more sophisticated, giving one response if the first condition is met and a different response if the second condition is met. For example, we can replace the final line of code in our program with a block so that the user receives different feedback if the number of sweets is 10 or less.

```
1  sweets = int(input('How many
   sweets have you eaten? '))
2  if sweets > 10:
3      print('That is a lot of
   sweets!')
4  if sweets < 10:
5      print('You deserve more than
   that!')
6      print('Have another one.')
```

Voting age

Copy and complete the program below. The program should ask the user how old they are. If they are under 18, it should tell them **Sorry. You are too young to vote.** If they are aged 18 or over, it should say **You are old enough to vote.**

```
1  age = int(input('How old are
   you? '))
2  if age < 18:
3      print('Sorry. You are too
   young to vote.')
```

Checking in

1. What is important about the condition used in an if statement?
2. How must an if statement end?
3. How can we tell which part of the program runs if the if statement is True?
4. What do you use Boolean operators for?

➡ 2 Decisions based on calculations

So far, we have simply printed out statements if the condition has been met. However, it is possible to include calculations in the if statement.

This program includes a calculation to tell the user how many years it will be until they can vote:

```
1  age = int(input('How old are you? '))
2  if age < 18:
3      print ('You will be able to vote in',(18-age),'
   year(s).')
```

The number of years until the user can vote is calculated by subtracting the user's age from 18 **(18-age)**. Note the use of commas to separate the strings and the numbers.

Passing your exam

Write a program that asks the user for their mark in a test. If the mark is greater than or equal to 60, the program should output **Well done! You have passed.** Otherwise, it should print out **Sorry. You have failed.** and then tell them how many more marks they needed to have got to pass.

For example:

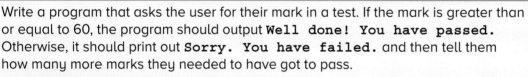

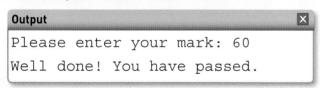

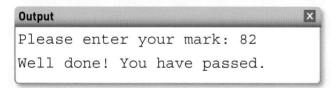

Positive or negative

Write a program that asks the user to enter an integer and then tells them
if the number they have entered is a positive number, a negative number or zero.

For example:

```
Output                                    ☒
Enter a number: 5
Your number is positive.
```

```
Output                                    ☒
Enter a number: -9
Your number is negative.
```

```
Output                                    ☒
Enter a number: 0
Your number is zero.
```

Checking in

① How do we tell a program what to do if the
condition in the if statement returns True?

② How do we tell a program what to do if the
condition in the if statement returns False?

③ Look at this program:

```
1  num = input('Enter a number: ')
2  if num >= 3:
3      print(num * 2)
4  print(num)
```

What is output if we input:

a 2?

b 4?

c 3?

➡ 3 If else

So far, we have used an if statement to check whether or not a condition has been met and, if it has, to do something. However, our programs would be more useful if we could also instruct the computer to do something different when the condition has not been met.

This program uses two separate if statements to instruct the computer to do one thing if the number of sweets input by the user is greater than or equal to 10 and to do something else if the number of sweets input by the user is less than 10.

```
1  sweets = int(input('How many
   sweets have you eaten? '))
2  if sweets > 10:
3      print('That is a lot of
   sweets!')
4  if sweets < 10:
5      print('You deserve more than
   that!')
6      print('Have another one.')
```

However, we can rewrite this program using an **else statement** instead of a second if statement:

```
if <<condition>>:
    <<code to be executed when the
    condition is true>>
else:
    <<code to be executed when the
    condition is false>>
```

```
1  sweets = int(input('How many
   sweets have you eaten? '))
2  if sweets > 10:
3      print('That is a lot of
   sweets!')
4  else:
5      print('You deserve more than
   that!')
6      print('Have another one.')
```

Using an if statement and an else statement rather than two if statements does not allow us to do anything new, but it does make the code easier to read, write and maintain. For example, if you wanted to change the number of sweets to 5, you would only have to change the value once, in the condition.

Ride height

Write a program that asks the user to enter their height in centimetres.

If their height is less than 140 the program should print out: **Sorry, you are too short for this ride.**

Otherwise, it should print out: **Welcome aboard the ride.**

The program should always end by saying: **Have a nice day!**

You should use a single if with a single else. You should not use two individual if statements.

For example:

```
Output                                    ☒
Please enter your height in cm:
140
Welcome aboard the ride.
Have a nice day!
```

```
Output                                    ☒
Please enter your height in cm:
139
Sorry, you are too short for
this ride.
Have a nice day!
```

```
Output                                    ☒
Please enter your height in cm:
190
Welcome aboard the ride.
Have a nice day!
```

Using else after more than one if

You can use more than one if statement before an else statement, for example:

```
1  temperature = int(input('Enter
   the temperature: '))
2  if temperature > 20:
3      print('It must be summer.')
4  if temperature < 5:
5      print('It must be winter.')
6  else:
7      print('Nice weather for the
   time of year.')
```

Python works through the program sequentially. The first if condition is checked and, if it is True, the indented code immediately below it is run. Then the second if condition is checked and, if it is True, the indented code immediately below it is run. If it is False, the else condition is executed. The else condition will always be executed when the if condition immediately above it is False.

If a temperature of 25 is entered, the output will be:

It must be summer.

Nice weather for the time of year.

The first condition has been met and so the first sentence is printed. The program then checks the second condition, which is not met, and so the program executes the else code as well.

Bigger or smaller

Write a program that asks the user to enter an integer and then enter a second, different, integer. The program should then check which number is the largest and output either **The first number is bigger.** or **The second number is bigger.**

If and else calculations

Write a program that asks the user to enter a number between 1 and 20.

If the user's number is greater than 10, the program should divide the number by 2, add 3 to it and print out the result.

If the user's number is less than or equal to 10, the program should multiply the number by 2, subtract 3 from it and print out the result.

As a reminder, the most common operators are:

Operator	Meaning	Example
+	addition	3 + 8 = 11
-	subtraction	8 - 5 = 3
*	multiplication	3 * 5 = 15
/	division	15 / 3 = 5

Checking in

Copy and complete the program by filling in the gaps. It asks the user to print a number between 5 and 10 and outputs **Too small** if the number is below 5, **Too big** if the number is above 10 and **You chose** followed by the number if it is between 5 and 10.

```
1  num = int(input('Enter a
   number between 5 and 10: '))
2  if num __ 5:
3      print('Too small')
4  if num > ____:
5      print('_____')
6  _____
7      print('You chose', _____')
```

➡ 4 Comparing strings and numbers

Up until now, we have concentrated on comparing the value of a number to a condition. However, it is also possible to look at the value of a string and see whether this matches a preset value.

We can use an if-else statement and the equal to (==) Boolean operator to create a simple program to check whether a password is correct, for example:

```
1  realPassword = 'computer'
2  userPassword = input('Please
   enter the password: ')
3  if userPassword == realPassword:
4      print('The password is
   correct.')
5  else:
6      print('Wrong password.')
```

The correct password has been set to 'computer'. The user is asked to enter the password and the program checks to see if the two strings match. The user is then told whether they have entered the correct password or not.

Note that the correct password, **'computer'**, is enclosed within quotation marks. This is necessary to make Python treat it as a string. In Python, you may use either single quotation marks or double quotation marks, so either **'computer'** or **'computer'** is acceptable.

Favourite colour

Write a program that asks the user what they think the computer's favourite colour is. If they enter **yellow**, they should receive a message telling them **Well done! My favourite colour is yellow.** If they enter any other colour, the message should say **Sorry. That is not my favourite colour.**

Adding a random element to your program

Many programs, especially games, can be made more interesting if some of the choices are random.

Python has a random module that can be imported into a program to add extra functions that enable the computer to do things such as generate a random number or pick a random element from a list.

To use the random module, we need to include the following line of code at the beginning of the program: **import random**.

We can then use the function **random.randint(x, y)** to generate a random number between the lowest number **(x)** and the highest number **(y)** inclusive. You need to state what values you want to use for x and y when writing the program.

For example, to generate a random number between 1 and 10, and then output it, we would use the following Python code:

```
1  import random
2  number = random.randint(1, 10)
3  print(number)
```

Guess the random number

Write a program that:

- ▶ asks the user to enter a number between 1 and 10
- ▶ randomly generates a number between 1 and 10 and prints it out
- ▶ compares the two numbers.

If the numbers are the same, the output should be **Both numbers are the same.** If the numbers are different, the output should be **The two numbers are different.**

For example:

Output   ×
Enter a number between 1 and 10:
6
The random number is 6.
Both numbers are the same

Output ☒

```
Enter a number between 1 and 10:
3
The random number is 7
The two numbers are different.
```

Remainder after whole number division

Most of the time, when we divide numbers, we use the / operator. This results in what is called 'true division' and returns the answer we would normally expect to see, for example: 19/5 gives the result 3.8.

Remainder after whole number division uses the % operator and returns the remainder when one integer is divided by another. For example, 19 % 5 gives the result 4, because 19 divided by 5 equals 3, remainder 4.

Remainder after whole number division is very useful if we want to see if an integer is odd or even. We can divide the integer by 2 and if there is a remainder then the number must be odd.

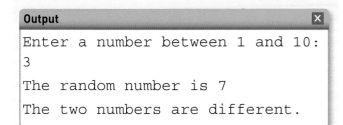

Odd or even

Write a program that asks the user to enter an integer and then tells the user if the number is odd or even.

Checking in

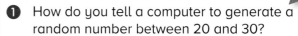

1. How do you tell a computer to generate a random number between 20 and 30?

2. Copy and complete the program by filling in the gaps. It asks the user to enter an integer and decides if it is divisible by 5 or not.

```
1  num = ___ (input('Enter a
   number: '))
2  if _____ __ __ _____ 0:
3      print('Number is divisible
   by 5')
4  _____
5      print('_____
   _____')
```

➡ 5 Elif

So far, we have used if to check whether a condition has been met. If the condition has been True then our program has done one thing, and if it has been False then our program has done something else.

We can make our programs even more useful and interesting by checking several different conditions in a row. We do this using an **elif statement**: 'elif' is short for 'else if':

```
if <<condition1>>:
    <<code to be executed when condition1
    is true>>
elif <<condition2>>:
    <<code to be executed when condition1
    is false but condition2 is true>>
else:
    <<code to be executed when all previous
    conditions are false>>
```

For example, this program asks the user to input two numbers and then compares them and says which is the biggest:

```
1 number1 = int(input('Please
  enter a number: '))
2 number2 = int(input('Please
  enter another number: '))
3 if number1 > number2:
4     print('The first number is
  the biggest.')
5 else:
6     print('The second number is
  the biggest.')
```

However, it runs into a problem if both numbers are the same. It can only, incorrectly, state that **The second number is biggest.** if both numbers are the same. We can correct this using an elif statement.

```
1 number1 = int(input('Please
  enter a number: '))
2 number2 = int(input('Please
  enter another number: '))
3 if number1 > number2:
4     print('The first number is
  the biggest.')
5 elif number2 > number1:
6     print('The second number is
  the biggest.')
7 else:
8     print('The numbers are the
  same.')
```

The program first checks to see if **number1** is bigger than **number2**. If it is, then the output is **The first number is biggest.**

If not, it then checks to see if **number2** is bigger than **number1**. If it is, then the output is **The second number is biggest.**

If neither the first condition nor the second condition is True, the output is **The numbers are the same.**

Age restrictions

Write a program that asks the user to enter their age as an integer. If they are aged 12 or under, the output should be **You are a child.** If they are aged 13 to 19, the output should be **You are a teenager.** Otherwise, the output should be **You are an adult.**

For example:

Output   ✕
Please enter your age: 12 You are a child.

Weather forecast

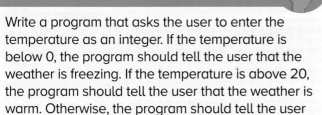

Write a program that asks the user to enter the temperature as an integer. If the temperature is below 0, the program should tell the user that the weather is freezing. If the temperature is above 20, the program should tell the user that the weather is warm. Otherwise, the program should tell the user that the weather is nice for the time of year.

You should assume that your user will supply temperatures rounded up to the nearest whole number and that they will not enter temperature readings with decimal points.

For example:

```
Output                                    ×
Enter the temperature: -5
It is freezing.
```

```
Output                                    ×
Enter the temperature: 25
The weather is warm.
```

```
Output                                    ×
Enter the temperature: 14
The weather is nice for the time
of year.
```

Multimaths

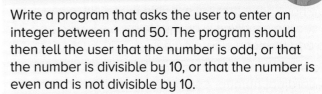

Write a program that asks the user to enter an integer between 1 and 50. The program should then tell the user that the number is odd, or that the number is divisible by 10, or that the number is even and is not divisible by 10.

For example:

```
Output                                    ×
Enter a number between 1 and 50:
23
That number is odd.
```

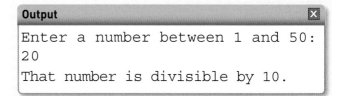

```
Output                                    ×
Enter a number between 1 and 50:
20
That number is divisible by 10.
```

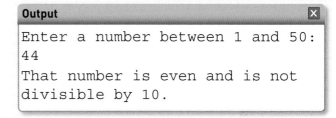

```
Output                                    ×
Enter a number between 1 and 50:
44
That number is even and is not
divisible by 10.
```

Checking in

Copy and complete the program by filling in the gaps. It selects a random number between 1 and 10, asks the user to enter a number and compares the random number with the number entered by the user. If the number entered by the user is bigger than the random number, the output is **My number is smaller.** If the number entered by the user is smaller than the random number, the output is **My number is bigger.** If the number is guessed correctly, the program outputs **Well done!**.

```
1  import _____
2  num = random.randint(1, 10)
3  guess = _____(input('What
   number am I thinking of? '))
4  if _____ > num:
5      print('My number is
   smaller.')
6  _____ guess __ num:
7      print('My number is
   _____')
8  _____
9      print(_____)
```

➡ 6 Multiple elifs

We have seen that it is possible to use elif to check for a second condition in an if statement. It is also possible to add as many elif statements as you want so that any number of different conditions can be checked.

A cardinal number says how many there are of something, for example, 1, 2, 3. An ordinal number says what position something is in a list, for example, 1st, 2nd, 3rd. The program below asks the user to input a cardinal number between 1 and 9, and then outputs the related ordinal number.

```
1  number = int(input('Please enter
   a number between 1 and 9: ')
   entered)
2  if number == 1:
3      print(str(number) + 'st')
4  elif number == 2:
5      print(str(number) + 'nd')
6  elif number == 3:
7      print(str(number) + 'rd')
8  else:
9      print(str(number) + 'th')
```

The numbers 1, 2 and 3 all need a different ending when they are written as ordinal numbers. Therefore, we need to check for each of these numbers separately using an if statement and then two different elif statements.

In contrast, the remaining numbers (4 to 9) all need the same ending, which can be added using the else statement.

Notice how the answer is cast back to a string so that it can be output in the print statement.

Ready for the weekend

Write a program that asks the user to enter the day of the week, and then tells them:

▶ **It is the weekend.** if the day is Saturday or Sunday

▶ **It is almost the weekend.** if the day entered is Friday

▶ **It is a weekday.** if the day entered is Monday, Tuesday, Wednesday or Thursday.

Time of day

Write a program that asks the user to enter the hour of the time of day using the 24-hour clock (using, for example, 14 for 2 p.m. or 15 for 3 p.m.). The program should then greet the user appropriately:

▶ Up to 11: **Good morning**

▶ 12 to 17: **Good afternoon**

▶ 18 to 22: **Good evening**

▶ 23 or later: **Good night**

For example:

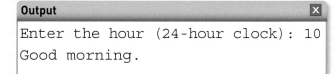

```
Output                              ✕
Enter the hour (24-hour clock): 10
Good morning.
```

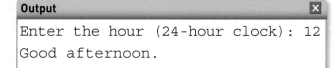

```
Output                              ✕
Enter the hour (24-hour clock): 12
Good afternoon.
```

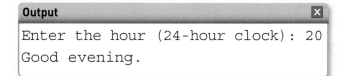

```
Output                              ✕
Enter the hour (24-hour clock): 20
Good evening.
```

```
Output                              ✕
Enter the hour (24-hour clock): 23
Good night.
```

Exam grades

Write a program that asks the user to enter the number scored in a test. The program should then output the grade that has been achieved, as a single letter. The grade boundaries are:

▶ Mark of 75 or more: A

▶ Mark of 65–74: B

▶ Mark of 55–64: C

▶ Mark of 45–54: D

▶ Mark of less than 45: U

For example:

Output ☒

```
Enter the test score: 87
A
```

Output ☒

```
Enter the test score: 56
C
```

Output ☒

```
Enter the test score: 34
U
```

Checking in

① Which keyword do we use to check just one condition?

② Which keyword do we use to check multiple conditions?

③ Complete the program by filling in the gaps.

- If a person is 15 or over, they are old enough to use the fairground ride.
- If they are not 15 or over but are 1.5 m or taller, they are tall enough to use the fairground ride.
- If they are not 15 or over and not 1.5 m or taller, they are not old enough and not tall enough to use the fairground ride.

```
1  age = _____ (input('Enter age:
   '))
2  height = _____
   (input('Enter height: '))
3  if age ____ 15:
4      print('Old enough to
   ride.')
5  _____ height _____ :
6      print(_____
   _____)
7  _____
8      print('Sorry not old
   enough and not tall enough to
   ride.')
```

The internet has become an essential part of our daily lives. People of all ages rely on the internet for communication, file sharing, entertainment, online shopping, banking and much more.

It is important to make sure people can keep themselves safe and keep their data secure. They can do this by, among other things, being conscious of the impact of social media, using anti-malware software and understanding the importance of encryption, which scrambles important data so that others can't understand it.

→ 1 Digital footprint

Social media

When considering who to give a job to, most employers now look at applicants' **social media profiles** and check for anything that might be concerning. Companies want to employ hard-working, responsible people to work for them. People are on their best behaviour in a job interview and looking at someone's social media posts can help an employer find out what a person is really like.

Social media platforms

1 Name as many social media platforms as you can.
2 For each social media platform, think about who typically uses it and how they use it.

Here is an example of a post that had serious consequences for the person who posted it:

James' boss saw the post and he was fired. His employer clearly concluded he was a poor ambassador for their business and may have been personally offended too. Future employers are likely to call James' judgement into question and pass him over for better candidates.

The dos and don'ts of social media

The best way to make sure your digital footprint is good and reflects well on you is to avoid posting anything unpleasant. And remember the human: the person who posted something angry might be lovely most of the time but be having a bad day. Take a breath and don't respond straight away. Getting into an argument on the internet is always a bad idea.

Here are five top tips to help protect your digital footprint (and yourself!).

▶ Use **privacy settings** so that only people you allow can see your posts.
▶ Keep some information to yourself, including your address, school and phone number and your real name, if possible.
▶ Use a picture of anything except yourself as your **avatar**.
▶ Block and report people who are mean, unpleasant or nasty.
▶ Ask permission before you post photographs of other people.

Job applications

Imagine that you work for the International Space Organisation. The ISO has received the applications for the next batch of trainee astronauts and, before it considers which applicants to hire, it needs you to look at two candidates' social media profiles and check for anything that might be concerning. One of the applicants is Harry Iqbal, another is LC Johnson. If you can't find anything to worry about, or you can't find anything about them at all, they should go through to the next stage. Otherwise, they should be rejected.

Copy and complete the following table for each applicant:

Description of post	Comments
Continue to next stage?	

Harry Iqbal is with **Henry Iqbal**
Yesterday at 4.15 p.m.

Thanks @Henry for the photoshoot. Need this for my #InternationalSpaceOrganisation training!

😊😊👍 437

21 Comments 10 Shares

👍 Like   ➦ Share

View 16 more Comments

Henry Iqbal ✔ Any time bro!
Like Reply 1h   👍 1

LC Johnson
Yesterday at 11.55 a.m.

So bored! Gotta make up fake hobbies for this stupid astro thing my parents are making me do. Pretty sure this is what all scientists look like, rite?
View 5 more comments

👍😊😊 7

21 Comments 10 Shares

👍 Like   ➦ Share

HenryIqbal
HIqbal97

No more cheap bikes for the next few months.
Hit me up when I'm back on the streets.

4.17 p.m. 14 Aug 2020

3 Reposts 7 Likes

Checking in

❶ Describe a social media post that could get the person posting it into trouble.

❷ Suggest ways you can protect yourself from damaging your digital footprint.

➡ 2 Passwords and phishing

Secure passwords

Most people now have at least one online account, and online accounts are protected by passwords. Passwords are vulnerable to **hacking**. The most commonly used passwords are:

password	12345
qwerty	11111
password1	

The names of local football teams and celebrities are also commonly used passwords.

People use these passwords because they are easy to remember and quick to type. But it is a terrible idea to use one of the most commonly used passwords because they are easy to guess and can be quickly identified with a **brute force attack**.

If someone wants to log into your account but doesn't know the password, they can use a computer program to try hundreds of passwords per second. This is called a brute force attack because the software will eventually try every possible combination of letters, numbers and symbols until it breaks in. The software will try the most common passwords first so, the more common your password, the quicker it will be identified.

A password is much harder to identify if it is a mixture of the following:

▷ upper case letters (A B C D E etc.)

▷ lower case letters (a b c d e etc.)

▷ digits (1 2 3 4 5 etc.)

▷ special characters (! £ $ % etc.)

Passwords that are harder to identify are also harder to remember, so a good technique to create a strong but memorable password is to base it on a phrase or song lyric.

For example, the song lyrics:

Twinkle twinkle little star

How I wonder what you are

can become the password: `Ttls,Hiwwya`.

Using the same password for several websites means that, if one website is compromised, a hacker can access your other accounts. Remembering dozens of unique passwords is

almost impossible though, and writing passwords down somewhere is a big risk. One strategy to protect your password is to make sure that you use unique passwords for key accounts (banking, email, social media and so on) and worry less about websites that don't include any payment information. Another strategy is to use a password manager, a piece of software that you can use to store and retrieve passwords for different websites.

There are two other threats to passwords:

▷ **publicly accessible information:** if you use the name of a favourite musician or sports personality, the name of your pet or your brother, or a key date like your birthday as part of your password, then a hacker can surf your social media to find out information about you that will help them guess your password.

▷ **shoulder surfing:** it is surprisingly easy for someone to look over your shoulder as you enter your password. This is why you should be especially careful entering passwords into your devices in public places.

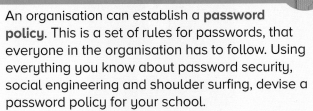

Password policy

An organisation can establish a **password policy**. This is a set of rules for passwords, that everyone in the organisation has to follow. Using everything you know about password security, social engineering and shoulder surfing, devise a password policy for your school.

Phishing

Phishing is a common scam.

Someone sends you an email that pretends to be from a legitimate source, such as a bank or a big trusted company like Amazon or BT. The emails usually use a pressure tactic, for example threatening to close your account, and contain a **hyperlink** for the user to click on. This hyperlink will take you to a fake website that looks real, where you will be asked to log in. The scammers have now discovered your password and can use it to log in to your real account.

Common features of phishing emails include:

- a generic greeting, when the real company knows your name

- spelling and grammar mistakes

- a suspicious email address; the email has obviously not come from the real company

- high pressure tactics; for example, telling you that your account will be closed unless you click on the hyperlink

- exploiting greed; for example, offering you a free iPhone if you click on the hyperlink

- a hyperlink to click on, which may look legitimate but hovering over shows that it will not take you to the real company.

If you suspect an email is a phishing email, ignore it. DO NOT click on the link.

Mega-Tee Newsletter newsletter@mega-tee.com Unsubscribe
To: Shauna MacPherson

Having trouble seeing this email click here

Mega-Tee Newsletter

AMAZING SUMMER SALE FINAL CHANCE!!!

Final 24 hours!!!

It's the LAST 24 HOURS of our unbelievable summer sale. All T-shirts reduced, up to 70% off and free shipping on all orders over £20! We've never had a sale this big so order quickly. When they're gone, they're gone!
https://www.mega-tee.co.uk

Phishing or genuine?

Look at the emails below. For each email:

1. state whether you think the email is genuine or a phishing email.

2. identify at least three features of the email that helped you make your decision.

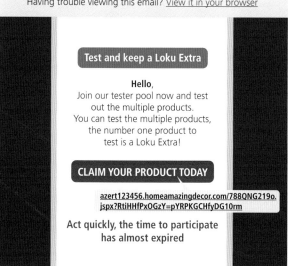

Loku Offer 4U663EFLQ@4u663eflq.us 1.37 a.m (15 hours ago)
to me

Having trouble viewing this email? View it in your browser

Test and keep a Loku Extra

Hello,
Join our tester pool now and test out the multiple products.
You can test the multiple products, the number one product to test is a Loku Extra!

CLAIM YOUR PRODUCT TODAY

azert123456.homeamazingdecor.com/788QNG219o.jspx?RtiHHfPxOGzY=pYRPKGCHfyDG10rm

Act quickly, the time to participate has almost expired

Checking in

1. Describe a secure password.

2. What is a password manager?

3. What features of an email might suggest it is part of a phishing scam?

➡ 3 Malware

Malware comes from the words **mal**icious (meaning 'bad') and soft**ware** (meaning 'computer programs'). The word 'malware' is used to describe computer programs designed to do something bad.

Viruses, trojans and worms can do a lot of different things. Depending on the code that has been inserted into a computer system, they can delete or damage user files. They can corrupt a computer system so it won't start any more. They can even allow the creator of the worm to take control of a computer system.

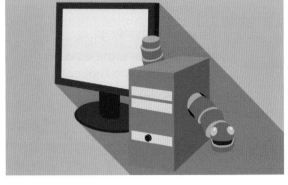

➡ Back in the year 2000, the ILoveYou worm was so effective that it infected over 50 million computers within 10 days. That was about 10% of all the internet-connected computers in the world at that time!

Viruses

The phrase 'computer virus' is sometimes used to describe all types of malware, but a virus is a very specific type of malware.

Viruses are inserted into programs that are then passed on. Viruses are often spread via email attachments, but they may also be spread through files, programs or games downloaded from a web page or an external storage device.

Trojans

A trojan is a special type of malware that tricks users into thinking it is a helpful piece of software. For example, it might be a program that says it can tell you who has looked at your social media profile or it might pretend it is an anti-malware program!

Spyware

Spyware is the name for software that lets other people spy on your activities. A common way for a program to infect a computer system is to claim to be an anti-spyware program, when actually it contains spyware! This is a type of trojan attack.

Once infected, the spyware monitors, records and transmits everything a user does. It captures passwords, browsing history, web searches and much, much more. This information is often sold to advertisers or used to hack into the victim's online accounts.

Adware

Adware is all about getting users to see adverts. There are many ways to get adware onto a user's computer, but one of the most popular methods is to include it as part of a bundle of free software. When the user downloads and installs the software, they are given the option to install other 'useful' programs at the same time. Many users just click through the options without checking them carefully.

In order to make money, the creators of the adware make pop-up messages appear on the victim's computer and can take control of their web browser, redirecting the user to sites filled with adverts. The advertisers will pay the adware creators for ensuring people see the adverts.

Malware

Ransomware

Ransomware is a type of malware that can attack individuals but is mostly aimed at large organisations. It encrypts (scrambles) the files on a computer and then demands money in order to unlock the files. If the victim doesn't have a recent backup, then they could end up losing everything.

There are several ways to get ransomware onto someone's computer, but one of the main methods is through a file attached to a phishing email. This is one reason why you should always be wary of files attached to emails if you aren't expecting them.

Worms

A worm is a particularly nasty piece of malware. While most malware needs the user to run a program, a worm can copy itself automatically and send itself over a network connection to another computer. Because of this, worms can infect a large number of computers very quickly.

Malware posters

Choose one type of malware and produce a poster or presentation slide describing it. Your poster or presentation slide can contain images and should contain no more than 10 words.

Measures to protect against malware

Anti-malware software
Often called anti-virus software, anti-malware software scans computer programs and emails for malicious code. If it finds anything suspicious it puts it into quarantine so it cannot infect or damage the computer system. The user can then decide whether or not to trust the file, or delete it.

Backups
Regularly backing up your files (saving a copy of all your files) means that damaged or deleted files can be quickly replaced with little or no loss of data.

Measures to protect against malware

Firewalls
Firewalls block connections into or out of a computer system unless they are authorised. Firewalls stop spyware and keyloggers from sending data back to the creators of the malware and they stop worms from spreading automatically.

Avoid file-sharing websites
File-sharing websites are a common place to pick up malware. Stay away from dodgy websites and illegal downloads and stick to legal and official websites. This will reduce your risk of infecting your computer system with malware.

Updates
Installing system updates fixes security flaws identified by the company that makes your computer's operating system. Installing program updates fixes the security flaws identified by the companies that make the software programs your computer uses. New flaws are found all the time, so it's really important to install updates whenever they are available. These updates make your computer, phone and console much hard to attack. Putting off a security update is a major security mistake!

➡ Regularly backing up limits the impact of viruses, trojans, worms and ransomware

Checking in

❶ What could be wrong if someone says their computer 'has a virus'?

❷ Explain how anti-malware software can protect you against the threat of malware.

❸ What is the simplest thing you can do to protect your own computer or phone from malware?

➡ 4 Encryption

Why use encryption?

Encryption is a method of scrambling a message so that it cannot be understood if someone else reads it.

Decryption means unscrambling an encrypted message so that it makes sense again. Hopefully, only the intended recipient is able to successfully decrypt the message.

Simple decryption

Try to decode the following secret messages:

1 Int hism essagea llt hes pacesh aveb eenm ovedb yo nep lace.

2 Rmvng ll th vwls cn mk ths mssg mch hrdr t rd.

3 It dseno't mttaer in waht oderr the lterets in a wrod are. The olny irpoamtnt tihng is taht the frsit and lsat ltteers are in the rhgit pclae.

4 Nac uoy llits daer a egassem fi I etirw yreve drow sbrawkcab?

5 ?redrah ro reisae taht sI ?sdrawkcab egassem elohw eht etirw I fi tuoba woH

Messages sent between computers are passed across a network and any computer on that network is able to read the messages. People often send sensitive information across the internet and encryption makes it harder to read an encrypted message if it is intercepted. Encryption helps keep sensitive information secret.

Whenever you buy something on the online, you enter sensitive information – such as your debit or credit details and your address – onto a web page and it is sent across the internet. It is, therefore, important to check that the data is encrypted before it is sent. Web addresses that begin with https:// use encryption; web addresses that begin with http:// don't. This is sometimes hard to spot, so always look for the padlock and *never* send personal or private information to a website without the padlock!

🔒 https://www.hoddereducation.co.uk

Ciphers

Encryption algorithms are often called **ciphers**. When encrypting a message, the original message is called **plaintext** and the encrypted message is called **ciphertext**.

There are lots of different ciphers. Some are very simple and some are extremely complex. The ciphers we will look at are fairly simple, and certainly not complex enough for transmitting sensitive data over the internet.

The Atbash Cipher

One of the oldest ciphers in the world is the Atbash Cipher.

The alphabet is written twice, once forwards and once backwards:

Plaintext	A	B	C	D	E	F	G	H	I	J	K	L	M
Ciphertext	Z	Y	X	W	V	U	T	S	R	Q	P	O	N

Plaintext	N	O	P	Q	R	S	T	U	V	W	X	Y	Z
Ciphertext	M	L	K	J	I	H	G	F	E	D	C	B	A

To encrypt a message, the original letter is identified in the plaintext row and the encrypted letter is taken from the ciphertext row directly below it. 'BAD' is encrypted as 'YZW'.

The Caesar Cipher

The most famous encryption algorithm was invented by Julius Caesar. He needed to send instructions

The Atbash Cipher

1 Encode these messages:
  a HELLO WORLD
  b DOGS CHASE CATS
  c SECRET MESSAGE

2 Decoded these messages:
  a OLT RM MLD
  b HGZB SRWWVM
  c HZYLGZTV GSV VMTRMVH

to his armies but didn't want his enemies to find out what the instructions were if the messengers were caught. He came up with the idea of shifting the alphabet sideways.

Here is the alphabet written with the ciphertext shifted sideways by one letter:

Plaintext	A	B	C	D	E	F	G	H	I	J	K	L	M
Ciphertext	B	C	D	E	F	G	H	I	J	K	L	M	N

Plaintext	N	O	P	Q	R	S	T	U	V	W	X	Y	Z
Ciphertext	O	P	Q	R	S	T	U	V	W	X	Y	Z	A

To encrypt a message, the original letter is identified in the plaintext row and the letter is taken from the ciphertext row directly below it. In this case, the letters in the ciphertext row have been shifted 1 place to the left, meaning that each plaintext letter is shifted up by 1. This means that the plaintext message, 'BAD' is encrypted as 'CBE'.

How many letters you shift the alphabet sideways is called the **key**.

▶ With a key of 5, the letters are shifted 5 places to the left.

▶ With a key of 25, the letters are shifted 25 places to the left.

▶ With a key of 26, the letters are shifted 26 places to the left. A key of 26 is, therefore, the same as a key of 0.

The Caesar Cipher

Find out what a cipher wheel is, make your own and use it to encode and decode the messages that follow.

1 Encode these messages:
  a HELLO WORLD Key: 4 (A becomes E)
  b JULIUS CAESAR Key: 12 (A becomes M)
2 Decode these messages:
  a PJCN XYNW Key: 9 (A becomes J)
  b OHHOQY OH ROKB Key: 14 (A becomes O)

Decrypting a message with the Caeser Cipher is easy if you have the key. It is also relatively easy if you don't know the key, although it can be time consuming. The simplest method is brute force, trying all 26 possible combinations.

Cracking the Caesar Cipher

Use brute force to decrypt these messages. Try each key, one at a time, to decrypt the first word. If it makes sense, you've found the key and can decrypt the rest of the message. If it doesn't make sense, move on to the next key.

1 YMJ XJHZWNYD ITTW BNQQ GJ ZSQTHPJI FY YJS UR
2 AYK ZNK VGYYCUXJ 'YVGIKOYIUUR'

The Keyed Caesar Cipher

To make the Caesar Cipher harder to crack, the Keyed Caesar Cipher has been designed. It uses two keys: a word and a number.

First, the word is inserted as ciphertext with duplicate letters removed. For example, the word key is 'password', but the second 's' has not been included.

The rest of the alphabet is then filled in, skipping the letters already used in the key word so there are no duplicate letters:

Plaintext	A	B	C	D	E	F	G	H	I	J	K	L	M
Ciphertext	**P**	**A**	**S**	**W**	**O**	**R**	**D**	B	C	D	E	F	G

Plaintext	N	O	P	Q	R	S	T	U	V	W	X	Y	Z
Ciphertext	H	I	K	L	M	N	Q	T	U	V	W	Y	Z

Finally, as with the Caesar Cipher, the number key shifts the ciphertext left by the number of places given.

The Keyed Caesar Cipher

Use the Keyed Caesar Cipher to encrypt and decrypt the following messages, using 'CIPHER' as your word key and '0' as your number key. You will need to draw a grid, like the ones on this page, to help you.

1 Encrypt this message: WELCOME
2 Decrypt this message: QDELH

Checking in

❶ Which of the ciphers we have looked at is the easiest to crack?

❷ Which of the ciphers we have looked at is the hardest to crack?

➡ 5 Automating encryption

Automating encryption – programming a computer to do it for you – is much quicker than doing it manually. While the time taken to make the spreadsheet function correctly will initially slow the process down, encrypting and decrypting a large number of long messages is much easier with an automated solution.

The Atbash Cipher: automated encryption and decryption

You are going to create a spreadsheet that automates the encryption and decryption of the Atbash Cipher.

1 Create a look-up table in cells A1 to B27 and a decoding table in cells A29 to K30, like this:

	A	B	C	D	E	F	G	H	I	J	K
1	Plaintext	Ciphertext									
2	A	Z									
3	B	Y									
4	C	X									
5	D	W									
6	E	V									
7	F	U									
8	G	T									
9	H	S									
10	I	R									
11	J	Q									
12	K	P									
13	L	O									
14	M	N									
15	N	M									
16	O	L									
17	P	K									
18	Q	J									
19	R	I									
20	S	H									
21	T	G									
22	U	F									
23	V	E									
24	W	D									
25	X	C									
26	Y	B									
27	Z	A									
28											
29	Plaintext	H	E	L	L	O	W	O	R	L	D
30	Ciphertext										

2 Write a **VLOOKUP** function in cell B30 to find the first ciphertext letter for the plaintext letter in cell B29. Remember to use absolute cell referencing ($) when referencing the lookup table. If you need a reminder about how to write a **VLOOKUP** function, turn back to page 22.

3 Use the fill handle to replicate the function in cell B30 to cells B30 to K30.

4 Encrypt this message by typing the plaintext letters into cells B29 to K29 one word at a time and inputting the ciphertext letters from cells B30 to K30 on to a separate sheet of paper: COMPUTERS ENCRYPT QUICKLY.

5 Decrypt this message: RMRGRZORHV OZFMXS HVJFVMXV. The Atbash Cipher is symmetrical, so you can type the ciphertext into cells B30 to K30 and input the resulting plaintext letters from cells B29 to K29.

The Caesar Cipher: automated encryption

You are going to create a spreadsheet that automates the encryption of the Caesar Cipher.

1 Create two tables like this:

	A	B	C	D	E
1	**Key**				
2					
3					
4	**Plaintext**	**Value**	**Shifted value**	**Adjusted value**	**Ciphertext**
5	H				
6	E				
7	L				
8	L				
9	O				
10	W				
11	O				
12	R				
13	L				
14	D				

2 Use the CODE function to convert the plaintext letter in B5 to its ASCII value in C5, for example: `=CODE(B5)`.

3 Write a formula using an absolute cell reference in cell C5 to add the key to the ASCII value to get the shifted value.

4 Write an IF function in cell D5 so that 26 is subtracted from the shifted value if the shifted value is larger than 90. If you need a reminder about how to write an **IF** function, turn back to page 84.

5 Use the CHAR function to convert the adjusted value to ciphertext, for example: `=CHAR(E5)`.

6 Use the fill handle to replicate the functions and formulae to complete the table.

7 Encrypt this message by typing the plaintext letters into column A and inputting the ciphertext letters from column E onto a separate sheet of paper: SPREADSHEETS CAN BE HELPFUL ONCE PROGRAMMED.

Secret message

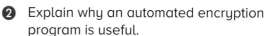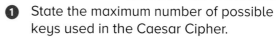

Imagine you work for the International Space Organisation. An email has been sent from one of the computers inside the ISO with a garbled message attached. The Chief Security Officer thinks it might be an encrypted message and has asked you to decrypt it and work out if security has been compromised.

You need to work out if it was encrypted with the Atbash Cipher or the Caesar Cipher and, if it is the Ceaser Cipher, what key was used.

Has the security of the ISO been compromised?

Here is the message:

U tmhq ftq zqi daowqf xmgzot oaybgfqd bdasdmy. Uf ue rmd nqffqd ftmz iq qhqd qjbqofqp mzp iuxx qzegdq ftq UEA payuzmfqe ftq ebmoq fagduey ymdwqf rad kqmde fa oayq. U omz etmdq uf iuft kag ur kag mdq iuxxuzs fa oaybqzemfq yq.

Checking in

1 State the maximum number of possible keys used in the Caesar Cipher.

2 Explain why an automated encryption program is useful.

3 Explain one problem with using an automated encryption program.

→ 6 Keeping yourself safe online

Understanding how to use social media appropriately, how to choose secure passwords and keep them safe, how to protect yourself from different types of malware and will be useful to you throughout your life, so it's important you fully absorb them.

Knowledge organisers

Complete knowledge organisers, like the one below, for the following topics.

▶ Social media

▶ Passwords

▶ Phishing

▶ Malware

▶ Encryption

Topic: Social media		What we should know:
Vocabulary:		
Key word	Meaning	
		Why we should know it:

What do you know?

1 Which one of the following describes an avatar?

  a A profile picture.

  b An online bully.

  c A type of social media.

2 Which one of the following describes phishing?

  a Downloading files illegally.

  b Trying to guess someone's password.

  c Tricking someone into giving away their password.

3 Which one of the following describes malware?

  a Software designed to protect a computer.

  b Software designed to do harm to a computer.

  c Expensive software.

4 Which one of the following describes encryption?

  a Unscrambling a message so it can be understood.

  b Blocking unwanted messages from a computer system.

  c Scrambling a message so it cannot be understood.

5 Which one of the following is the opposite of encryption?

  a Decryption

  b Unencryption

  c Cybercryption

6 Which one of the following describes a cipher?

  a Someone who cracks encrypted messages

  b An algorithm for encrypting and decrypting messages

  c Someone who comes up with encryption algorithms

7 True or false? Before offering a candidate a job, employers will often search for them online to see what their digital footprint says about them.

8 True or false? Using privacy settings can ensure that anything you post is totally secure and can never be copied or shared with anyone else.

9 True or false? Social media posts cannot be used in a court of law as evidence against you.

10 True or false? People are more likely to post or say something they regret when they are angry.

11 Which one of the following describes a brute force attack?

   a A hacker tries to find out information about you to try and guess your password.

   b A hacker threatens to hit you if you don't give them your password.

   c A hacker uses a program that tries every possible combination of passwords to identify your password.

   d A hacker looks over your shoulder while you log in and sees your password.

12 Which one of the following describes shoulder surfing?

   a A hacker tries to find out information about you to try and guess your password.

   b A hacker puts a secret tracker on your shirt collar.

   c A hacker uses a program that tries every possible combination of passwords to identify your password.

   d A hacker looks over your shoulder while you log in and sees your password.

13 Write down the words missing from these sentences:

   a A typical _____ scam will try to redirect a user to a _____ website.

   b Common features of phishing scams include _____, a _____ greeting and pressure to do something quickly.

   c If you are not sure if an email is genuine you should _____.

   d A computer _____ is when a piece of malicious code is inserted into an existing program.

   e A _____ is a whole program that pretends to do something that people will want to trick them into installing it.

   f A _____ doesn't need to be run by the user; it can copy itself from one machine to another automatically.

   g Software that watches and records a user's actions and sends them back to the creator is called _____.

   h Some malware will encrypt a user's files and demand a payment to unlock them. This type of malware is called _____.

   i One of the key methods of keeping devices safe from malware is to use a _____. This software blocks connections into or out of a computer system unless they are authorised. In this way, it can help combat spyware and worms.

   j Using _____ software is important because it scans programs for malicious code and prevents it from running.

   k Running _____ means that any holes in your online security are fixed as soon as possible, making it harder for malicious coders to gain access.

14 Use the Atbash Cipher to decrypt this ciphertext message: 'HMZRO'.

Plaintext	A	B	C	D	E	F	G	H	I	J	K	L	M
Ciphertext	Z	Y	X	W	V	U	T	S	R	Q	P	O	N

Plaintext	N	O	P	Q	R	S	T	U	V	W	X	Y	Z
Ciphertext	M	L	K	J	I	H	G	F	E	D	C	B	A

15 Use the Caesar Cipher to encrypt this plaintext message with a key of 3: 'HACK'.

Plaintext	A	B	C	D	E	F	G	H	I	J	K	L	M
Ciphertext	D	E	F	G	H	I	J	K	L	M	N	O	P

Plaintext	N	O	P	Q	R	S	T	U	V	W	X	Y	Z
Ciphertext	Q	R	S	T	U	V	W	X	Y	Z	A	B	C

16 Use the Caesar Cipher to encrypt this plaintext message with a key of 1: 'DPEF'.

Plaintext	A	B	C	D	E	F	G	H	I	J	K	L	M
Ciphertext	B	C	D	E	F	G	H	I	J	K	L	M	N

Plaintext	N	O	P	Q	R	S	T	U	V	W	X	Y	Z
Ciphertext	O	P	Q	R	S	T	U	V	W	X	Y	Z	A

This chapter provides an insight into how a digital processor works. All data stored, processed and generated by a computer is represented by just two digits, a 1 and a 0. When you type 'Hello' on your keyboard, the computer receives this data as a string of 1s and 0s. How exactly? You are going to find out …

➡ 1 Logic gates

Animal sorting gate

A zookeeper has installed a digital sorting gate between two animal enclosures, to control which animals leave the first enclosure and enter the second enclosure. The gate is programmed to allow only big cats with stripes through, so two things must happen for an animal to enter the second enclosure:

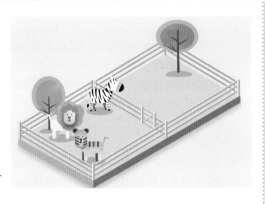

1 the animal must be a big cat.

2 the animal must have stripes.

The lion approaches the gate.

Is the animal a big cat?
    YES

Does the animal have stripes?
    NO

The lion cannot enter the second enclosure.

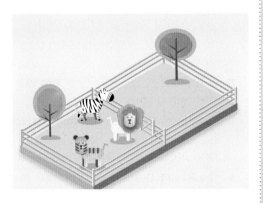

The tiger approaches the gate.

Is the animal a big cat?
    YES

Does the animal have stripes?
    YES

The tiger can enter the second enclosure.

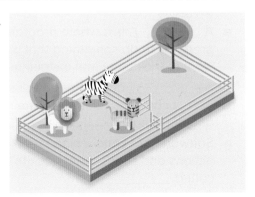

Input describes data going into a processing system and output describes data leaving a processing system.

Our animal sorting gate receives two inputs, which are the Boolean responses to two questions:

1 Is the animal a big cat?

2 Does the animal have stripes?

Think of each input like a **switch**. If the answer to the question is YES, the switch is turned on and this is represented by a 1. If the answer to the question is NO, the switch is turned off, and this is represented by a 0.

These two switches combine to create a logic gate. **Logic gates** process two or more inputs and produce the correct output.

The animal sorting gate requires two conditions to be met before it will open: the animal must be a big cat AND the animal must have stripes. This logic gate is called an **AND gate** because both condition 1 and condition 2 must be met for the gate to open.

If both inputs are a 1, the gate between the enclosures opens and this is represented by a 1.

If only one input is 1 or both inputs are 0, the gate between the enclosures remains closed and this is represented by a 0.

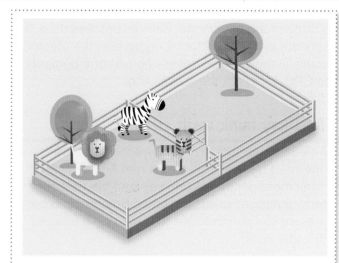

The tiger approaches the gate.

Is the animal a big cat?
    YES (represented by a 1)

Does the animal have stripes?
    YES (represented by a 1)

What is the state of the gate?
    OPEN (the output is 1 so the gate opens)

The tiger can enter the second enclosure.

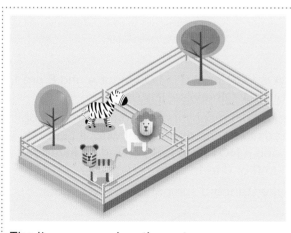

The lion approaches the gate.

Is animal a big cat?
    YES (represented by a 1)

Does the animal have stripes?
    NO (represented by a 0)

What is the state of the gate?
    CLOSED (the output is 0 so the gate remains closed)

The lion cannot enter the second enclosure.

Animal sorting gate

The zebra approaches the gate, but the gate remains closed. Why?

Electrical circuits

To understand how digital devices process data, it is essential to know a little bit about how the electrical circuits in the central processing unit of a computer, the CPU, carry out the processing.

Two-key bank vault circuit

An electronic safe has two switches that are operated by two keys, Key A and Key B. The bank manager keeps one key and the assistant bank manager keeps the other. Both have to be present to open the safe. The motor (M) unlocks the safe door.

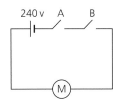

Key A closes switch A and Key B closes switch B. The circuit diagram shows that both switch A *AND* switch B have to be closed to turn on the motor that unlocks the safe door. The logic gate in this circuit is an AND gate, just like the logic gate in the animal sorting gate.

Automatic shop door circuit

An automatic shop door has a sensor switch, A, outside the shop to detect people wanting to come in and another sensor switch, B, inside the shop to detect people wanting to leave. The motor (M) opens the door.

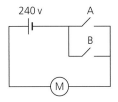

It does not matter which sensor switch detects a customer. The circuit diagram shows that if just one switch is closed, A *OR* B, the motor will operate to open the door. The logic gate in this circuit is an **OR gate**.

The central processing unit of a computer, the CPU, is built from millions of electrical circuits containing logic gates. When a computer is processing, each one of the millions of electrical circuits compares two items of data (the inputs) and makes a decision (the output). The output from one electrical circuit often becomes one of the inputs for another electrical circuit. The outputs result in the actions you can see on screen.

Logic gates

The logic gates in a computer's CPU are represented by standard symbols.

This is the standard symbol for the AND gate:

The inputs come in the form of two electrical currents, A and B. Each current flows into a switch. When an input switch in the logic gate is open, the electrical current flows and this is represented by a 1. When an input switch in the logic gate is closed, the electrical current does not flow and this is represented by a 0. If input A is 1 *AND* input B is 1, the output is 1. Otherwise, it is 0.

This is the standard symbol for the OR gate:

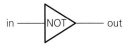

If input A is 1 *OR* input B is 1 *OR* input A and B are 1, the output is 1. Otherwise, it is 0.

If the input from a sensor or the output from a logic gate needs to be the opposite of what it currently is, we can add a **NOT gate** (also called an **inverter**) to switch 1 to 0 or 0 to 1.

Here is the standard symbol for the NOT gate:

in ——▷NOT▷—— out

Logic gates are so called because their operation is entirely logical and predictable. The operation of a particular gate can, therefore, be summarised in a table, known as a truth table. Truth tables describe how a computer processes data.

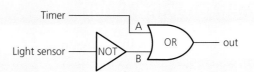

Truth tables

1 Copy the table below and use the circuit diagram of the two-key bank vault circuit to help you complete the truth table for the AND gate. You will need to work out all the possible combinations of inputs A and B and decide on the output for each combination.

A	B	Out
1	1	1

2 Copy the table again and use the circuit diagram of the automatic shop door circuit to help you complete the truth table for the OR gate. You will need to work out all the possible combinations of inputs A and B and decide on the output for each combination.

The timer is connected to input A. The timer switch is on between 6 p.m. and 6 a.m.

The light sensor is connected to input B. The light sensor switch is on when light shines on the sensor, and the input to the NOT gate will be on, or 1.

We do not want the street light to come on during daylight hours so the control system makes use of a NOT gate between the light sensor and input B of the OR gate.

Copy the table below and complete the truth table for the automated street light.

Timer	Light sensor	Street light

Street light

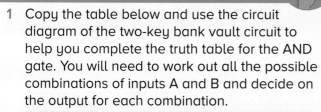

1 Copy the table below and complete the truth table for the NOT gate. Remember, the NOT gate inverts an input of 1 to an output of 0 and an input of 0 to an output of 1.

In	Out
0	
1	

2 An automated street light is connected to two switches: an input from a timer and an input from a light sensor. An OR gate is used to control the street light. Input A, input B, or both inputs A and B must be on for the street light to light up.

Checking in

1 In what form is data input into logic gates?

2 In what form is data output from logic gates?

3 If the inputs to an AND gate are 1 and 0, what is the output?

4 If the inputs to an OR gate are 1 and 0, what is the output?

➡ 2 Introducing binary

You should be familiar with the **decimal system**, which uses ten digits: 0, 1, 2, 3, 4, 5, 6, 7, 8 and 9. The decimal system is also known as the **denary system** or **base 10**.

In base 10, **place value** increases in multiples of 10. The units are followed by 10s, the 10s are followed by 100s and the 100s are followed by 1000s and so on.

The **binary system** uses just two digits: 0 and 1. The binary system is also known as **base 2**.

In base 2, place value increases in multiples of 2. The units are followed by 2s, the 2s are followed by 4s, the 4s are followed by 8s and the 8s are followed by 16s and so on.

1000s	100s	10s	1s	Place values	Denary number
			8	1×8	8
		2	5	$(2 \times 10) + (5 \times 1)$	25
	3	6	2	$(3 \times 100) + (6 \times 10) + (2 \times 1)$	362
1	0	4	0	$(1 \times 1000) + (4 \times 10)$	1040

16s	8s	4s	2s	1s	Place values	Denary number
				1	1×1	1
			1	0	1×2	2
		1	1	1	$(1 \times 4) + (1 \times 2) + (1 \times 1)$	7
	1	0	1	0	$(1 \times 8) + (1 \times 2)$	10
1	1	0	0	1	$(1 \times 16) + (1 \times 8) + (1 \times 1)$	25

Counting in binary

1 Copy and complete the table below to show how to count from 1 to 16 in binary.

2 Study your completed table carefully. Can you spot any patterns? These patterns will help you to spot possible errors in your table and knowing these patterns will help you when you work with binary numbers in the future.

16s	8s	4s	2s	1s	Place values	Denary number
				1	1×1	1
			1	0	1×2	2
						3

Binary to denary conversion

1 Make eight cards to help you convert binary numbers to denary numbers. The front of your eight cards should look like this:

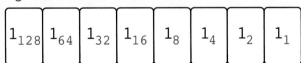

The back of your eight cards should look like this:

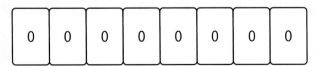

2 Lay out the cards with the denary numbers uppermost and in descending order, like they are in the first picture above. Without changing the order of the cards, turn each card over so that the 0 on the back is showing. Now use the cards to convert the following binary numbers to denary. Here are some examples to get you started.

To convert binary 1 to denary, turn over the card on the far right so it represents the binary number 1. The denary equivalent of the binary digit is the red number in the bottom left-hand corner of the card; in this case 1. Binary 1 is denary 1.

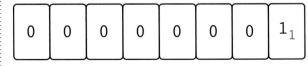

To convert binary 11 to denary, turn over the two cards on the far right so they represent the binary number 11. The denary equivalent is the sum of the red numbers; in this case 2 + 1 = 3. So binary 11 is denary 3.

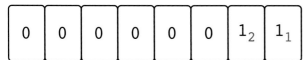

Working from right to left, turn over the cards that correspond to a 1 in the binary number 100110. Ignore the 0s on the left-hand side of the first 1; they have no numerical value. The six cards

on the right represent the binary number 100110. The denary equivalent is the sum of the red numbers; in this case 32 + 4 + 2 = 38. So binary 100110 is denary 38.

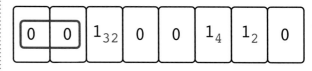

a 1	e 110010	i 10001000
b 10	f 11110000	j 01001110
c 1010	g 10011011	k 01000001
d 100110	h 10101010	l 11111111

Adding binary numbers

Adding binary numbers is similar to adding denary numbers, in that we carry a digit when the columns add up to more than one. To do this, you need to know that:

▶ 1 + 1 = 10 in binary (1 + 1 = 2 in denary and 2 is written as 10 in binary).

▶ 1 + 1 + 1 = 11 in binary (1 + 1 + 1 = 3 in denary and 3 is written as 11 in binary).

Here is how we add 110 + 111 in binary.

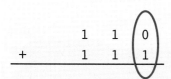

0 + 1 = 1 in binary, so we write down 1.

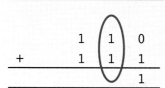

1 + 1 = 10 in binary, so we write down 0 and carry 1 to be added to the next column.

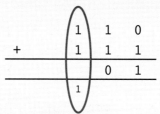

We just have 1 in this column, so we write down 1.

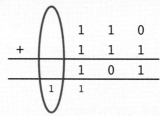

1 + 1 + 1 = 11 in binary, so we write down 1 and carry 1 to be added to the next column.

```
      1   1   0
+     1   1   1
  1   1   0   1
    1       1
```

Complete the following binary additions, showing all your working.

1   10 + 111

2   1101 + 1011

3   10011 + 10001

4   11100 + 10001

5   10011 + 110001

6   1001011 + 1111011

Checking in

1   What is the binary system also known as?

2   What is the denary system also known as?

3   What is the binary number 1001101 in denary?

→ 3 Creating an app

To help you consolidate your understanding of logic gates or binary, you are going to code an **app** that will teach students your age or slightly younger about logic gates or the binary system. The app must be programmed in Scratch and it can take the form of a game, an animation, a quiz or a combination of all three. You only have about an hour to code your app so don't be over ambitious!

Planning an app (Part 1)

Answer the questions below to plan your app.

1 What topic will your app be about, logic gates or the binary number system?

2 What type of app will you create, a game, an animation, a quiz or a combination of all three?

3 How will your app work? Describe what it will do.

Planning an app (Part 2)

You have decided what your app is about, what it will do and how it will work. Now, before you begin coding, you need to write an algorithm for your app.

For example, an algorithm for a game in which the user has to click on the binary number equivalent to the denary number the cat calls out might start off like this:

▶ The user clicks on the green flag to start the game.

▶ The score variable is set to 0.

▶ Five binary numbers are displayed on screen.

▶ The cat calls out a denary number.

▶ The user clicks on a binary number.

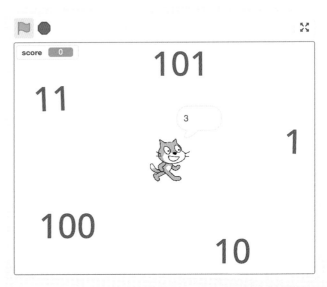

You can write your algorithm using text or as a flow diagram.

Coding your app

Go to https://scratch.mit.edu/, select 'Create' and code the app you have planned in Scratch. Remember to save your app to your computer at the end of the lesson, by selecting 'File' and choosing 'Save to your computer'.

Checking in

❶ The CPU of a computer is built from millions of electrical circuits containing what?

❷ Study the diagram. What will the output be?

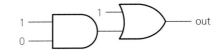

❸ What is base 2 number 101010 in base 10?

→ 4 Testing and reviewing an app

An error in a computer program is known as a **bug** and **debugging** is the activity of finding and correcting errors. Once you have fixed the bugs in a program, you should test it to make sure it does exactly what you want it to do.

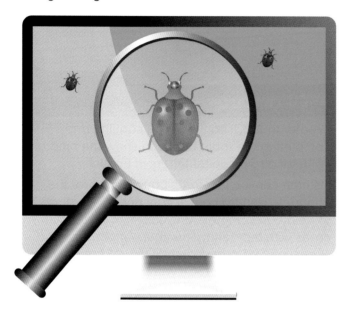

Debugging and testing

Debug and test your app. Consider the following questions when you are testing your app.

▶ Do you provide instructions for the user and do you give them enough time to read the instructions?

▶ Is the game play correctly sequenced? Do things happen in the right order?

▶ If you planned a quiz app with five questions, does your app ask the user five questions?

▶ Does the app increment the user's score correctly?

Peer review

Look at two other students' apps and give them feedback. Use the questions below to structure your feedback.

▶ What type of app is it?

▶ Which topic does it teach?

▶ How well is the app suited to the intended audience?

▶ Are there clear instructions to explain how to use the app?

▶ What are the most successful features of the app?

▶ What could be done to improve the app?

▶ Give the app a score out of 10 (with 10 indicating that it completely fulfilled the design brief and 1 indicating that it did not fulfill the design brief at all).

Evaluation

Return to your computer and look at the feedback your peers have given you. Reflect on your app in light of the feedback and answer the following questions in as much detail as you can.

▶ What do you like about your app? What do you not want to change?

▶ What would you improve about your app if you had more time to work on it?

Checking in

Complete the truth table for the AND gate by giving the correct binary value for a, b, c and d.

A	B	Out
a	1	1
1	0	b
0	c	0
0	0	d

➡ 5 Representing text

All the processing that takes place inside a computer is done using binary code, using 1s and 0s.

When you press a key on the keyboard, it uses a keyboard map to identify the character and return a binary code to the CPU. The standard English alphabet characters, numbers and symbols are represented using seven bits. For example, H can be represented by 1001000. Seven-bit binary code can be tricky for humans to work with, so we convert the binary numbers to denary. In this case, H can be represented by the denary number 72.

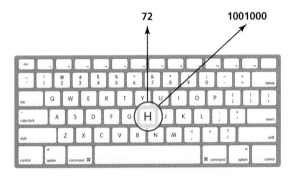

The American Standard Code for Information Interchange (**ASCII**) was invented to standardise the denary numbers assigned to each character on a keyboard. Standardisation is essential because we cannot assign the same denary number and binary string to two different characters if applications are to work on a range of different devices and on a global scale.

Here are some characters and their ASCII denary values:

space	32
!	33
"	34
#	35
$	36
%	37

@	64
A	65
B	66
C	67
D	68
E	69

'	96
a	97
b	98
c	99
d	100
e	101

The denary number we humans use to define a character is the equivalent of the 7-bit binary number the computer uses. So, 1000001 is the equivalent to 65 in denary, which we use to refer to the character A. Computers work with groups of 8 bits, so an additional 0 is added to the left of the binary number to make it a byte:

Letter	ASCII denary value	Binary value
A	65	01000001

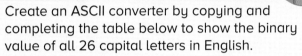

ASCII converter

Create an ASCII converter by copying and completing the table below to show the binary value of all 26 capital letters in English.

Use the conversion cards you created for the 'Binary to denary conversion' activity on page 128 to help you complete this activity. Lay out the cards with the denary numbers uppermost and in descending order. Identify the denary numbers that add up to the ASCII value you are converting and turn the rest of the cards over, revealing the binary value. For example, 64 + 1 = 65.

0	1_{64}	0	0	0	0	0	1_1

Character	ASCII denary value	Binary value (as a byte)
A	65	01000001
B	66	01000010
C	67	

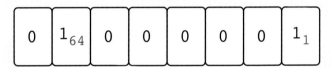

Processing a character like a computer

Use the ASCII converter you created to write a short message of one or two words and convert it to a series of bytes.

Swap your message with a partner and convert your partner's message from a series of bytes into text.

Hexadecimal

Computers work in binary, so programmers often have to work with binary numbers, such as 11011100 and 11011000.

These numbers can be very difficult to recognise and remember and mean it is easy to make errors when using them.

However, these two binary numbers can be represented in hexadecimal as DC and D8.

Hexadecimal is used by programmers because:

▶ hexadecimal numbers are easier to recognise and remember than binary numbers

▶ they make fewer mistakes working with hexadecimal numbers than they do working with binary numbers

▶ it is easy to convert hexadecimal numbers to and from binary.

Because hexadecimal is base 16, we need 16 symbols to represent the digits. We use 0 to 9, as in the decimal system, but add A to F to represent the values 10–15.

In hexadecimal each digit represents four bits (half a byte) and is known as a nibble.

Denary (base 10)	Binary (base 2)	Hexadecimal (base 16)
0	0000	0
1	0001	1
2	0010	2
3	0011	3
4	0100	4
5	0101	5
6	0110	6
7	0111	7
8	1000	8
9	1001	9
10	1010	A
11	1011	B
12	1100	C
13	1101	D
14	1110	E
15	1111	F

The following the binary code will process the characters THIS CODE HAS BEEN CONVERTED:

01010100 01101000 01101001 01110011 00100000 01100011 01101111 01100100 01100101 00100000 01101000 01100001 01110011 00100000 01100010 01100101 01100101 01101110 00100000 01100011 01101111 01101110 01110110 01100101 01110010 01110100 01100101 01100101

The first letter in the binary code above is 01010100. This is divided into two nibbles: 0101 and 0100. The first nibble is converted to hexadecimal 5 and the second nibble to the hexadecimal 4, giving the hexadecimal value 54.

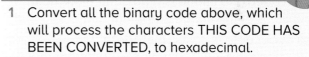

Hexadecimal

1 Convert all the binary code above, which will process the characters THIS CODE HAS BEEN CONVERTED, to hexadecimal.

2 What are the advantages of hexadecimal over binary code?

Unicode

ASCII can only represent 256 characters. This is because there are only 256 different ways 8 bits can be arranged into a byte.

This is adequate to represent characters when writing in English, but it is not adequate to represent all the characters in all the languages in the world.

This is why **Unicode** was developed. Each character is represented by 4 bytes, which means Unicode supports roughly 1,000,000 different characters.

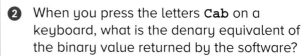

Checking in

1 What must data be converted to so that it can be processed by a digital device?

2 When you press the letters **Cab** on a keyboard, what is the denary equivalent of the binary value returned by the software?

3 Convert the character @ to binary.

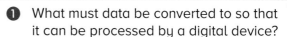

➡ 6 Representing images

Just like text, photographs are stored in the computer's memory and processed by the CPU as binary code.

As you know, bitmap graphics store an image as a matrix of pixels. When we can see the pixels in an image, it is **pixelated**. The colour of every pixel is stored, and every different colour in the picture has its own unique binary code.

The quality of a bitmap image depends on its resolution. This is the number of pixels the image contains. The size of a bitmap graphic file depends on the resolution of the image, the size of the image and how many unique colours it contains. Bigger images contain more pixels and images that contain lots of different colours require more bits to store each colour.

Converting text, images and sound into binary, so they can be processed by a computer, is known as **data representation**.

Extra data must accompany the binary string representing an image so that, when it is decoded, the image is represented correctly. This extra data specifies the dimensions of the image (the width and height of the image).

Data about data is called **metadata**. The metadata for the dimensions of the tick sprite image is 4 × 4. This tells the computer that the image is 4 pixels wide and 4 pixels high.

➡ Here is a bitmap image. If you look at the 'Details' in the image's 'Properties', it shows you the metadata, including data such as file type and size, dimensions, the name of the photographer, the date and time it was taken and copyright

Writing an algorithm to encode an image

Imagine that you are coding a video game and you want to use this tick sprite:

For the game console to store, process and display the tick sprite image, it must be turned into a string of binary code.

1 Write an algorithm for turning the image into a string of binary code.

2 Use your algorithm to write a string of binary code to represent the image.

Encoding and decoding a colour image

1 Look at the image and answer the questions below.

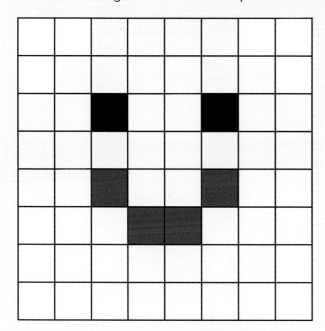

This table gives you the pairs of bits that have been used to encode each of the coloured pixels found in the image.

Colour	Binary code
white	00
black	01
red	10
yellow	11

   a What are the dimensions of the image in pixels?

   b How many pixels make up the image?

   c How many colours are there in the image?

   d How many bits are used to code each pixel?

2 Use an 8 × 8 grid to encode the image, placing the pairs of bits representing each pixel in the corresponding squares in the grid.

3 Using only four colours – white, black, red and yellow – use a spare sheet of paper to design a sprite with the dimensions 8 × 8 pixels.

4 Encode your sprite using in an 8 x 8 grid.

5 When you have finished encoding your sprite, ask your partner to decode and recreate your sprite using another 8 × 8 grid.

What do you know?

1 Study the two simple electrical circuits.

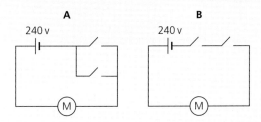

a Which circuit – A, B or neither – behaves like an OR gate?

b Which circuit – A, B or neither – behaves like a NOT gate?

c Which circuit – A, B or neither – behaves like an AND gate?

d Which circuit – A, B or neither – could be used in the control system for a shop door?

2 Study the logic gate symbols.

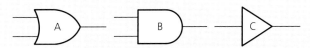

a Which symbol – A, B or C – is used to represent an AND gate?

b Which symbol – A, B or C – is used to represent a NOT gate?

c Which symbol – A, B or C – is used to represent an OR gate?

3 Study the inputs to the logic gate symbols.

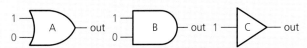

a What is the output from logic gate A?

b What is the output from logic gate B?

c What is the output from logic gate C?

4 Complete the truth tables by giving the correct binary values for A–J.

AND gate		
A	B	Out
1	1	A
0	1	B
1	0	C
0	0	D

OR gate		
A	B	Out
1	1	E
0	1	F
1	0	G
0	0	H

NOT gate	
In	Out
1	I
0	J

5 What is the output from this combination of logic gates?

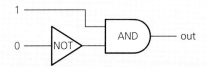

6 What base are denary numbers?

7 What base are binary numbers?

8 Convert the binary number 100 to a denary number.

9 Convert the binary number 10 to a denary number.

10 Convert the binary number 101 to a denary number.

11 Convert the binary number 1011 to a denary number.

12 Convert the denary number 10 to a binary number.

13 Convert the denary number 21 to a binary number.

14 What do the letters ASCII stand for?

15 What denary value is given to 'A' by ASCII?

16 What is the byte of data used to represent the letter 'c' in ASCII? ASCII gives the letter 'c' the denary value 99.

17 Look at these three black and white images. They have been enlarged to make their individual pixels visible.

A

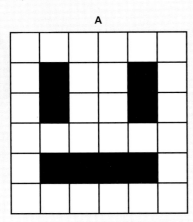

B

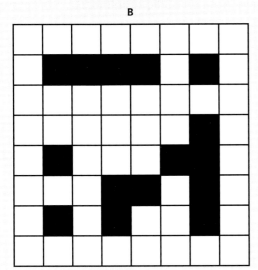

C

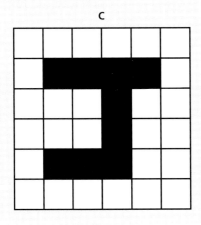

a What term is short for 'picture element'?

b What term to we use to describe an image that has been enlarged so its pixels are visible?

c Which image – A, B or C – has nine black pixels?

d Which image has the following metadata: dimension 8 × 8?

e Which image, with dimension 6 × 6, is represented by the following binary string: 000000010010010010000000001110000000?

18 Study the binary grid for an image of a smiley face.

00	00	11	11	11	11	00	00
00	11	11	11	11	11	11	00
11	11	01	11	11	01	11	11
11	11	11	11	11	11	11	11
11	11	10	11	11	10	11	11
11	11	11	10	10	11	11	11
00	11	11	11	11	11	11	00
00	00	11	11	11	11	00	00

Two bits are used to represented each coloured pixel in the image:

Colour	Binary code
white	00
green	01
blue	10
red	11

a What colour are the eyes?

b What colour is the mouth?

Knowing how to create and edit your own sound and video content opens up a whole world of creativity. In this chapter, you will learn how to use sound-editing software, including audio effects, to create soundtracks, and how to use video editing software to combine audio and video to create a video advert. After you have completed this chapter, you will have the tools to create your own audio and video content to share with friends.

➡ 1 Introduction to sound editing and Audacity®

Separate sounds

How many separate sounds can you hear when you listen to a radio advert? You should be able to hear a loud voiceover, but can you also hear other quieter sounds like cheering or the noise of a drill? Lots of different sounds make up one audio track, one advert or one song. This is why audio is often referred to as multi-track.

A DAW (a Digital Audio Workstation) is used to record and edit different sounds together to make an audio track. You will be learning how to use **Audacity**, which is free and can be downloaded from www.audacityteam.org, but other DAWs work in a similar way.

To ensure all the sounds come together to form something you want to listen to, sound designers work from an audio **timeline**. Here is an example:

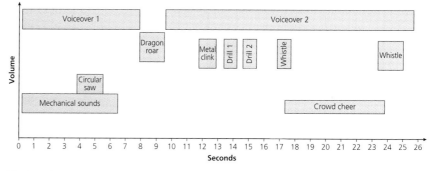

Notice how the audio timeline moves chronologically from left to right and that louder sounds are at the top and quieter sounds are at the bottom. And notice how specific sounds are played at specific times.

Importing audio tracks

When you open Audacity, you are presented with a blank template.

Click on 'File', 'Import' and 'Audio' to **import** sounds into Audacity. Then click on 'View', 'Track size' and 'Fit to Height' to resize the sounds so you can see them all on your screen at the same time.

Importing audio tracks

You will be creating a radio advert based on this timeline:

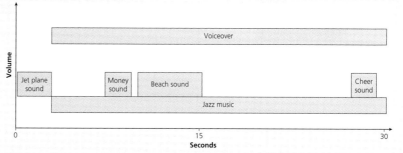

Begin by importing 'Sounds 1.1', which contains the sounds you need to create your advert, into Audacity.

Arranging the composition

Now that you have imported your audio tracks, you can start to **arrange** them according to the audio timeline. Use the 'Time Shift Tool' to move the audio files around. And press and hold 'CTRL' (or 'CMD' if you are using a Mac) on your keyboard and use the mouse to expand or contract the tracks.

If you want to trim one of the audio tracks, you can use the 'Selection Tool' to select the audio you want to delete and then press the 'Delete' key on your keyboard.

Arranging the composition and trimming

Arrange the audio tracks you imported according to the audio timeline and trim them if necessary.

Recording the voiceover

Now that your audio tracks are roughly in the right place, you need to use the script to record a **voiceover**.

To record a voiceover, click on 'Tracks', 'Add New' and 'Stereo Track'. Make sure your microphone is positioned properly and click the 'Record' button. When you have finished click the 'Stop' button. It's a good idea to mute all the other tracks when you are recording so you can concentrate on reading the script.

Use the 'Selection Tool' to trim your voiceover track and the 'Time Shift Tool' to move it into the right place.

Recording the voiceover

Record your voiceover using the following script:

Welcome to Hachette Travel. [Pause]

Right now, we're offering half price travel for anyone who buys tickets with us before July. [Pause]

Just imagine … [Pause]

You could be sat back on a sunny beach, paying half the price of the person sat on the sun lounger next to you. [Pause]

For more information, visit us in-store.

Adjusting the levels

You may have noticed that, when you press 'Play', all the audio tracks are at the same volume. You can adjust the volume, or **level**, of each track using the fader on each of the tracks.

Adjusting the levels

Change the volume of each track, so that levels match the audio timeline. It is important to ensure the voiceover is clear and easy to hear because the voiceover is the most important part of the advert.

Checking in

True or false?

1. An audio track is bigger on a timeline if it is louder.
2. An audio track on the far left of a timeline will appear later in the track.
3. A timeline shows how long the final audio track will last.

➡ 2 Audio effects

An **audio effect** is something that is used to enhance or process audio, to make it sound different. There are four main audio effects: fade in/fade out, reverb, compression and envelope.

Fade in/fade out

A **fade in** is added to the beginning of a track and a **fade out** is added to the end of a track so that it starts and stops playing smoothly, without pops or crackles. Some tracks, such as background music, might have a longer fade in and fade out than other tracks, such as a voiceover. Voiceovers need to be heard clearly almost straight away, but background music can be overpowering if it is too loud at the beginning.

You add a fade in and a fade out in Audacity by selecting the part of the track you want to apply it to and then clicking on 'Effect' and 'Fade in' or 'Effect' and 'Fade out'. Zooming in will make it easier to control the length of time over which the fade occurs.

Reverb

Reverb is used to make a sound feel like it is in a different space. For example, you can record a voiceover into a microphone in your classroom and then use reverb to make it sound like it was recorded in a tunnel!

You can add reverb in Audacity by selecting the part of the track you want to apply reverb to and then clicking on 'Effect' and 'Reverb …'. Reverb can get quite complicated, but you can test it out by moving the sliders on the effect and 'previewing' the output before applying it.

Applying fade in and fade out

You have created a radio advert. Now you will apply audio effects to the audio tracks in Audacity to make the advert sound more professional.

Experiment with fade in and fade out and then apply a fade in and a fade out to all the tracks that make up your advert.

Applying reverb

Experiment with reverb and then apply reverb to the voiceover and crowd cheer tracks in your advert. Remember that it is particularly important that you can hear what the voiceover is saying, so don't go crazy with the reverb!

Compression

Compression is a tool used to make sure that no parts of a sound are too quiet or too loud. It makes the quiet sounds slightly louder and the loud sounds slightly quieter.

You can add compression in Audacity by selecting the part of the track you want to apply compression to and then clicking on 'Effect' and 'Compressor ...'. Like reverb, compression can get quite complicated, but you can test it out by moving the sliders on the effect and 'previewing' the output before applying it.

Applying compression

Experiment with compression and then apply compression to the voiceover and jet plane tracks in your advert.

Envelope

Envelope allows you to make a track quieter and louder at certain points. For example, you might want the voiceover to be louder when the background music is playing and quieter when it is not, and you can use envelope to do this.

In Audacity, click on the 'Envelope Tool' and then use your cursor to increase or decrease the volume.

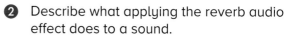

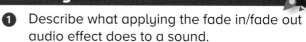

Applying envelope

Experiment with envelope and then apply envelope to the voiceover and beach tracks in your advert.

Checking in

1. Describe what applying the fade in/fade out audio effect does to a sound.
2. Describe what applying the reverb audio effect does to a sound.
3. Describe what applying the envelope audio effect does to a sound.

→ 3 Planning a video advert

Combining sounds and visuals

An advert is a short video designed to persuade you to do something, like buy a bar of chocolate or give up smoking. The sounds and visuals in an advert are carefully designed with the purpose of the advert in mind. For example, fast sounds combined with fast-moving visuals create tension and slower sounds combined with slower visuals create calm.

Like sound designers, people creating videos use timelines to ensure all the sounds and visuals come together to form something you want to watch.

Planning a video advert (Part one)

Hachette Travel organises holidays for families abroad, including flights. It would like to sell more holiday packages and it thinks a video advert will help it get more customers. It plans to show the advert online.

The marketing department of Hachette Travel has contacted you and asked you to create the advert. It will supply you with audio and video files, as well as a voiceover script, and you need to create the timeline for the advert and edit together the files provided. The advert must:

▶ be no longer than 30 seconds

▶ include a voiceover

▶ include background music

▶ include at least three audio effects

▶ include at least five different video clips

▶ include Hachette Travel's logo, which should be on screen throughout

▶ include at least three visual effects.

Listen to the audio files and look at the video files and voiceover script that you have been provided with by Hachette Travel; these are contained in 'Sounds and visuals 3.2'. You can download background music of your choice from www.bensound.com. Decide which sounds and images to use in your advert and create a timeline using a copy of the template below.

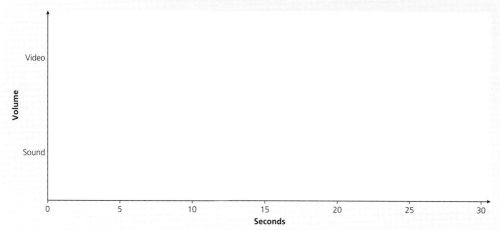

Planning a video advert (Part two)

You know how to add the following audio effects when designing sound:

▶ fade in/fade out

▶ reverb

▶ compression

▶ envelope

Annotate your timeline to include at least three audio effects. Do this by adding a text box containing the name of each audio effect and why you want to use it next to the sound you want to apply it to.

Checking in

True or false?

1. It is important to consider sounds when planning a video.
2. Having a detailed plan means you are able to produce a video more quickly.
3. Lagging is an audio effect that can be added to a sound.

➡ 4 Creating a soundtrack for a video advert

A **soundtrack** is the collection of sounds that accompany the visuals in a video.

Soundtrack

Record the voiceover and use your sound-editing skills to create the soundtrack for your video advert using Audacity.

Use your timeline to help you create your soundtrack. You can depart from your plan, but if you do something different make sure you save a new version of your timeline and change your timeline to match.

Exporting your soundtrack

When you have created your soundtrack, you need to **export** it so that you can import it into video editing software next lesson.

There are a number of different options for exporting sound files in Audacity, but you should click 'File', Export, 'Export as WAV' because most video editing software works well with WAV files and they are good quality.

Export your soundtrack

Now it is time to export your soundtrack.

Peer-assessing the soundtracks

Swap computers or share your work with somebody and listen carefully to their soundtrack.

▶ Is it 30 seconds or shorter?

▶ Does it include a voiceover?

▶ Does it include background music?

▶ Does it include at least three audio effects?

Give your partner one point for each success criteria they meet and tell them which success criteria they have yet to meet.

Checking in

State whether each image is a fade in or a fade out.

1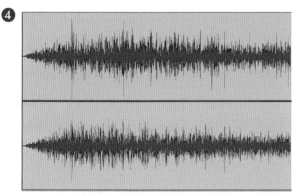

5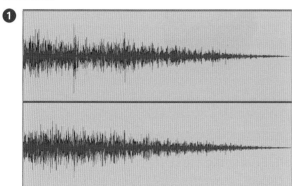

2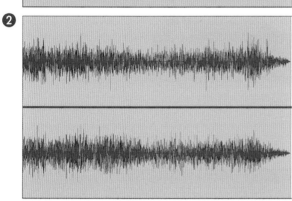

6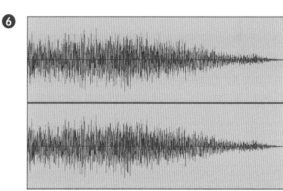

3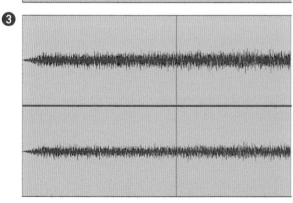

7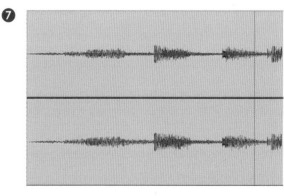

4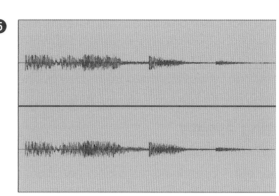

8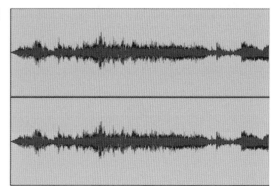

➡ 5 Introduction to video editing and OpenShot

Video-editing software

Just as a soundtrack is created by editing different sounds together, a video is made by editing different visuals together with the soundtrack using video editing software.

You will be learning how to use **OpenShot™ Video Editor**, which is free and can be downloaded from www.openshot.org, but other video editors work in a similar way.

Importing assets

When you open OpenShot, you are presented with a blank template.

Open the folder containing the assets you would like to import. Select the files and drag them into the 'Project Files' window.

Importing assets

Look at your timeline and import the assets you have decided to use in your advert into OpenShot. Your assets will consist of the video clips you have chosen to use, the soundtrack you have made and Hachette Travel's logo.

Arranging and editing assets

In OpenShot, you can drag assets to the stage and arrange them and trim them according to your timeline. The stage is layered, with a higher track playing over the tracks below it, so if the logo is placed above a video clip, it plays over the top of the video clip, but, if the logo is placed below a video clip, you can't see it because the video is layered over the top of it.

Click on the right-hand side or the left-hand side of an asset and drag to adjust how long it plays for.

To cut a video clip, position the playhead in the place you want to cut the clip, right-click on the clip and select 'Slice' and 'Keep Both Sides', 'Keep Left Side' or 'Keep Right Side'.

You can position the logo where you want it on screen by right-clicking on the logo, selecting 'Layout' and choosing one of the options available.

Press the spacebar to play the video. It will play from wherever the playhead is positioned and you can move the playhead by clicking and dragging it or by clicking in the timeline. If the outline of a video is red, it is still processing and may not play back until it has processed and the outline has turned blue.

Arranging and editing assets

Arrange the soundtrack, video clips and logo according to your timeline. Then use your timeline to help you edit your video advert.

You can depart from your plan, but if you do something different make sure you save a new version of your timeline and change your timeline to match.

Checking in

True or false? Video-editing software lets you:

1. combine sound, images and video clips.
2. import text files and record voiceovers.
3. layer assets so that an image can be displayed over a video.

Peer-assessing the video adverts

Swap computers or share your work with somebody and watch their video advert carefully.

▶ Is it 30 seconds or shorter?

▶ Does it include at least five different video clips?

▶ Does it feature Hachette Travel's logo on screen throughout?

Give your partner one point for each success criteria they meet and tell them which success criteria they have yet to meet.

➡ 6 Visual effects

A **visual effect** is something that is used to enhance or process video, to make it look different. Visual effects include transitions, other visual effects such as the wave effect and titles.

Transitions

You can apply **transitions** between video clips to add some excitement when the video changes from one scene to the next and smooth the passage between clips.

In OpenShot, click on the 'Transitions' tab, choose a transition, drag it to the appropriate track and trim it.

Applying transitions

Experiment with different transitions and then apply at least one transition to your video advert for Hachette Travel. Remember to update your timeline to show the transitions added.

Other visual effects

You can apply other visual effects, such as the wave effect, to your video advert to make it more interesting and exciting to watch.

In OpenShot, click on the 'Effects' tab, choose an effect and drag it to the appropriate track. Then click on it and adjust the values of each property of the effect.

Applying other visual effects

Experiment with different visual effects and then apply at least one to your video advert. Remember to update your timeline to show the visual effects added.

Titles

You can add **titles** (extra words) to your video advert to tell the viewer something important.

In OpenShot, click on 'Title' in the menu bar, then 'Title' and choose a template. Type in the text and adjust the font, text colour and background colour and click 'Save'. Finally, drag the title to a new track and trim it according to your timeline.

Adding titles

Do you want to add titles to your video advert? Perhaps you could emphasise half-price travel until the end of July by displaying '50% off' at the appropriate time. Remember to update your timeline to show any titles added.

Exporting your video

When you have finished your video advert, you need to export it in a high-quality video format so you can deliver it to Hachette Travel.

In OpenShot, click on 'File' in the menu bar, 'Export Project' and 'Export Video'. Type in the file name and choose where you want the exported video to save to in the 'Folder Path:' box. Then make sure the following options are selected and click 'Export Video'.

Export your video advert

Now it is time to export your video advert.

Checking in

1. What is the purpose of visual effects?
2. Describe what applying a transition does to a video clip.
3. Describe what applying titles does to a video clip.

Websites are an integral part of modern life and the most important part of the internet. Almost all businesses have a website, as do many individuals and organisations. Websites are used to sell products and services, raise awareness about issues and provide access to entertainment and gaming.

While it is possible to use drag-and-drop-style software and templates to create a website, it is far more powerful to create your own by writing the source code yourself. This module looks at how HTML and CSS interact to define and display a website, together with the principles of good website design.

➡ 1 Basic styling using CSS

Web pages

A web page is effectively a document that can be viewed using a web browser. As well as text and images, it can contain sound, videos and links to other web pages and websites.

Here is an HTML file that contains details of the structure and content of a web page:

```html
<!DOCTYPE html>
<html>
  <head>
    <title>Designing websites Lesson 1</title>
    <link rel="stylesheet" href="lesson1_style.css">
  </head>
  <body>
    <h1>This is the main heading</h1>
    <p>This is a paragraph.</p>
    <p>This is another paragraph.</p>
    <p>
      "Lorem ipsum, or Lipsum, is dummy text used to fill a space without actually
      saying anything meaningful. It is useful when setting up the layout and styling
      for a web page to give an idea of what the finished page will look like"
    </p>
    <p>
      "Lorem ipsum dolor sit amet, consectetur adipiscing elit. Vivasmus vel urna ut
      nulla lobortis egestas quis eu eros. Nullam ullamcorper orci a pharetra
      venenatis. Donec at consequat eros, vitae varius erat. In eget elit sem. Mauris
      euismod sollicitudin nulla, in luctus sapien molestie in. Pelentesque rutrum
      risus nulla, eget consequat ipsum facilisis ac. Vivamus in cursus sapien. Fusce
      ante nisl, tempor eu tellus sed, dictum ultricies nibh. Suspendisse sem nulla,
      lobortis vitae lobortis eu, ultrices volutpat dolor."
    </p>
  </body>
</html>
```

Here is a CSS file that defines the styling to be used when the web page is displayed:

```css
body {
    background-color: Snow;
}
h1 {
    color: MidnightBlue;
    font-family: "Times New Roman";
}
p {
    color: Indigo;
    font-family: Arial;
    font-size: 16px;
}
```

And here is the web page displayed by the code:

This is the main heading

This is a paragraph.

This is another paragraph.

Lorem ipsum, or Lipsum, is dummy text used to fill a space without actually saying anything meaningful. It is useful when setting up the layout and styling for a web page to give an idea of what the finished page will look like

Lorem ipsum dolor sit amet, consectetur adipiscing elit. Vivasmus vel urna ut nulla lobortis egestas quis eu eros. Nullam ullamcorper orci a pharetra venenatis. Donec at consequat eros, vitae varius erat. In eget elit sem. Mauris euismod sollicitudin nulla, in luctus sapien molestie in. Pelentesque rutrum risus nulla, eget consequat ipsum facilisis ac. Vivamus in cursus sapien. Fusce ante nisl, tempor eu tellus sed, dictum ultricies nibh. Suspendisse sem nulla, lobortis vitae lobortis eu, ultrices volutpat dolor.

HTML

Hyper Text Markup Language (**HTML**) is used to describe the structure of a web page. Each page of a website is written as a separate .html document and this consists of a series of elements. These elements use **tags** to label their content as a heading, a paragraph, an image or a hyperlink. Browsers such as Chrome™, Microsoft Edge™, Safari® and Firefox™, use these tags to determine how content should be displayed.

An HTML tag is a word or letter surrounded by angle brackets: < and >. Most elements have an opening tag and a closing tag, with the content placed between the two tags. The closing tag has a forward slash / in front of the word or letter. For example, **<p>** and **</p>**.

CSS

CSS stands for Cascading Style Sheet. **CSS properties** are used to format the layout of a web page, including:

- the colour of the text
- the size of the text
- the font used
- the background colours and images
- how elements are positioned
- the spacing between elements.

An **external style sheet** is a single document, saved with a .css extension, that sets out the styling to be used for all the main elements on every page of a website. This allows you to change the styling of an entire website by editing just one file. Each HTML page includes a link to the external style sheet that it needs to use, for example: **<link rel="stylesheet" href="styles.css">**.

A CSS style rule consists of a **selector** and a **declaration** block. The selector indicates which HTML element the styling refers to. The declaration includes the CSS **property name** and a value, separated by a colon.

It is possible to have more than one declaration in a block, in which case each declaration is separated using a semicolon. It is usual to put each declaration on a separate line so that it is easy to see which properties have been styled. The declaration block is surrounded by curly brackets.

```
body {
    background-color: Snow;
}
h1 {
    color: MidnightBlue;
    font-family: "Times New
Roman";
}
p {
    color: Indigo;
    font-family: Arial;
    font-size: 16px;
}
```

Selector • Declaration block • Property name • Value

➡ A style sheet with styling for several different aspects of a web page. Styling added to the **body** selector will be applied to the whole web page. The main heading is defined using the **h1** selector, and paragraphs are defined using the **p** selector

The most common CCS properties are as follows:

- **color** (note the American spelling) sets the colour of the text. The easiest way to specify a colour is to use one of the 140 standard colour names and a full list can be found online.

- **background-color** sets the background colour. Again, the colour name can be used for the value.

- **font-family** sets the font. The value is the name of the font that you want to use, such as Arial or Courier New. If the name of the font family has more than one word then it must be put in quotation marks, for example, **"Times New Roman"**.

- HTML tags have predefined font sizes for six heading levels (**h1** to **h6**) and for the normal text in paragraphs. To change the size of the font we use the property **font-size** and the value is, for example, **16px**.

CSS classes

So far, we have applied the same styling to all elements on a web page that share the same tag. For example, all of the paragraphs defined by **<p>** have had the same styling.

However, it is possible to apply different styling to specific HTML elements using the **CSS class** selector. The styling is defined in the style sheet with a full stop followed by your chosen class name; for example, the following code changes the text colour of all elements that have been assigned the class **black-text** to black.

```
.black-text {
    color: Black;
}
```

The class is assigned in the HTML document by adding **class=** followed by the class name inside quotation marks, for example:

```
<p class="black-text">
```

A class can be applied to as many elements in an HTML document as required. It is also possible to assign more than one class to an HTML element, by placing additional class names inside the quotation marks separated by spaces.

Editing HTML and CSS files

All the HTML files, the CSS file and any images for a website that you are creating need to be saved to the same folder on your computer. To edit these files, you will need to use a text editor such as Notepad++ (Windows) or Brackets (MacOS). Open the editor and then click on 'File', then 'Open' to select the file you wish to edit.

To view the web page, double click on the HTML file, or right-click on it and choose 'Open with' and select your browser.

Challenge exercise

Recreate the following web page:

> ## Challenge exercise
>
> The page has a background colour of "Whitesmoke" and uses the font "Courier New"
>
> The main heading has a background colour of "LightGrey". It uses the font "Arial" and the text colour is "Navy".
>
> The paragraph have a font-size of 16px and the text colour is "SlateGrey".
>
> This paragraph uses a class called "black-text" to change the text colour.

Remember to save both your .html file and your .css file regularly and open/refresh the .html file in a browser to see how the web page looks.

Checking in

❶ What is CSS used for?

❷ What is HTML used for?

❸ What is a CSS class?

→ 2 Images and lists

Embedding an image on a web page

It is very important that any images you wish to use on your web pages are saved to the same folder as the HTML and CSS files for that web page.

The `<img>` tag is used to embed an image in an HTML page and there are two attributes that must be included inside the tag:

▶ `src`: the link to the source image. Usually, this is the image's filename and extension.

▶ `alt`: alternative text that describes the image, to be used if the image cannot be displayed. It is also used by screen readers.

It is also advisable to specify the `width` and the `height` of the image.

The following code has been used to add a picture of a red flower to a web page:

```
<img src="redFlower.png" alt=
"Picture of a red flower" width=
"200" height="350">
```

Adding images

Here is a picture of a flower.

Adding images

Here is a picture of a flower.

Picture of a red flower

The web page has displayed correctly.	The browser could not locate the image because it was not stored in the correct folder. An icon and text is shown instead.

If you add code to an HTML file to embed an image but the image does not display correctly, check that you have saved the image to the correct folder and that the filename and extension of the image are exactly the same as the code in the HTML document.

Embedding an image

Create a folder called 'Designing websites' and save 'lesson2_index.html' and 'lesson2_style.css' to it.

Browse the internet for an image of a computer. Find one that you can use without infringing the creator's copyright and then save a copy to your 'Designing websites' folder by right-clicking on the image and choosing 'Save image as'.

If the image's filename is long or complicated, rename it to something that will be easier to use. Be careful not to change the file extension.

Add code to 'lesson2_index.html' to insert the image below the heading and above the first paragraph. Your code should have the following format:

```
<img src="file name" alt="description"
width="250" height="250">
```

▶ The file name in the code should match the filename of the image you have chosen.

▶ The description in the code should describe the image.

▶ The width and height will vary depending on the image chosen. If necessary, use trial and error to choose suitable values. Right-clicking on the file and looking at its properties will show you the dimensions of the original file for you to use as a guide.

Using `float` to position an element

The CSS `float` property is used to position and format content and it can be used to position an image alongside text.

Creating a class called `float-right` means that this styling can be applied to any HTML element to position it to the right of other elements:

```
.float-right {
    float: right;
}
```

It is also possible to float an element to the left of the screen or to the centre of the screen using the values **left** and **center**. Note that the American spelling of 'center' is required.

Using `clear` to prevent floating

The CSS **clear** property is used to prevent other elements from floating to the left or right of a specific paragraph element.

▶ Using the value **right** will stop elements from floating on the right-hand side.

▶ Using the value **left** will stop elements from floating on the left-hand side.

▶ Using the value **both** will stop elements from floating on both the right- and left-hand sides.

The **clear** property is commonly used after the **float** property has been used, to return the layout to normal. The value used for the **clear** property should be the same as that used for the **float** property; for example:

```
.float-clear-right {
    clear: right;
}
```

Floating an image

1 Edit 'lesson2_style.css'.
  a Create a class called **float-right** to float elements to the right.
  b Create a class called **float-clear-right** to prevent elements floating to the right.
  c Save 'lesson2_style.css'.
2 Edit 'lesson2_index.html'.
  a Add the class **float-right** to the image attributes.
  b Add the class **float-clear-right** to the final paragraph.
  c Save 'lesson2_index.html'.

Using `margin` to add space around elements

The CSS **margin** property is used to create space around elements. If you want to add the same size margin to all sides, use **margin** and one value, for example:

```
.margin {
    margin: 25px;
}
```

Use **margin-top**, **margin-right**, **margin-bottom** and **margin-left** to add a specific margin to a specific side.

Adding a margin

1 Edit 'lesson2_style.css' to create a class called **margins** that adds a margin of 25 pixels.
2 Edit 'lesson2_index.html' to add the **margins** class to the image attributes.

Lists

Lists are used to present information in an ordered way.

Unordered lists use bullet points to mark each item. They are used when the order of the items is not important. The **<ul>** tag is used to define an unordered list and each item in the list is preceded by the **<li>** tag; for example:

```
<p>Here is a list
of colours:</p>
<ul>
   <li>red</li>
   <li>blue</li>
   <li>green</li>
</ul>
```

Here is a list of colours:

- red
- blue
- green

In an **ordered list**, each item is marked by a number. They are used when the items need to be presented in a particular order. The `<ol>` tag is used to define an ordered list, and each item in the list is preceded by the `<li>` tag; for example:

```
<p>Here is
a list of
instructions:
</p>
<ol>
   <li>Get into
bed</li>
   <li>Turn off
the light</li>
   <li>Go to
sleep</li>
</ol>
```

Here is a list of instructions:

1. Get into bed
2. Turn off the light
3. Go to sleep

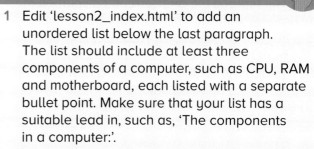

Creating lists

1 Edit 'lesson2_index.html' to add an unordered list below the last paragraph. The list should include at least three components of a computer, such as CPU, RAM and motherboard, each listed with a separate bullet point. Make sure that your list has a suitable lead in, such as, 'The components in a computer:'.

2 Below the list of computer components, add an ordered list of instructions for making a cup of tea. Make sure that your list has a suitable lead in and that the instructions are presented in the correct order.

Checking in

❶ Which tag is used to embed an image?

❷ Which two attributes have to be included inside the `<img>` tag?

❸ What else should you define when embedding an image?

3 Hyperlinks and navigation

Hyperlinks are found on nearly all web pages. They allow users to move from page to page within a website, or to move to a page on another website. The anchor tag `<a>` is used to define a hyperlink.

```
<a href="destination">Link text</a>
```

The **hyperlink reference** attribute `href` is used to identify the destination that the hyperlink will take you to; if this is an external web page, you need to give the full URL. The **link text** is what is shown on the screen. When the mouse moves over this text, the mouse pointer turns into a hand. Clicking on the link text takes you to the linked page.

Here is an example of a hyperlink included within a sentence in an HTML document:

```
<p>Here is a hyperlink to <a
href="https://www.hoddereducation.
co.uk">Hodder Education</a>.</p>
```

Adding an external hyperlink

Edit 'lesson2_index.html' to add a hyperlink to your favourite search engine. The hyperlink should be included in a suitable sentence.

The target attribute

When a user clicks on a hyperlink, the linked page will replace the one currently displayed in the browser window. This is ideal when moving from page to page within a website. However, if the hyperlink is to an external web page, it is often preferable for this to open in a new browser window. This is done by adding `target="_blank"` after the `href`; for example:

```
<a href="https://www.
hoddereducation.co.uk" target="_
blank">Hodder Education</a>
```

Opening the linked web page in a new window

Edit 'lesson2_index.html' so that the hyperlink to your favourite search engine opens in a new browser window by adding `target="_blank"` after the hyperlink reference.

Naming web pages and adding internal hyperlinks

The default name for the home or start page of a website is `index.html`. Other pages are usually given a name that is the same as, or very similar to, the title of the page. Page names must:

▶ only use lower-case letters

▶ contain no spaces, punctuation or symbols (although dashes may be used for spaces)

▶ be as short as possible, using keywords that make it clear what the page is about.

For example, `biscuit-recipes.html` or `footballers.html`.

An internal hyperlink, a link to a page on the same website, is created in exactly the same way as an external hyperlink, but the file name of the page is used instead of the full URL.

Adding an internal hyperlink

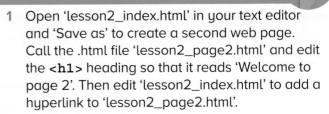

1 Open 'lesson2_index.html' in your text editor and 'Save as' to create a second web page. Call the .html file 'lesson2_page2.html' and edit the `<h1>` heading so that it reads 'Welcome to page 2'. Then edit 'lesson2_index.html' to add a hyperlink to 'lesson2_page2.html'.

2 Edit 'lesson2_page2.html' to add a hyperlink to 'lesson2_index.html'.

Using an image as a clickable hyperlink

To use an image as a hyperlink, replace the link text with the `<img>` tag containing the `src`, `alt`, `width` and `height` attributes of the image; for example:

```
<p>Click on the image to go to the
Hodder Education website.</p>
<a href="https://www.
hoddereducation.co.uk" target="_
blank"><img src="Hodder-Education-
logo.png" alt="Hodder Education
logo" width="210" height="140"></
a>
```

Using an image as a clickable hyperlink

Edit 'lesson2_index.html' to turn the image of a computer into a hyperlink to the Hodder Education home page at https://www.hoddereducation.co.uk. Users should click on the image of a computer to be taken to the Hodder Education home page. The Hodder Education home page should open in a new browser window.

Creating a navigation bar

A **navigation bar** is essentially a set of hyperlinks, but by adding formatting it is possible to make a website look much more professional. The **<nav>** tag should be used to create a series of navigation links, with the individual hyperlinks defined in the usual way using the anchor tag **<a>**; for example:

```
<nav>
    <a href="index.html">Home</a>
    <a href="page2.html">Page 2</a>
</nav>
```

Styling is applied via the style sheet to all **<a>** elements within the **<nav>** tag; for example:

display: block; creates a block around each hyperlink, with the whole block clickable, not just the text.

color, **background-color** and **text-align** are used to control the text colour, background colour and text alignment.

text-decoration: none; removes the underlining that is normally added to a hyperlink.

```
nav a {
    display: block;
    color: White;
    background-color: MidnightBlue;
    text-align: center;
    text-decoration: none;
    margin: 0px;
    padding: 16px;
    float: left;
}
```

margin: 0; ensures that the hyperlinks are displayed starting at the left-hand edge of the page.

padding: 16px; adds some padding around each hyperlink so that they are spaced appropriately. The amount of padding can be adjusted.

float: left; ensures that the hyperlinks appear next to each other.

We can also add styling to the **nav** tag itself. To make the links appear side by side in a row we use **display: flex**. This creates a flexible container that the hyperlinks are placed inside in a row. Adding the same background colour for the container as you have used for the hyperlinks ensures the navigation bar fills the width of the page; for example:

```
nav {
    display: flex;
    background-color: MidnightBlue;
}
```

To make the navigation bar look even more professional, it is possible to change the background colour and/or text colour of a hyperlink when the mouse hovers over it; for example:

```
nav a:hover {
    background-color: White;
    color: MidnightBlue;
}
```

Creating and styling a navigation bar

1 Add a navigation bar to 'lesson2_index.html' and add hyperlinks to 'lesson2_index.html' and 'lesson2_page2.html'.
2 Add a navigation bar to 'lesson2_page2.html' and add hyperlinks to 'lesson2_index.html' and 'lesson2_page2.html'.
3 Edit 'lesson2_style.css' so that the background colour:
   • of the navigation bar and the hyperlinks are the same
   • and the text colour of the navigation bar and hyperlinks change when the mouse hovers over them.

Checking in

1 Which tag is used to insert a hyperlink?
2 What does **href** stand for?
3 What is the name of the text shown on the screen that the user clicks on to move to a new page?
4 What is the effect of adding **display: block;** to a hyperlink?

➡ 4 Layout elements and web page design

HTML document structure

An HTML document sets out the structure and content of a web page, and there are certain things that it must contain. It needs to start with `<!DOCTYPE html>`, which defines it as an HTML5 document, so that the browser displays it correctly. Immediately below this is `<html>` and the document ends with `</html>`.

The rest of the document is divided into two main elements, the `<head>` and the `<body>`.

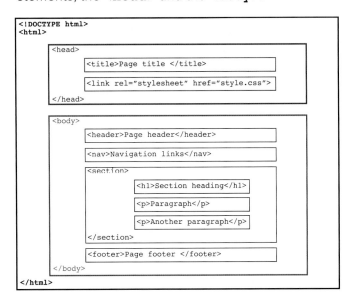

The `<head>` element contains information about the page. There are two elements that we are going to use here:

1 `<title>`: This is the title of the document that is displayed in the browser's title bar or page tab. It can only contain text and is used by search engine algorithms when listing pages in search results; for example: `<title>Favourite biscuit recipes</title>`.

2 `<link>`: This links the document to an external style sheet. The `<link>` element does not have a closing tag; for example: `<link rel="stylesheet" href="styles.css">`.

The `<body>` element contains all the content of the web page, including text, images, videos and hyperlinks to other pages and websites. Only the content inside the `<body>` element will be displayed by the browser.

HTML semantic elements

Various **semantic elements** are used within the `<body>` element. Each one is like a box and its name describes its purpose and content:

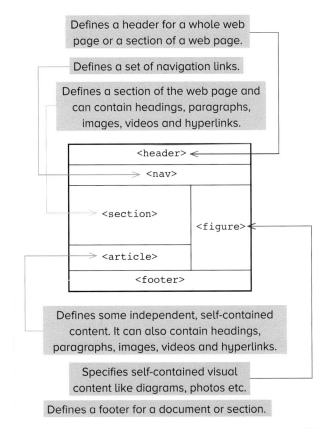

Semantic elements

Have a look at 'lesson4_index.html' to see how these semantic elements are coded.

Defining the width of an element

By default, most elements take up the full width of the screen. However, setting the width allows you to control the layout. The width can be defined as a percentage of the total width, which is better if your website will be viewed on different-sized screens, or as a set value in pixels, for example:

```
section {
    width: 70%;
}
```

```
section {
    width: 714px;
}
```

The height of an element automatically adjusts to fit its contents, so it is only necessary to define the height if a specific height needs to be maintained.

Setting the width and layout of elements

Save 'lesson4_index.html', 'lesson4_style. css' and 'birthdayCake.png' to your 'Designing websites' folder. Then edit 'lesson4_style.css' to:

1 define the width of the section element. Each small square in the diagram below represents 10% of the width of the screen

2 ensure the figure floats to the right of the screen and is cleared from the article.

				<header>					
				<nav>					
		<section>				<figure>			
		<article>							
				<footer>					

Adding borders and padding

To add a **border** to an element we use the CSS property **border**. There are three attributes of a border that can be defined:

▶ width: a value in pixels, or simply **thin**, **medium** or **thick**

▶ style: **solid** for a line

▶ colour: a colour name to complement the background colour.

For example: **border: 2px solid Black**

> A paragraph with a 2px solid black border.

Padding is used to add space between the border and the contents of the box it defines.

For example: **padding: 25px**

> A paragraph with a 2px solid black border and 25px padding.

This improves the layout and makes text inside the border easier to read.

To maintain the width and height of an element so it doesn't get wider and deeper when you add a border and padding, add the following property to the styling: **box-sizing: border-box;**.

Adding borders and padding

Edit 'lesson4_style.css' to add:

1 borders to the header and footer. The borders should be 2px wide, solid and coloured black.

2 padding of 16px to the header, footer, section and article. Remember to add **box-sizing: border-box;** to each of these elements so that the width of the padding and border are included in the total dimensions of the element.

Checking in

❶ What must the first line of an HTML document contain? Why?

➡ 5 and 6 Web page design (parts 1 and 2)

Planning your own website

You are going to develop your own website. It should be aimed at people of your own age and should tell them about your hobbies and interests. It should consist of a home page and at least two other pages.

Before starting to write the code for your website, you need to plan out the content that you intend to include.

Planning the content of a website

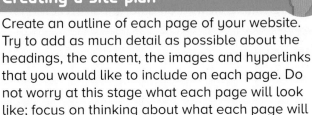

Write down all your ideas about what you could include on your website. The following questions should help to guide your thinking.

1 What activities do you enjoy doing in your spare time?

2 Why do you enjoy these activities?

3 What facts can you tell your audience about these activities that they may not already know?

4 Where could they find out more if they are interested in trying the activities themselves?

Creating a site plan

The next stage is to decide what information will go on each page of your website. This is known as the **site plan**. The home page should explain what your website is about and include general information about the topic you have chosen. Ideally, each of the other pages should have a separate theme.

For example, a website about your baking adventures might have some information about you and how you started baking on the home page and then have one page for biscuit recipes and another page for cake recipes.

Creating a site plan

Create an outline of each page of your website. Try to add as much detail as possible about the headings, the content, the images and hyperlinks that you would like to include on each page. Do not worry at this stage what each page will look like; focus on thinking about what each page will include.

Designing the page layout

Here are eight golden rules for designing the page layout of a website:

1 It is generally best to keep the same basic layout and colour scheme for every page of a website.

2 Avoid using too many different colours. Use one colour as the dominant colour and choose a second complementary colour as an accent colour.

3 Avoid using brightly coloured or 'busy' backgrounds as it can make text hard to read. Aim for a good contrast between the text and background colours.

4 Avoid using more than two different fonts. Sans-serif fonts generally look clearer on screen than serif fonts.

Serif fonts have features on the ends of strokes.

Sans-serif fonts do not have features on the ends of strokes.

5 Put the most important information in the top half of the screen.

6 Text is easiest to read when it is left-aligned, not centred.

7 Divide your content into logical bite-size blocks.

8 Avoid excessive line lengths, because long lines can be hard to read.

Designing the page layout

Use a 10 x 10 grid to design the page layout for your website.

Identify the semantic elements and include details of the styling to be used, such as the text colours, background colour, font names and font sizes, as well as the width of each `<section>` and `<article>` you have decided to include.

Setting up the style sheet

Using the page layout design you have sketched out, create some empty. html documents and a style sheet to define the layout and colours you wish to use for your website. Save all the files to a folder called 'My website'.

Remember to use classes for any colour or styling that you want to apply to specific elements.

Don't forget to save your CSS file and to open/ refresh your HTML files regularly to see what your website will look like and to make sure that your desired layout and styling is achieved.

Locating images and URLs

Locate and save the images you intend to use on your website and the URLs of any external web pages you intend to link to from your website.

Completing your website

When you have identified content for your website, planned the layout and page design and set up your style sheet, you can start adding text and images to the HTML documents.

Completing your website

Add the content to your HTML documents. Complete the home page first and then work on the other pages of your website.

Make sure that the images and words you use are suitable for your audience, and check that all of the hyperlinks work and that images are displayed correctly. Remember that all the images for your website need to be stored in the same folder as the HTML and CSS files.

Checking in

Here is screenshot of the home page of Yale School of Art's website, taken in the Autumn of 2020.

Which of the eight golden rules for designing the page layout of a website does it break and how?

Computer networks are a fundamental part of modern computer systems, and standalone systems are, now, almost unheard of. In this chapter, you will learn about some of the everyday practicalities of networking, such as understanding the pros and cons of using public Wi-Fi and mobile data when away from home, as well as more fundamental concepts such as IP addressing, DNS and packet switching. This will help you understand the digital world around you.

➡ 1 IP addressing and switches

IP addresses

Each device on a network has a unique **IP address**, just like each home has a unique address and each phone has a unique phone number, so that data can be sent to the correct place.

IP stands for 'Internet Protocol'. A **protocol** is a set of rules, and the Internet Protocol is a specific set of rules for how to transmit data from one device to another. All IP addresses must contain four numbers between 0 and 255, separated by full stops; for example:
`217.83.0.12`

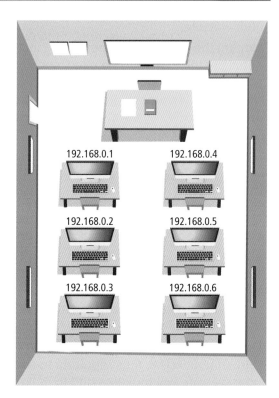

192.168.0.1   192.168.0.4

192.168.0.2   192.168.0.5

192.168.0.3   192.168.0.6

IP address format

Which of the following IP addresses are valid and which are invalid?

1 172.168.13.83.250

2 192.168.32.6

3 217.0.85.7

4 256.842.16.370

5 18.27.3.9

6 153.81.7

You can find your IP address on a Windows computer by pressing the 'Windows' key and typing **cmd** to open the Command Prompt (CMD), then typing the command **ipconfig** and pressing the 'Return' key.

Look for your IPv4 address:

```
Wireless LAN adapter Local Area Connection* 11:

   Media State . . . . . . . . . . . : Media disconnected
   Connection-specific DNS Suffix  . :

Ethernet adapter Local Area Connection:

   Connection-specific DNS Suffix  . :
   Link-local IPv6 Address . . . . . : fe80::61fb:7871:b05f:5ca4%13
   IPv4 Address. . . . . . . . . . . : 192.168.0.44
   Subnet Mask . . . . . . . . . . . : 255.255.255.0
   Default Gateway . . . . . . . . . : 192.168.0.1
```

You can find your IP address on a MacOS computer or a Linux computer by going to the 'Utilities' folder inside the 'Applications' folder and opening the Terminal application, then typing the command `ipconfig getifaddr en0` if you're on a Mac or `ifconfig` on Linux and pressing the 'Return' key.

Public and private IP addresses

The IP protocol allows for a little over 4 billion possible IP addresses. This means there are not enough IP addresses for every device in the world. Consequently, IP addresses are divided into public IP addresses and private IP addresses. **Public IP addresses** are unique and allow devices to access the internet directly. **Private IP addresses** allow devices to connect to the network, which then connects to the internet.

Private IP addresses work like an internal phone network with extension numbers. Two different networks can use the same private IP addresses, reducing the need for unique IP addresses. Private IP addresses start with one of the following numbers:

▶ 192.168.x.x (usually used for home networks)

▶ 172.x.x.x (typically used for larger networks, like an office or school network)

▶ 10.x.x.x (typically used for larger networks, like an office or school network)

Public or private?

Which of the following IP addresses are public and which are private?

1 An IP address that starts with 192.168.x.x
2 An IP address that starts with 172.x.x.x
3 An IP address that starts with 10.x.x.x
4 217.16.32.8
5 192.168.0.1
6 17.35.184.203
7 10.173.83.104
8 193.18.41.6
9 174.16.52.221
10 172.16.213.42

Switches

Devices on a network need to connect to each other. But, if they connected to each other directly, we would need *a lot* of cable. We, therefore, use a switch to connect the devices on a network.

▶ Data is sent from a device to the switch.

▶ The switch reads the destination IP address of the data and sends it to the right device.

▶ Large networks may have more than one switch so the data passes through more than one switch on its way to the destination IP address.

If the destination IP address is a public IP address, the switch passes the data to the internet connection. If the destination IP address is a private IP address, the switch passes the data directly to the device.

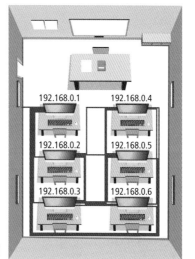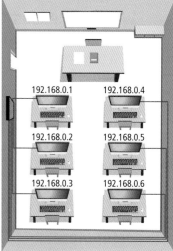

⟹ Switches enable devices in a network to connect to each other without the need for a lot of cable

Checking in

❶ Describe the format of an IP address.

❷ Explain the purpose of an IP address.

❸ Explain the purpose of a switch.

❹ How can a switch identify whether the data is intended for a computer on the network or for the internet?

➡ 2 Domain names and DNS

Web browsers

A **web browser** is the software used to view and interact with web pages.

➡ This is Hodder Education's home page viewed with the Firefox web browser. Other popular browsers include Chrome, Safari, Edge and Internet Explorer

Web addresses

You can visit a website by typing its address into the web browser's address bar. For example, you can open a web browser and type in www.hoddereducation.co.uk/computing to go straight to the Computing page on Hodder Education's website. This is the quickest and easiest way to go to a website if you know the web address; much quicker and easier than searching for the wesbite.

A web address has two parts:

www.hoddereducation.co.uk/computing

Domain name   Path

The **domain name** indicates the organisation that runs the site. Domain names end with a top level domain name, for example, .org (for an organisation), .com (for a company) and .co.uk (for a company based in the UK). Anything after the domain name is called the path. It indicates which part of the website the user is viewing.

Domain names

1 Look at the web address www.bbc.co.uk/ bitesize.

   a Which part is the domain name?

   b Which part is the path?

IP addresses

Computers use IP addresses to send data to other computers. For example, you can open a web browser and type 142.250.31.17 into the web browser's address bar and you will be taken to the Google home page.

When you type a domain name into a web browser, the web browser looks up the IP address for the website using the Domain Name System, known as **DNS**. DNS works in the same way as your contacts on your phone works: you look up the name of the person you want to call, and your phone dials their number.

DNS lookup

You can find an IP address by carrying out a DNS lookup.

Search for a DNS lookup tool online, and find the IP address for each of the following websites. Some websites will return more than one IP address as a backup in case one IP address stops working. You only need to find one valid IP address for each site.

1 microsoft.com

2 bbc.co.uk

3 boohoo.com

4 fifa.com

5 wikipedia.org

6 apple.com

7 Pick two websites that you like to visit.

DNS servers

There are DNS servers all around the world and web browsers ask them to find IP addresses. Most internet service providers run their own DNS servers.

This is what happens when a user wants to load a web page using a web address:

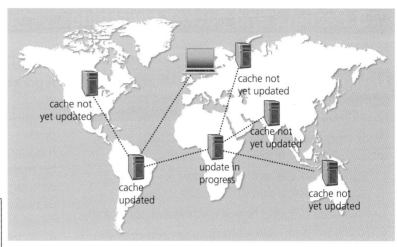

➡ The user types the web address into the web browser and the web browser sends the domain name to the DNS server.

➡ When a website changes its IP address it tells the nearest DNS server, which passes the information on to other DNS servers. It can take up to 24 hours for all DNS servers to be updated

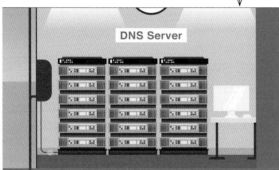

DNS Server

➡ The DNS server looks up the IP address for the website and sends it back to the web browser.

➡ The web browser contacts the IP address it has been given and asks for the web page named in the path.

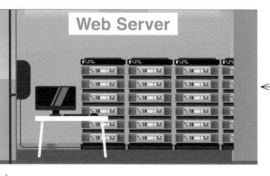

Web Server

➡ The website receives the required and sends the data for the web page back to the web browser.

➡ The web browser displays the web page for the user.

Checking in

❶ Explain why we use domain names instead of IP addresses.

❷ What does DNS stand for?

❸ Explain how a web browser uses a DNS server to communicate with a website.

→ 3 Packets and packet switching

Modelling packets and packet switching

Work as a class to complete this activity, which models packets and packet switching.

1 Take an A4 piece of paper and fill the page with a drawing of a spider.

2 Fold your drawing in half and then in half again.

3 Use the fold lines to cut or tear your drawing into four equal-sized packets.

4 Fold each packet to hide to hide its contents, number the packets from 1 to 4 on the outside and write the name of the person in your class you want to send it to on the outside of all four packets.

5 Pass the packets to the intended recipient following these rules:

- You must stay in your seat.
- You must pass the packets, not throw them.
- You can only pass *one* packet at a time.
- You must pass the packet towards the recipient.

6 When you have received all four packets, open them, put them in order and check that the message looks OK.

Packets

A **packet** is a small chunk of data. When a file or an email message is sent over a network, it is split into equal-sized packets. Just like your spider drawing, each packet is numbered and addressed to the recipient. If a whole file or a whole email message was to go missing or was damaged, then the whole thing would have to be resent. If a packet goes missing, or is damaged, then just one packet needs to be re-sent. Having the packet numbers makes it easy to identify which one is missing. This is a big advantage because it is much less work!

Each packet must have a **header** added to it which includes the packet number, the IP address of the recipient and the IP address of sender. Adding this data to every packet increases the total amount of data sent by about 3%. Despite this disadvantage, using packets is better than sending files or emails in one go.

Packet switching

Each packet travels independently, like the parts of your spider drawing. If there is a traffic jam, then different packets can take different routes. Because each packet is numbered, it doesn't matter if they arrive in the wrong order. They can be put into the correct order when they all arrive. This is called **packet switching**.

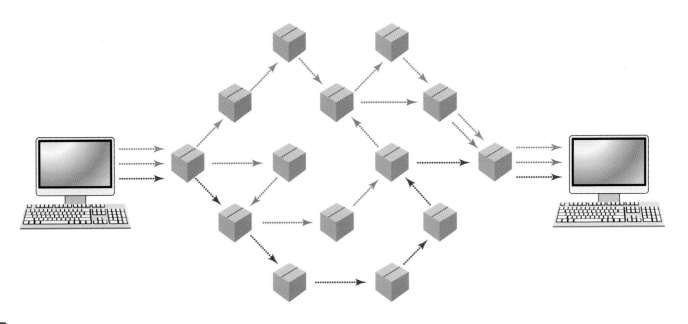

Packet switching can be demonstrated with a traceroute. A traceroute shows you the hops a packet makes as it travels across the internet.

Below is an example of a traceroute. A starred hop is a hop that failed because it timed out; the packet then tried a different route.

```
PS C:\Users\T430> tracert google.com

Tracing route to google.com [172.217.169.14]
over a maximum of 30 hops:

  1      5 ms      4 ms      5 ms   192.168.0.1
  2     15 ms     14 ms     11 ms   10.13.128.1
  3     23 ms     17 ms     13 ms   midd-core-2b-xe-833-0.network.virginmedia.net [62.252.167.69]
  4      *         *         *      Request timed out.
  5     31 ms     29 ms     29 ms   tcl5-ic-4-ae5-0.network.virginmedia.net [62.252.192.246]
  6     30 ms     28 ms     28 ms   74.125.146.216
  7     32 ms     32 ms     31 ms   209.85.249.149
  8     31 ms     32 ms     33 ms   209.85.241.95
  9     32 ms     29 ms     28 ms   lhr25s26-in-f14.1e100.net [172.217.169.14]

Trace complete.
```

Traceroute

1 Go to https://tools.keycdn.com/traceroute and type in www.hoddereducation.co.uk. Choose five locations from the locations provided and, for each one, find out how many hops the packet had to make to reach the location and how many packets timed out. Packets that timed out are indicated with three question marks. Record your findings in a table like this:

Location	Total number of hops	Number of hops that timed out

2 Go to https://geotraceroute.com/new.php? and type www.hoddereducation.co.uk in the 'Site/IP' field. Choose five locations from the locations provided in the 'Source' field and, for each one, find out how many hops the packet had to make to reach the location. Record your findings in a table like this:

Location	Total number of hops

3 Explain which website you think is more useful, and why.

Checking in

❶ Explain how a file is sent using packets.

❷ What extra data must be added to each packet?

❸ Give one advantage and one disadvantage of using packets.

❹ Explain how packet switching can help keep the internet running smoothly.

➡ 4 The internet

A global collection of computer networks

Most schools, offices and homes have a network. These networks join together to form the internet, which connects over 50 billion devices worldwide.

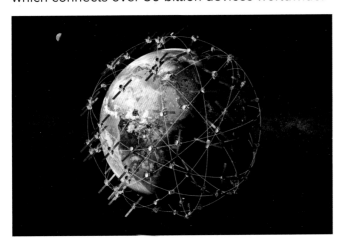

The simplest method of joining networks together is using cables. It isn't practical to run cables between all the schools, offices and homes in a country, so existing telephone cables are used.

➡ Telephone cabinets contain the cables that connect networks to the internet

Special submarine (under-sea) cables are used to connect networks across seas and oceans. These cables carry very high volumes of data at very high speed. They are very expensive and very important. If the cables are damaged, then whole countries can lose their internet connection.

Submarine cables

Hundreds of cables run under the seas and oceans, connecting countries and continents together. Go to www.submarinecablemap.com and find answers to these questions.

1 A cable in the Black Sea connects Bulgaria and which other country?

2 How many cables connect the island of Iceland to the rest of the world?

3 Which group of islands in the South Atlantic Ocean rely on just one cable to connect them to the rest of the world?

4 How many cables connect Tasmania's internet to Australia?

5 Look at the list of submarine cables on the right. Find and click on the 'ALPAL-2' cable. How long is the cable? Click on an empty part of the sea to return to the full list of cables.

6 Find and click on the 'SeaMeWe-3' cable. How long is the cable? Click on an empty part of the sea to return to the full list of cables.

7 Find the landing point for the cable that is closest to your home. Where does the cable go to?

Online services

Connecting computers over the internet means that many services are available online. An online service set up and run in one country can be accessed by anyone, anywhere in the world.

Online services

Imagine the history department at your school is putting together a time capsule, which will stay buried for 100 years. Each subject area has been asked to describe one aspect of life in the early twenty-first century and you have been asked to describe the advantages and disadvantages of each of the following five online services.

> Online service: Streaming
>
> Examples: YouTube, Netflix, Spotify

> Online service: Communication
>
> Examples: Email, Messenger, WhatsApp, Zoom, social media

> Online service: Online learning
>
> Examples: BBC Bitesize, Khan Academy, Duolingo

> Online service: Online gaming
>
> Examples: Minecraft, Animal Crossing, Rocket League, FIFA, Fortnite

> Online service: Online shopping
>
> Examples: Amazon, eBay, Etsy

Cloud computing

Cloud computing means running programs and storing files on the internet. Cloud computing involves taking things that would be traditionally done on a local computer and hosting them online so that they can be accessed from anywhere.

Cloud storage

Many business back up their files online and many people back up their photos online. Using cloud storage has many advantages. You can access your data on any device from anywhere in the world if you have an internet connection. You will not lose your data if your device is lost, stolen or damaged. There is, potentially, unlimited storage and you can easily share your data with other people.

However, there are disadvantages to using cloud storage. You can store only a relatively small amount of data for free. Monthly fees for extra storage can be expensive. Perhaps most troubling, cyber criminals can potentially access your files from a cloud server without accessing your computer or phone. They can then ransom them, delete them or steal sensitive information.

Cloud software

Many people and business now use online software, including word-processing, spreadsheet and photo and video-editing software. Using cloud software has many advantages. You do not need to install software on your computer and you never have to worry about software updates. You're less likely to be affected by malware because the data and programs are not stored on your computer. You can work on your files anywhere using any device if you have an internet connection, and you don't need a powerful computer because the processing is done by the server running in the cloud. Some of the most popular online software, including Google Docs, Google Sheets and Open Office, is free.

However, there are also disadvantages of running software in the cloud. You can only access online software if you have an internet connection. Online image editing and video-editing software is getting better, but it can be very slow and online versions of software often have fewer features than the downloadable versions. The software developer may earn money selling advertising, so you may be distracted by a lot of adverts. Additionally, the software company may have access to your work and could sell this information to someone else.

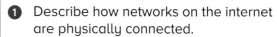

Checking in

1. Describe how networks on the internet are physically connected.
2. Describe one type of online service.
3. Explain what is meant by the term 'cloud computing'.

➡ 5 Connecting to the internet

Network connections

There are two main ways to connect to a network.

Wired: Ethernet cables	Wireless: Wi-Fi
Offices and classrooms usually use a cabled network connection.	People usually use a wireless network connection in their homes.

Wired connections are stable, reliable and fast, but you need to buy and install cabling and you cannot move around and stay connected to the network.

Wi-Fi uses radio waves transmitted to and from a wireless access point to send data through the air. Any device that is connected to the network and in range of the wireless access point can send and receive data using Wi-Fi.

You can turn a wired network into a wireless network by adding a wireless access point.

All devices in range can pick up a Wi-Fi signal. This means anyone nearby can eavesdrop on the data communicated over a Wi-Fi network. This is why you must make sure your home Wi-Fi is encrypted; encrypted data can still be intercepted, but the eavesdropper is unlikely to understand it. This is also why you must password-protect your home Wi-Fi network, so that only people with the password can gain access to the network.

Wi-Fi signals are generally less stable, less reliable and slower than wired connections. They are relatively short-range, so you may not get a good signal in all rooms without a Wi-Fi repeater boosting the signal. Thick walls and electronic devices, such as fridges and microwave ovens, can interfere with a Wi-Fi signal.

Connecting to the internet wirelessly

There are three main ways to connect to the internet wirelessly:

1 **Private Wi-Fi:** You can usually connect to private Wi-Fi at home, work or school. It is secure; access to the network is password protected and the data is almost always encrypted. Unfortunately, as soon as you leave home, work or school, you lose the connection.

2 **Public hotspot:** Public hotspots are found in public places like hotels, coffee shops and trains. Everyone can access them and access is usually free, although sometimes you must sign in by entering your details via a web page. Connection is usually slow, although some public hotspots offer a free low-speed service and a paid-for high-speed service. As with private Wi-Fi, as soon as you leave the hotel or coffee shop, you lose the connection.

Public hotspots can be dangerous. Many are unencrypted so anyone nearby can intercept your data and steal your passwords! Cyber criminals set up public hotspots, using names like 'CoffeeShopWifi', to entice you to connect to them and share your personal data. If your device is set to automatically connect to a hotspot, it will connect to any hotspot with that name, regardless of whether it's genuine or not.

3 Mobile data: This is when you use a SIM card to connect to the internet using the mobile phone network of cell towers. 2G, 3G, 4G and 5G are all types of mobile data. Mobile data is encrypted and very secure, and most people can get a good signal in most locations. However, mobile data is expensive, especially when you use more than your contracted allowance. Connection speeds can also slow considerably if lots of people use mobile data in a small area, at a festival or a sporting event. It can also be impossible to get a signal underground.

Top tips for using public hotspots safely

1. Look for the padlock to see if the hotspot is encrypted before deciding whether or not to use it.
2. Never use a public hotspot to make online purchases, do online banking or send personal information.
3. Never set your device to automatically connect to a public hotspot.

Choosing how to connect

Sheila works for a large company and she has been asked to work in a different office for a couple of days. In the following situations, suggest how Sheila should connect to the internet and why she should choose the method you suggest.

1. Sheila has just got off the train and needs directions to the office. She takes out her mobile phone and is about to turn on her mobile data when she notices there is a public hotspot called 'TrainStationFreeWifi'. It doesn't need a password to connect.

2. Sheila arrives at the office and takes out the laptop she uses for work. She notices there are several Wi-Fi networks, including 'OfficeWiFi' (which needs a password) and 'VisitorWiFi' (which doesn't need a password).

3. At lunchtime Sheila goes to a local café. While she is there, she gets a phone call telling her that there is a problem with her hotel and she will need to book somewhere else to stay. She takes her phone out to find a nearby hotel and sees there is a sign on the wall with the password for the free Wi-Fi. She could use the free Wi-Fi or she could use her mobile data.

Design a poster

Design a poster for your school to remind people of the key security concerns when using public hotspots.

Checking in

1. Describe the advantages of using a wired network connection compared to a Wi-Fi network connection.
2. Describe the advantages of using a Wi-Fi network connection compared to a wired network connection.
3. Describe the disadvantage of using mobile data compared to other ways to connect to the internet wirelessly.

6 A community guide to the internet

Frequently Asked Questions (FAQs)

Imagine your school is launching a project to help students, their parents and members of the wider community become more confident using online technology. The school has asked people what they struggle with and what they want to know more about and has collected together a list of Frequently Asked Questions (FAQs).

A community guide to the internet

Write answers to the following FAQs. Use this as an opportunity to show off everything you have learnt, but, remember, the people the answers are supposed to help are not experts, so try to explain technical terms in language that everyone can understand.

IP addresses and website addresses

Try to remember what you have learnt about IP addresses, domain names and DNS.

▶ To connect to the internet, I have been told I need to connect my laptop to a switch. What is a switch and what does it do?

▶ I have heard the term 'IP address'. What is an IP address and what does it look like?

▶ I don't think I can remember the IP addresses for all my favourite websites. Isn't there something easier I can use?

▶ How does the computer know which website to go to when I type in the website address?

Packets and packet switching

This section is probably a bit complicated for your average user, so focus on showing off what you have learnt.

▶ What are packets and what are they used for?

▶ What is a header, and what goes into it?

▶ When I send my packets off, what happens if they get stuck in a traffic jam?

Online services

'I already use some online services but are there any I'm missing out on?'

▶ Describe three online services.

Connecting to the internet

'When I got my phone, they told me to keep my Wi-Fi and mobile data turned off. When should I turn them on?'

▶ When should I use private Wi-Fi?

▶ When should I use a public hotspot?

▶ When should I use mobile data?

A community guide to the internet: self-assessment

Now you have finished writing the community guide to the internet, self-assess your work. What have you done well and what could be better? Copy and complete the following table:

Strengths	Areas for improvement

Checking in

A student has designed a card game, but they have not named four of the cards.
Can you work out the title of each card?

1

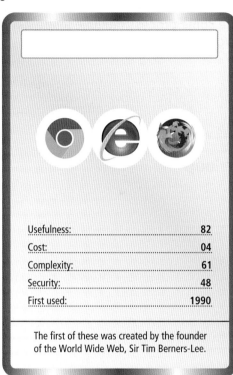

Usefulness:	82
Cost:	04
Complexity:	61
Security:	48
First used:	1990

The first of these was created by the founder of the World Wide Web, Sir Tim Berners-Lee.

2

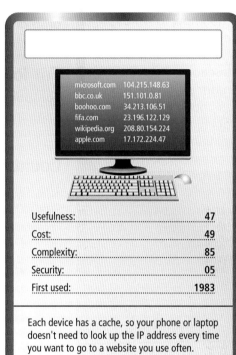

microsoft.com	104.215.148.63
bbc.co.uk	151.101.0.81
boohoo.com	34.213.106.51
fifa.com	23.196.122.129
wikipedia.org	208.80.154.224
apple.com	17.172.224.47

Usefulness:	47
Cost:	49
Complexity:	85
Security:	05
First used:	1983

Each device has a cache, so your phone or laptop doesn't need to look up the IP address every time you want to go to a website you use often.

3

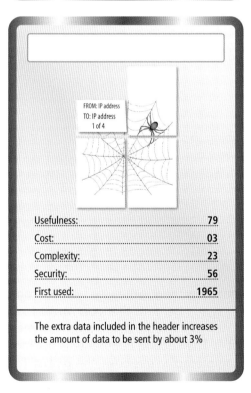

FROM: IP address
TO: IP address
1 of 4

Usefulness:	79
Cost:	03
Complexity:	23
Security:	56
First used:	1965

The extra data included in the header increases the amount of data to be sent by about 3%

4

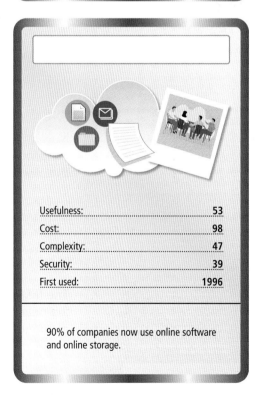

Usefulness:	53
Cost:	98
Complexity:	47
Security:	39
First used:	1996

90% of companies now use online software and online storage.

Programming in Python: iteration

Computers are excellent at repeating the same process over and over again and this chapter will teach you how to write programs that contain loops to repeat sequences of instructions. This will make your programs more professional. The key programming construct underpinning all the work in this chapter is iteration.

➡ 1 Repeating instructions

What is iteration?

Iteration is when a set of instructions is repeated. It is used when a program needs to complete the same process multiple times. Iteration can also be referred to as using a loop.

For loops

For loops are programming constructs that allow us to perform repetitive tasks that might otherwise require lots of lines of code. We use them when we know how many times we want to do something.

Counting up with a for loop

The following code shows how we might simulate closing our eyes and counting to ten in a game of hide and seek.

```
1   print('1')
2   print('2')
3   print('3')
4   print('4')
5   print('5')
6   print('6')
7   print('7')
8   print('8')
9   print('9')
10  print('10')
11  print('Coming, ready or not!')
```

Now imagine that the code is going to simulate counting to 20. If we wrote the program in the same way, we would need to write 21 lines of code. But, if we use a for loop instead, we can reduce repetitive lines of code.

```
1   for i in range(1, 21):
2       print(i)
3   print('Coming, ready or not!')
```

The first line of code tells the loop how many times we want to complete the action within the loop. The first number tells the loop where to start counting, in this case at 1. If this number is left out, the loop assumes the value is **0** and starts counting at 0. The second number tells the loop how many times the action will be completed. In this case, the **print(i)** action will be completed 20 times. On the twenty-first visit to the loop, the program will bypass the loop and continue with code outside the loop: **print('Coming, ready or not!')**. This means that, in Python, the second number in the range (in this case **21**) must always be one higher than the number of times you wish to repeat the action within the loop.

i is a variable. In this program, it is an integer that will change each time the loop is entered. It will start as **1**, the first number in the range, and will then become **2**, **3**, **4** and so on until it reaches **20** and the program bypasses the loop.

The numbers in the brackets are known as **parameters**. These are rules that we give the for loop. In this case, they tell the program when to start counting and when to stop counting.

The colon at the end of the for statement signals the start of the loop, and the code that you wish to repeat should appear on the next line and should be indented.

Counting backwards with a for loop

We use for loops to count up, as in the hide and seek scenario above, but we can also use them to count backwards. To do this we need to include another parameter which tells the for loop that we wish to take a backwards step each time the loop is run:

```
1 for i in range(10, 0, -1):
2     print(i)
3 print('We have lift off!')
```

The **-1** tells the for loop to count backwards, in this case from 10 to 0. If we didn't include the **-1**, the program would start counting at 10 and then count up (11, then 12, then 13 and so on), never finding the value **0**. This would create an endless loop. The program would never stop!

The race is on

Write a program that uses a for loop to count down to a race. The output should look like this.

```
Output                          ✕
3
2
1
Go!
```

Counting down, counting up

Create a program that counts down from 5 to 0 and then counts up from 1 to 5.

Use the following code to help you complete the challenge.

```
1 for i in range(  ):
2     print(i)
3 for i in range(  ):
4     print(i)
```

Stepping more than once

By changing the size of the third parameter, it is possible to jump every second number, or every third number, or every fourth number, and so on. This enables you to output times tables:

```
1 for i in range(2, 22, 2):
2     print(i)
```

The first parameter in the range tells the program to start counting at 2, the second parameter tells the program to loop until **i** reaches 22 and the final parameter tells the loop to go up by 2 each time.

Five times table

Write a program that uses a for loop to output the five times table up to 50.

Checking in

What will the following code output?

```
1 for i in range(2, 14, 3):
2     print(i)
```

➡ 2 User-defined for loops

Using for loops with user-defined variables

So far, the for loops we have been working with have made use of a range that has been defined by the programmer, for example, the range in this program from is **1** to **6**.

```
1  for i in range(1, 6):
2      print(i)
3  print('Once I caught a fish
   alive.')
```

Programs like this provide the same output every time they are run. However, by incorporating values from variables input by the user, for loops can be used to provide a more custom or dynamic experience, for example:

```
1  count = int(input('What number
   would you like to count up
   to?'))
2  for i in range(1, ( count + 1)):
3      print(i)
4  print('Coming, ready or not!')
```

School trip

The program below was supposed to ask the user how many students were going on a school trip, then count each student and display the text 'All present and correct'. However, the code is not quite right.

```
1  count = int(input('How many
   students are going on a
   school trip? ') )
2  for i in range(1, count):
3      print(i)
4  print('All present and
   correct.')
```

Copy and amend the program so that it counts all of the students going on the school trip.

Using for loops to output simple drawings

If we use print statements to output symbols within a for loop, it is possible to create some simple drawings.

Flamingo

The code below is supposed to draw a flamingo with the height of the flamingo's legs decided by the user. Unfortunately there is a problem with the code. Copy the program and debug the code so that it draws the flamingo to the height instructed by the user.

```
1   height = int(input('Enter the
    height of the flamingo: '))
2   print('            __')
3   print('           /(\ 'o')
4   print('        ,-, // \\')
5   print('         (,,,)|| v')
6   print('  (,,,, )\//')
7   print('   (,,,/w)-')
8   print('   \,,/w)')
9   print('   \'V/uu')
10  print('     /|')
11  print('     ||')
12  print('     ||')
13  for i in range(1, height + 1):
14  print('     ||')
```

Often, when we run code, the output is not exactly as we expect it to be. Finding the problem and fixing it is known as debugging code and it isn't always easy. Sometimes we have to use trial and error. For example, we might increase a number in a for loop to see if it has the desired effect. If the adjustment leads us further away from the result we were expecting, we can change the number in the for loop again, this time reducing it to see what happens. And so on until we have the output we want.

Skyscraper

Write a program that uses a for loop to draw a skyscraper like the one below. The program should ask the user to input how tall the building should be. Your skyscraper should be six stars wide at the top. The input and output should look like this:

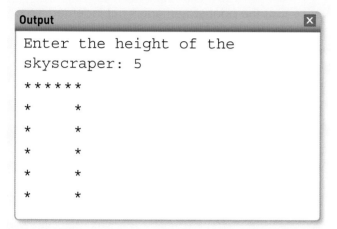

```
Output                                    ×
Enter the height of the
skyscraper: 5

* * * * * *

*         *

*         *

*         *

*         *

*         *
```

Combining loops with concatenation

Strings of characters can be combined using concatenation. The **+** symbol adds together the strings inside quotes and the strings stored as variables. For example:

```
1  name = 'Frank'
2  print('Hello ' + name)
```

```
Output                                    ×
Hello Frank
```

The flamingo and skyscraper programs output one string multiple times. However, if we use concatenation, it is possible to combine multiple inputs in one print line using **+**, and this allows us to vary the output on each line.

Look at this program:

```
1  triangle = ' '
2  height = int(input('Enter the
   height of the triangle: '))
3  for i in range(1, height + 1):
4      triangle = triangle + '*'
5      print(triangle)
```

The first line of code creates an empty variable. This is called on in the for loop and the concatenated data is added to it.

We use the **triangle = triangle + '*'** to add an asterisk to the string **triangle** each time the for loop runs. After an asterisk is added to the end of the string, the string is output creating a triangle.

It is important that the print statement, **print(triangle)**, is placed within the for loop. If it is placed outside the for loop, the program would only print the last line of however many asterisks the user entered.

Steps

Write a program that uses a for loop and concatenation to display a staircase made up of asterisks (star * symbols). Each 'step' should be four asterisks wide, which means the input and output should look like this:

```
Output                                    ×
Enter the number of steps: 4
* * * *

* * * * * * *

* * * * * * * * * * *

* * * * * * * * * * * * * * *
```

Checking in

How can we use a for loop to print out multiples of a number entered by the user, starting with the number entered by the user and going up to another number entered by the user?

3 For loops and strings

Combining with string manipulation

We have been using for loops and strings to output simple images, including a skyscraper and some steps. If we use a wider range of string manipulation skills, it is possible to do even more.

This program will output the phrase, **One small step for man, one giant leap for mankind.** with a space between each letter:

```
1 phrase = 'One small step
  for man, one giant leap for
  mankind.'
2 newphrase = ' '
3 for i in range(0, len
  (phrase)):
4     newphrase += phrase
  [i] + ' '
5 print(newphrase)
```

The **len()** function returns the number of characters in a string, including spaces and other special characters. The length of the string **phrase** is 51.

The **len()** function takes the place of the second parameter in the range. It inserts the number of characters in the string, in this case 51, into the range.

In Python, a string is simply a list of characters and we can refer to each individual character by an index value that reflects its position in the string. The first position in a string is 0 because we start counting at 0 in Python.

The square brackets used inside the for loop indicate that we wish to call a character in the string using its index value. Since the first character in a string always has the index value 0, **phrase[0]** is O and **phrase[4]** is **s**. In this program, we are calling each character in the string in turn – starting with the character with the index value **0** and ending with the character with the index value given to us by the **len()** function – and adding a space after each character using concatenation.

We often need to add something to a value to change it. For example, if we have a variable,

count, and we wish to increment it by one we can use **count = count + 1**. We can also use the **+=** symbol, which adds a value to the original variable. This means that **count += 1** adds one to count, just like **count = count + 1**.

Notice that the print statement is not indented, so it is outside the loop. This means that the **newphrase** variable, with the spaces between the characters, is output just once, after the spaces have been added between all of the characters.

Keep calm

Write a program that asks the user to enter a message and then outputs each character of the message followed by a full stop. For example:

```
Output                          ✕
Enter a message: KEEP CALM
K.E.E.P. .C.A.L.M.
```

Secret message

Write a program to hide a secret message entered by the user. The program should take this message and change every character to an asterisk using a for loop and concatenation.

Looping backwards

We know how to use a for loop to work through a string character by character forwards. We also have the skills to use a for loop to step backwards.

Adding a third parameter, one that begins with a - to the for loop outputs the string backwards. Here's an example using numbers, that should be familiar to you:

```
1 for i in range(10, 0, -1):
2     print(i)
3 print('We have lift off!')
```

Here is an example using characters:

```
1  animal = 'pink flamingo'
2  for i in range(len(animal) -1,
   -1, -1):
3      print(animal[i])
```

There are 13 characters in the phrase **pink flamingo** including the spaces, so the first parameter in the range is 13. Because the first character in the string has the index value **0** and the last character in the string has the index value **12**, -1 is added to the first parameter so that the 13 characters in the string can be referred to by their correct index value.

The second parameter is also -1 because we want the for loop to stop looping after the first character in the string, which has the index value **0**.

Backwords

Copy the code below and modify it so that the word **robert** is output in reverse. Your program should output **trebor**, with each letter displayed on a new line.

```
1  word = 'robert'
2  for i in range(len(word) -1,
   -1):
3      print(word[i])
```

Palindrome

Write a program that asks the user to enter a word and checks to see if it is a palindrome. A palindrome is a word that reads the same backwards as forwards. For example, 'tacocat' is palindrome. The program should output the word forwards and then output the word backwards. It should check to see if both outputs are the same

and, if they are, it should tell the user that the word is a palindrome.

You will need to use an if statement and the equal to Boolean operator (**==**) to check if the original word and the word in reverse are the same.

The input and output should look like this:

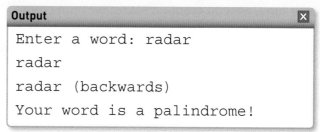

```
Output                              ☒
Enter a word: radar
radar
radar (backwards)
Your word is a palindrome!
```

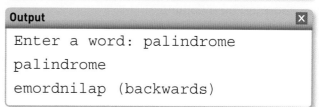

```
Output                              ☒
Enter a word: palindrome
palindrome
emordnilap (backwards)
```

Checking in

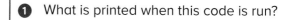

❶ What is printed when this code is run?

```
1  num1 = 3
2  num2 = 5
3  num1 += num2
4  print(num1)
```

❷ What is printed when this code is run?

```
1  text = 'cat'
2  for i in range(1, 3):
3      text += 'dog'
4  print(text)
```

➡ 4 For loops and lists

For loops with lists

For loops can be used to check through a list, output a list and sort a list.

When we have a large number of items of the same type, we can create a list rather than create a variable for each item, for example: **animals = ['duck', 'lizard', 'dog', 'turtle']**.

A list uses a single identifier such as **animals** to create a container for a set of variables.

▶ Each variable is known as an element and the list stores the elements one after another separated by a comma.

▶ The elements in a list are identified by the identifier and an index value in square brackets. The first element in a list has the index value **0**.

The code below contains a list of animals and print statements to output each animal in the list:

```
1  animals = ['duck', 'lizard',
   'dog', 'turtle']
2  print(animals[0])
3  print(animals[1])
4  print(animals[2])
5  print(animals[3])
```

This piece of code wouldn't take too long to write out, but imagine you were trying to output a list of 1000 different animals. That would require many lines of code. This is when for loops come in handy. With a for loop, you can tell the computer to print out a range of items in the list. For example, this program will print all four animals in the list:

```
1  animals = ['duck', 'lizard',
   'dog', 'turtle']
2  for i in range(0, 4):
3      print(animals[i])
```

Ice cream

Write a program that creates a list of eight different ice-cream flavours, then uses a for loop to print each of them out on a new line.

Adding to lists with for loops

If we want to add another four animals to our list, we can adjust the range in the for loop so that the code is now:

```
1  animals = ['duck', 'lizard',
   'dog', 'turtle', 'goat',
   'shrew', 'hedgehog', 'mouse']
2  for i in range(0, 8):
3      print(animals[i])
```

However, although changing the range from **(0, 4)** to **(0, 8)** works, it means that we need to update the for loop every time we extend the list. Instead, we can make use of the **len()** function to find the length of the list:

```
1  animals = ['duck', 'lizard',
   'dog', 'turtle', 'goat',
   'shrew', 'hedgehog', 'mouse']
2  for i in range(0, len
   (animals)):
3      print(animals[i])
```

Looping with multiple lists

If we want to store more data about each animal, we can create another list and concatenate each animal and its colour using a comma between them in the print statement:

```
1 animals = ['duck', 'lizard',
  'dog', 'turtle', 'goat',
  'shrew', 'hedgehog', 'mouse']
2 colours = ['black', 'green',
  'brown', 'green', 'grey',
  'brown', 'white']
3 for i in range(0, 8):
4     print(animals[i] + ', ' +
  colours[i])
```

Musicals

A program contains three lists, **show**, **theatre** and **popularity**:

```
1 show = ['Cats', 'The Lion
  King', 'Les Miserables', 'The
  Phantom of the Opera', 'Mamma
  Mia']
2 theatre = ['Apollo Victoria',
  'Lyceum Theatre', 'Drury Lane
  Theatre', 'Prince Edward
  Theatre', 'Prince of Wales
  Theatre']
3 popularity = [1, 2, 5, 3, 4]
```

Copy the lists and add to the program so that the output looks like the output shown.

Rather than just writing print statements with the lines of text hard-coded, you should use a for loop to loop through the lists and combine the items into a single output line.

If you decide to use concatenation to solve this problem, note that Python expects the variables being concatenated to be strings, but the data in the **popularity** list are integers. We cannot concatenate strings and integers so, to create the outputs required, we need to cast the integers as strings in the print statement using the **str** command. For example, **age = 13** makes **age** a numeric value but **str(age)** casts **age** as a string that can be concatenated with other strings in a print line.

Output ☒

The show Cats can be seen at the Apollo Victoria and is ranked 1 in popularity.

The show The Lion King can be seen at the Lyceum Theatre and is ranked 2 in popularity.

The show Les Miserables can be seen at the Drury Lane Theatre and is ranked 5 in popularity.

The show The Phantom of the Opera can be seen at the Prince Edward Theatre and is ranked 3 in popularity.

The show Mamma Mia can be seen at the Prince of Wales Theatre and is ranked 4 in popularity.

Checking in

What will be output if this code is run?

```
1 fruits = ['Damson', 'Pear',
  'Orange', 'Apple', 'Kiwi']
2 print(fruits[len(fruits) -1])
```

→ 5 Searching using for loops

By combining for loops with selection in the form of if statements, it is possible to search for data in a list and even find out if something is in a list or not.

The following program contains a list of vehicles that pass a school. Using a for loop and an if statement we can output all of one type of vehicle from the list:

```
1  traffic = ['car', 'car',
   'lorry', 'car', 'van',
   'motorcycle', 'car', 'car',
   'van']
2  for i in range(0, len(traffic)):
3      if traffic[i] == 'car':
4          print(traffic[i])
```

Notice that:

▶ the for loop uses **len()** to find the number of elements in the list.

▶ the if statement uses the variable **i**, which is given a range in the for loop, in this case **0** through to the length of the **traffic** list. Each time the loop is entered, the value of the variable will go up by one, checking each element of the list, from the first element in the list through to the last element in the list.

▶ when checking each element, the if statement compares what is in that element with the word **car** and, if they match, it outputs **car**.

▶ the if statement is inside the for loop so the if statement checks every item in the list against the word **car**.

▶ the print statement is inside the if statement inside the for loop so it is indented eight spaces.

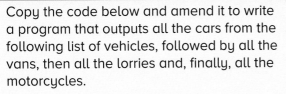

Identifying vehicles

Copy the code below and amend it to write a program that outputs all the cars from the following list of vehicles, followed by all the vans, then all the lorries and, finally, all the motorcycles.

```
1  traffic = ['car', 'car',
   'lorry', 'car', 'van',
   'motorcycle', 'car', 'car',
   'van']
2  for i in range()
3  for i in range()
4  for i in range()
```

Linear search

This program carries out a search to find out if a sport is included in the Olympic Games:

```
1  watersports = ['swimming',
   'diving', 'canoe sprint',
   'canoe slalom', 'rowing',
   'sailing', 'synchronised
   swimming', 'waterpolo']
2  for i in range(0,
   len(watersports) ):
3      if watersports[i] ==
   'waterpolo':
4          print('waterpolo is an
   Olympic water sport')
```

This search is known as a **linear search**. It looks at each element of the list and compares it to what we are searching for, in this case **waterpolo**.

Finding a specific item

The code could be improved, so the user can decide which water sport they want to search for, by including an input statement and a variable called **search**:

```
2  search = input('What Olympic
   watersport do you wish to
   search for? ')
3  for i in range(0,
   len(watersports)):
4      if watersports[i] == search:
5          print(search + ' is an
           Olympic watersport')
```

Commonwealth countries

Copy the code below and add to it to write a program that asks the user to enter the name of an Asian country and performs a linear search on the list of Asian Commonwealth countries provided. If the country appears in the list, then the program will output **Found**.

```
1  commonwealthasia =
   ['Bangladesh', 'Brunei
   Darussalam', 'India',
   'Malaysia', 'Pakistan',
   'Singapore', 'Sri Lanka']
```

Finding out if something is not in a list

By adding an else clause to the if statement, we can write a program that searches a list and tells the user if the data they are looking for is not in the list. Using if and else allows us to specify what happens if we do find a match for our condition and what happens if we do not find a match for a condition (else do that). For example:

```
3  for i in range(0,
   len(watersports)):
4      if watersports[i] ==
   search:
5          print(search + ' is an
   Olympic water sport')
6      else:
7          print(search + '  is
   not an Olympic water sport')
```

When a sport is not in the list, the program returns an output each time it checks an element in the list. There are eight items in the list so, if the user enters **kayaking**, the program outputs **kayaking is not an Olympic water sport** eight times. Logically this is correct, but it would be better if the program only output the statement once.

To improve the program, we can use a **Boolean variable** instead of an else statement. A Boolean

variable is a variable that is only **True** or **False**. For example:

```
3  found = False
4  for i in range(0,
   len(watersports)):
5      if watersports[i] == search:
6          found = True
7          print(search + ' is an
   Olympic water sport')
8  if found == False:
9      print(search + '  is not an
   Olympic water sport')
```

Notice:

▶ Line 3 sets the Boolean variable **found** to **False** and it will stay as **False**.

▶ If the sport input by the user is in the list, then line 6 of the program changes the Boolean variable found to True. This happens inside the if statement and the user is told that the sport they input is an Olympic water sport.

▶ Line 8 is another if statement, and is outside the for loop. When the loop has completed checking all of the items in the list, if a match has not been found the variable **found** will still be set to **False**. This will cause the program to output the print statement on line 9.

Checking in

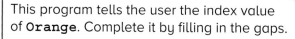

This program tells the user the index value of **Orange**. Complete it by filling in the gaps.

```
1  fruits = ['Damson', 'Pear',
   'Orange', 'Apple', 'Kiwi']
2  for i in range(0, _____):
3      if ____ ____ 'Orange':
4          print('Orange is found
          at index value', _____)
```

→ 6 While loops

While loops versus for loops

While loops are programming constructs that allow us to perform repetitive tasks that require lots of lines of code.

In this way, they are very much like for loops. However, while loops are often used when we do not know how many times we want to repeat something, whereas for loops are normally used when we want to repeat a task a set number of times. The following table provides some examples of when we might use a for loop and when we might use a while loop:

Task	Type of loop
Asking the user to enter a password and asking them again and again until they get it correct.	while loop
Asking the user to enter the number of students in a class then using a loop to collect that number of names.	for loop
Asking the user to keep entering numbers until they type 0, at which point all of the numbers entered so far will be added together.	while loop
Asking the user to enter ten numbers, at which point the ten numbers will be added together.	for loop

Avoiding infinite loops

A while loop must contain a condition. The colon at the end of the while statement signals the start of the loop and the code that you wish to repeat should appear on the next line and should be indented. The code inside the loop runs when the condition is met and the loop is bypassed when the condition is not met, for example:

```
1  answer = str(input('What is the
   tallest animal in the world? '))
2  while answer != 'giraffe':
3      print('Incorrect, try
   again.')
4      answer = str(input('What
   is the tallest animal in the
   world? '))
```

Notice how the input statement occurs twice, once at line 1 and again at line 4. Without the second input statement, the program would enter an infinite loop because the user would not be able to correct their answer if it was wrong.

We can improve the program by adding an output if the user answers the question correctly:

```
1  answer = str(input('What is the
   tallest animal in the world? '))
2  while answer != 'giraffe' :
3      print('Incorrect, try
   again.')
4      answer = str(input('What
   is the tallest animal in the
   world? '))
5  print('Correct, well done.')
```

Notice how the print statement containing the success message is not inside the while loop because it is aligned with the while loop condition. This means that if the while condition is not met at line 2 – if the user correctly enters **giraffe** – then the program will bypass the loop and print out the success message at line 4.

Highest mountain

Write a program that asks the user to answer the following question: What is the highest mountain in the world?

The program should continue to ask the question until the user answers it correctly. The correct answer is **Everest** (that's Everest with a capital E). Each time the user guesses incorrectly, it should print the response **Incorrect, try again.** and when they get it right it should print **Correct, well done.**

Making code more efficient

It is possible to create a while loop that has only one input statement. Consider the following simple password program:

```
1  password = ' '
2  while password != 'letmein!':
3      password = str(input
   ('Enter the password: '))
4  print('You are in!')
```

The variable **password** is set to empty at the start of the program and so is not equal to **letmein**. This means that the program always enters the while loop.

Creating a while loop with only one input statement is a more efficient solution, because it requires fewer lines of code.

Tallest animal

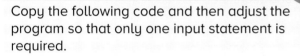

Copy the following code and then adjust the program so that only one input statement is required.

```
1  answer = str(input('What is
   the tallest animal in the
   world? '))
2  while answer != 'giraffe':
3      answer = str(input('What
   is the tallest animal in the
   world? '))
4  print('Correct, well done.')
```

Birth date

Write a program that validates a date of birth. The program should ask the user to enter their day of birth as a number, their month of birth as a number and the year they were born. The program should check each input and ask the user to re-enter the value if the following conditions are not met:

▶ the value of the day should not be more than 31

▶ the value of the month should not be more than 12

▶ the value for the year should not be less than 1900.

This means you will need three while loops, one for each value the user enters. For each value, if the number entered does not meet the condition, the program should display an error message that *must* include the word **Invalid** and continue to ask the user to enter the value until a valid number is entered. If the number does meet the condition, then the program should output **Accepted** and move onto the next value to be input.

The input and output should look like this:

```
Output                                    ☒

Enter your day of birth as a
number: 99
Invalid number entered. Your
day of birth must be 31 or
less.
Enter your day of birth as a
number: 31
Accepted
Enter your month of birth as a
number: 11
Accepted
Enter your year of birth as a
four-digit number: 1066
Invalid number entered. Your
year of birth must be 1900 or
more.
Enter your year of birth as a
four-digit number: 1902
Accepted
```

Checking in

1. When would you use a for loop?
2. When would you use a while loop?
3. What type of loop would you use if you want a user to input an unknown number of values?
4. How might you check that the user has finished entering values?

185

It's easy to think of modern information technologies in a wholly positive way, as tools that make our lives easier and more interesting. But they can have a darker side and this chapter will give you the opportunity to investigate some of the wider ethical issues, including the moral, environmental and legal issues that can arise in the digital age. Understanding these issues will help you make fully informed choices.

➡ 1 Sourcing content responsibly

Everything online has an owner

Every paragraph of text, image, video and sound on the internet was created by somebody.

More often than not, you are breaking the law if you copy material from the internet without **crediting** the person who created it. People own the **copyright** of material they create and you must not suggest that you created it yourself. You must say where you got it from.

To credit a source, you must state who created it, the title of the article or page it came from, the date it was published, the web address of the page you found it on and the date you accessed the web page. Credits should be placed as close as possible to the text, photograph or video.

For example, here's how you credit a quote from a web page:

> Source: World Animal Foundation, 'Zebras', 25 Apr 2021, https://www.worldanimalfoundation.com/advocate/wild-animals/params/post/1294331/zebras, (accessed 16/05/21)

For example, here's how you credit a photograph:

> Source: South African National Biodiversity Institute, 'Burchell's Zebra', May 2020, https://www.sanbi.org/animal-of-the-week/burchells-zebra/, (accessed 8/10/20)

For example, here's how to credit a video:

> Source: Real Wild, 'Striped Survivors: A tale of a zebra', 27 Jan 2018, www.youtube.com/watch?v=wmNandLRMcw, (accessed 8/10/2020)

Getting permission to use copyright material

Although it is good practice to credit all sources, you cannot use a lot of copyright material at all without first getting permission to use it from the person or company who created it. You need to identify the person who originally created the material in the first place and contact them to ask permission. Email addresses and contact forms on websites are the best way to make contact with people.

You can use Google to find out who wrote a specific piece of text, by going to www.google.com and pasting it into the search bar with speech marks around it. Google returns a list of links to web pages where the exact phrase is used and you need to use your common sense to work out where it most likely originated from.

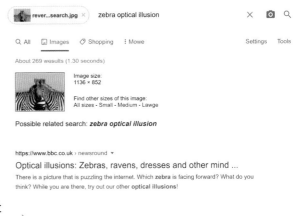

 The results of a Google reverse image search

You can also use Google to find out where a photo you have downloaded and saved to your computer comes from, by performing a reverse image search. Go to www.google.com, click on 'Images', click on the camera icon and on 'Upload an image' and then upload your image. As with a text search, Google returns a list of links where the image – or similar images – have been found. Click through to the websites to find the name of the photographer.

Save the tigers

While looking at the internet one day, you've come across a website raising money for a conservation project to save tigers. The website's home page can be found on 'The ethics of computing Worksheet 1.2'

1 Use Google to find out where the paragraph of text comes from and record:
- the name of the person or organisation that runs the website
- the title of the article or page it appears on
- the web address of the page you found it on
- the date you access the web page.

2 Use Google's reverse image search to find out where each of the photographs comes from and record your findings in the table. You will need to right click on the photo in the worksheet and save it to your computer in order to use the reverse image search.

3 Do you think the person who created the website should credit the author of the paragraph of text and the three photographers who took the photographs or do you think they should ask the content creators for permission to use their copyright material? Explain your answer.

Creative Commons

It can be difficult to know who is happy for you to use their copyright material as long as you credit them and who wants you to ask for permission to use it. **Creative Commons licences** have been created to help you work out what to do.

 Where you see these logos, you know that the content creator is happy for you to use their material with attribution (with a credit), even if you have adapted it.

 When you also see this logo, you know the content creator is happy for you to use their material with attribution, but they do not want you to adapt it.

 Where you also see this logo, you know that the content creator is happy for you to use their material with attribution, even if you have adapted it, but you have to let other people use it and adapt it too.

 Where you also see this logo, you know that the content creator is happy for you to use their material with attribution, but not for commercial use (you must not make money from it).

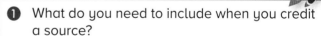

Checking in

1 What do you need to include when you credit a source?

2 What are the benefits of releasing your work under a Creative Commons licence?

3 Why do companies rarely release their content under Creative Commons licences?

➡️ 2 Using technology responsibly

When something is **illegal**, it is against the law. When something is **immoral**, it is not necessarily against the law but it is against acceptable standards of behaviour.

Is it illegal, immoral or both for a business to sell a customer's personal data without their permission?

It is, of course, illegal for a business to sell a customer's personal data without their consent. It is an offence under the **Data Protection Act 2018**. It is also immoral.

Is it immoral for a football club to monitor its player's heart rates and average speed while they train and play a match?

While this is another example of an employer using technology to monitor its staff, the difference here is that the football players know that they are being monitored. They have agreed to wear heart rate monitors and GPS trackers and know that the data collected will be used to improve their performance.

Is it immoral for a company to secretly monitor its staff with CCTV cameras and scan all the emails they send and receive while they are at work?

On the one hand, workers are paid to work and a company can argue it is simply checking its staff are doing what they are paid to do. On the other hand, workers can argue that being spied on is unacceptable, not what they agreed to when they signed their contract and against their human rights.

Technology itself cannot be immoral, but the way people use it can be. Lack of consent is a good indicator that something might be immoral.

Immoral or not?

1 Think about these questions on your own:
- Is it immoral for the boss of the company you work for to search for you on social media?
- Is it immoral for the boss of the company you work for to set up a fake profile and befriend you on social media to find out more about you?
- Is it immoral that people can never fully remove their **digital footprint** (the information about you on the internet)?

2 Discuss your answers to these questions with a partner. Do you agree? If not, can you persuade your partner to your point of view?

You're the boss

Imagine that you are the CEO of Via Electronics. One of your managers has come to you and told you that they have discovered some concerning information about two of your employees on social media. The manager would like you to fire both members of staff.

1 Look at the information collected by the manager and set out the manager's case for firing each member of staff.

2 Decide whether you are going to:
- fire the employee
- give the employee a formal warning
- have a quiet word with the employee
- reprimand the manager for wasting your time.

Explain the reasons for your decision.

Paul Derrick

Paul called in sick on 24 May 2020, telling his manager he had been up all night with a stomach upset. He was due to give an important presentation, which his team had spent weeks preparing, and the company lost a big contract as a result.

Paul Derrick
@PaulDerrick999

What an amazing night celebrating our win! Very tired 😴 but so happy!!

Sophie Waterman

Recently a prototype of a new microchip went missing from Via Electronics. Sophie was responsible for keeping it safe and her manager suspects she may have had something to do with its disappearance. Via Electronics' main competitor would pay a lot of money for the prototype.

FishBandit
@FishBandit

So pleased that both my Mum and Dad made it to my graduation today 🖤 🖤

FishBandit
@FishBandit

So you know I couldn't afford that holiday of a lifetime... I can now! Some money has 'fallen into my lap'. Whoop whoop!`

Yesterday, 03.34 p.m.

Checking in

True or false?
❶ Something that is immoral is always illegal.
❷ Something that is immoral can also be illegal.
❸ Something that is illegal is always immoral.

➡ 3 Technology and the environment

Here are some examples of how technology can damage the environment.

When people have finished with their digital devices, they generally end up in landfill. In 2019, we created 54 million tonnes of **e-waste** and only 17% of it was recycled.[1] The rest probably ended up in a rubbish dump in one of the poorest countries in the world, where it was burned. This has devastating consequences for the environment and for the health of the people who live and work nearby.

Coltan is an important mineral. It contains tantalum, which is needed to manufacture smartphones and other digital devices. Coltan is mined in the Democratic Republic of Congo and the huge profits gained from extracting this mineral have contributed to the devastating violence experienced in the country for decades. Coltan mining has also destroyed the habitat of the eastern lowland gorilla. Efforts are being made to ensure coltan traded on the international market is 'conflict-free', but the miners – many of them young children – work in appalling conditions.

Digital devices are powered by electricity. When electricity is generated by burning fossil fuels, the CO_2 emissions produced contribute to climate change. Streaming currently produces 0.3% of the world's CO_2 emissions and this is expected to rise.[2] Not only are you watching on a digital device, but servers around the world have to run to deliver content to you and they use electricity too. Experts calculate that the same amount of electricity was used to stream *Despacito*, a music video released in 2017, as was consumed by the countries of Chad, Guinea-Bissau, Somalia, Sierra Leone and the Central African Republic in one year![2] Visit www.internetlivestats.com to see the CO_2 emissions produced by people using the Internet today.

It is important to understand the negative enviromental impacts of technology so that efforts can be made to minimise them. Educating people will help them make better decisions about the digital devices they buy, how they use them and what they do with them when they no longer want them.

Minimising the environmental impact of your digital devices

Choose one environmental impact of technology and create an infographic that:

▶ outlines the environmental impact

▶ explains how the impact can be minimised.

If you need a reminder about infographics, look back at page 55. You will need to do some research to find out how the impact you choose can be minimised. Remember to credit all your sources!

1: *The Guardian*, '$10bn of precious metals dumped each year in electronic waste, says UN', 2/7/2020, https://www.theguardian.com/environment/2020/jul/02/10bn-precious-metals-dumped-each-year-electronic-waste-un-toxic-e-waste-polluting (accessed 6/1/2021)

2: BBC News 'Climate change: Is your Netflix habit bad for the environment?', 12/10/2018 https://www.bbc.co.uk/news/technology-45798523 (accessed 6/1/2021)

Checking in

Do you think it is right for mobile phone manufacturers to launch new models every year given the environmental impact of e-waste?

→ 4 Technology and the law

Companies collect information about you, including your name, address, data of birth, mobile phone number, email address and bank details. This data is usually stored electronically.

At the time of writing, there are two main laws that protect your personal data from exploitation in the UK:

▷ General Data Protection Regulation (EU) 2016/679, which is commonly referred to as '**GDPR**'

▷ Data Protection Act 2018

When companies break these laws, they are acting illegally. They can be prosecuted and fined.

The key principles of data protection law in the UK

Laws can be very difficult to read and understand but look at these extracts from GDPR and try and work out what the key principle of data protection law each paragraph describes.

Article 5(1) of GDPR

1. Personal data shall be:

(b) collected for specified, explicit and legitimate purposes and not further processed in a manner that is incompatible with those purposes; further processing for archiving purposes in the public interest, scientific or historical resources or statistical purposes shall, in accordance with Article 89(1), not be considered to be incompatible with the initial purposes.

(c) adequate, relevant and limited to what is necessary in relation to the purposes for which they are processed.

(d) accurate and, where necessary, kept up to date; every reasonable step must be taken to ensure that personal data that are inaccurate, having regard to the purposes for which they are processed, are erased or rectified without delay.

(e) kept in a form which permits identification of data subjects for no longer than is

necessary for the purposes for which the personal data are processed; personal data may be stored for longer periods insofar as the personal data will be processed solely for archiving purposes in the public interest, scientific or historical research purposes or statistical purposes.

(f) processed in a manner that ensures appropriate security of personal data, including protection against unauthorised or unlawful processing and against accidental loss, destruction or damage, using appropriate technical or organisational measures.

Is Google acting illegally?

Read this article about Google collecting personal data.

Google knows everywhere you go — here's how to stop it from tracking you and delete the logs

Todd Haselton

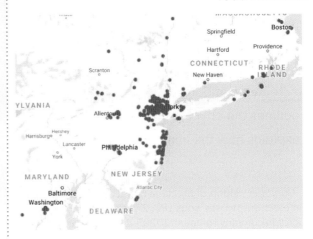

Google knows a lot about you and, if you use Google Maps or other Google apps, it stores a copy of everywhere you go. I recently performed Google's 'Privacy Checkup' to learn a bit more about what it knows about

me, and was pretty surprised at the level of detail it had on my exact locations.

I picked a random date: April 16, 2019. It knew everywhere I went, including that I took Interstate 95 to our office in northern New Jersey and that I arrived at 7:58 a.m. It knew that at 1:02 p.m. I drove to Jersey City and took a train in to Manhattan to the New York Stock Exchange before returning home at 4:38 p.m. And it has a copy of the pictures I took at each location.

It's a creepy level of detail.

Google says it uses location history to 'create a private map of where you go with your signed-in devices even when you aren't using a specific Google service.' It also says the 'map is only visible to you.' The data, it says, provides 'improved map searches and commute routes, as well as helping you to rediscover the places you've been and the routes you've travelled.'

I don't really care about that information. I know the roads I drove on April 16, and I can't see any reason why Google should store it, even if it's only for my use. I never know who might be able to access that data, even if Google promises it's private.

You can stop Google from storing your location history and delete what it has already stored. Here's how.

How to stop Google from tracking your location history

First, go to myaccount.google.com/privacycheckup. This is a good page to bookmark, since it gives you granular control over lots of privacy settings.

- Next, scroll down to 'Location History' and choose 'Manage Location History.'

- This is where you'll see everywhere you've been. It's a freaky level of detail.

- Tap 'Manage Location History' at the bottom of the screen again.

- Toggle the button to turn off Location History.

To delete your history, do this:

- Tap the settings button on the 'Location History' map.

- Select 'Delete all location history.'

That's not it, though.

Google will continue tracking your location unless you also turn off a separate 'Web & App Activity' tracker. Google says it tracks your location from apps to provide 'better recommendations, and more personalized experiences in Maps, Search, and other Google services.'

To turn off web and app activity, do this:

- Go to myaccount.google.com/activitycontrols

- Turn off the 'Web & Activity' toggle.

Source: CNBC, Todd Haselton 'Google knows everywhere you go — here's how to stop it from tracking you and delete the logs', 24/4/19, https://www.cnbc.com/2019/04/25/how-to-stop-google-from-storing-your-location-history.html (accessed 6/1/21)

1 Do you think Google should be collecting this data about you?

2 Is Google acting illegally, breaking UK data protection law? Think about each principle of UK data protection law you previously identified and decide if Google has broken it or not. Then justify your decision.

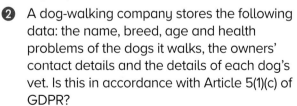

Checking in

1 Why do you think GDPR requires personal data to be 'accurate and, where necessary, kept up to date'?

2 A dog-walking company stores the following data: the name, breed, age and health problems of the dogs it walks, the owners' contact details and the details of each dog's vet. Is this in accordance with Article 5(1)(c) of GDPR?

➡ 5 Moral dilemmas (Part 1)

A thought-experiment

In 1967, the moral philosopher, Philippa Foot, created the Trolley Problem.

Imagine you are the driver of a runaway tram ('a trolley'). All you can do is steer from one narrow track to another.

Five men are working on one track and one man is working on the other track. Anyone working on the track when the tram enters it will be killed.

Which track do you choose?

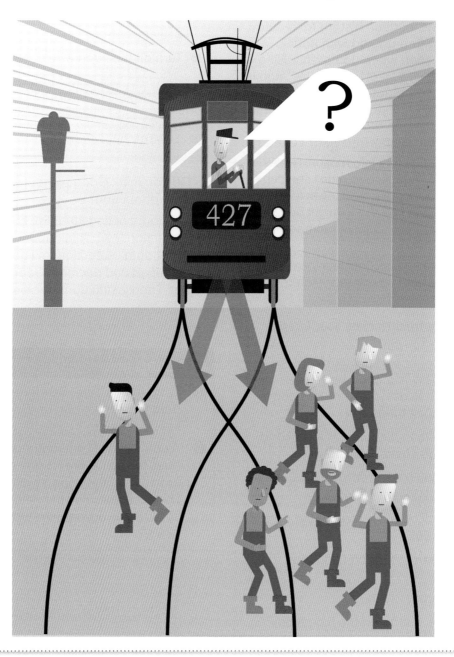

Driverless cars

When Philippa Foot came up with the Trolley Problem in 1967, driverless cars were the stuff of science fiction. Now they are a reality and the Trolley Problem has become a very real **moral dilemma**.

Driverless cars have to make decisions. They are computers and, as you know, computers can be programmed to make decisions using algorithms. This means that programmers are writing algorithms to govern what a driverless car does in lots of different situations. This is relatively simple when the car needs to turn left:

```
The programmed route identifies that
the car needs to take the next turning
on the left.

The left-hand indicator signals for
10 seconds.

The car steers left and continues on
down the new road.
```

But it gets a lot more complicated when the car has to make a moral decision. If somebody steps out in front of a driverless car, should the car swerve to avoid the person and potentially kill all the passengers? Or should the car kill the person who stepped out into the road? If you were driving the car, you would make a split-second decision and whatever happened would be called an accident. But a programmer must decide in advance what a driverless car will do.

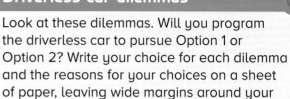

Driverless car dilemmas

Look at these dilemmas. Will you program the driverless car to pursue Option 1 or Option 2? Write your choice for each dilemma and the reasons for your choices on a sheet of paper, leaving wide margins around your writing.

Dilemma A

Two adults and two children are in a driverless car. A child, chasing a ball, runs out in front of the car.

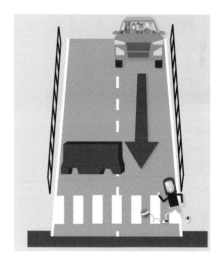

Option 1: The car continues driving and kills the child.

Option 2: The car swerves to avoid the child and kills all four passengers.

Dilemma B

You are in a driverless car. Two teenagers looking at their mobile phones step out in front of the car.

Option 1: The car continues driving and kills both teenagers.

Option 2: The car swerves to avoid the teenagers and kills you.

The counter arguments

Swap your answers to the driverless cars dilemma with a partner and use the space around the reasons for their choices to present the counter arguments in another colour. Why should the other option be chosen? You may agree with your partner's choice, but is there another way of looking at the dilemma?

A final decision

Look at your answers to the driverless-cars dilemma and your partner's annotations. Highlight the best arguments and decide, once and for all, which option you will program the driverless car to pursue.

Checking in

Can you think of another new technology that creates a moral dilemma for the programmer or the user?

➡ 6 Moral dilemmas (Part 2)

Programming driverless cars

You have looked at two driverless car dilemmas and decided, once and for all,
which options you will program the driverless car to pursue. Now it's time to
write an algorithm for your driverless car program.

Here is a reminder of the standard flow diagram symbols.

Symbol	Name	Function
(oval)	start/end	an oval represents a start or end point
→	arrows	an arrow shows the relationship between the two shapes it connects
(parallelogram)	input/output	a parallelogram represents input or output
(rectangle)	process	a rectangle represents a process
(diamond)	decision	a diamond represents a decision

Driverless cars algorithms

1 a Design an algorithm, as a flow diagram, to program the car to respond to Dilemma A.

   b Now justify your algorithm.

2 a Design an algorithm, as a flow diagram, to program the car to respond to Dilemma B.

   b Now justify your algorithm.

3 If you complete parts 1 and 2 of this activity, try and design one flow diagram that will apply to both dilemmas.

HINT: To justify your algorithms, you need to give reasons for the choices you have made. This could involve discussing and discounting the alternative choice.

Checking in

❶ What have you found most interesting about this module?

❷ Has this module changed the way you think about technology? And, if so, in what way?

This chapter contains three projects for you to complete to show off the computing skills you have worked so hard to acquire.

▶ Project 1 gives you the opportunity to use the Python programming skills you have developed to write two programs: an arithmetic quiz and a password-strength program.

▶ Project 2 gives you the opportunity to use the spreadsheets skills you have developed to build a finance system for a hotel.

▶ Project 3 gives you the opportunity to create an image and use the audio and video-editing skills you have developed to create a multi-media advert for a theme park.

➡ Project 1

The iterative approach to project development

You will be using the Python programming skills you have learnt to develop two computer programs. First, you will code an arithmetic quiz and then you will code a password-strength program. You will code a section of each program and then debug and test it before moving on to the next section. This is the **iterative approach to project development.**

Debugging

When you run each section of your program for the first time, it will probably contain errors. These errors are known as **bugs.** The bugs occur because Python cannot understand the program or because it is unable to carry out the instructions. You will usually be given a clue about the cause of the bug and you will need to read through the code carefully to work out how to fix or **debug** it.

Testing

When each section of your program is working without bugs, you need to **test** it to make sure it works as it should. To do this, you need to test the program with:

1 **normal data:** this is data you would expect to see if the program was being used normally. For example, **8** is entered in response to the question **What is 3 + 5?**

2 **abnormal data:** this is data you would not expect to see if the program was being used normally. For example, **Do not know** is entered in response to the question **What is 3 + 5?**

3 **boundary data:** this is data that checks that answers just within a range are accepted and those just outside a range are not. For example, if we wanted to check to see if someone was 10 or older, we would use **9** (just outside the range) and **10** (just inside the range) as the test values.

When testing a program, you must record what you do in a test table and provide accompanying evidence. You will focus on testing your programs with normal data so your test tables and evidence will look something like this:

Test data	Reason	Expected outcome	Actual outcome	Actions
What is 9 + 1 ? 10	Will I get the expected response to the correct answer?	Well done.	Well done.	None required
What is 5 + 5 ? 7	Will I get the expected response to an incorrect answer?	That is not right.	That is not right.	None required

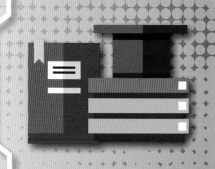

Evidence

```
Output                                    ☒
What is 9 + 1 ?
Enter the answer: 10
Well done.
What is 5 + 5 ?
Enter the answer: 7
That is not right.
What is 10 + 1 ?
Enter the answer:
```

Keeping versions

It is important to save a **version** of a program before you test and debug it. Saving multiple versions of a program means you can return to a working version if something goes wrong.

Remember to use logical file names, so that you know which version of the program is which.

IDLE

IDLE is Python's standard development environment.

When IDLE is loaded, it opens the Python shell. This is where the output from a program appears.

```
Python 3.8.5 Shell                        —  □  ×
File Edit Shell Debug Options Window Help
Python 3.8.5 (tags/v3.8.5:580fbb0, Jul 20 2020, 15:57:54) [MSC v.1924 64 bit (AMD64)]
on win32
Type "help", "copyright", "credits" or "license()" for more information.
>>>
= RESTART: C:\Users\kumar\OneDrive\Desktop\My_Work\22-04-2021\python_gopala\hello.py
Hello World
>>> |
```

To start coding a new program, click on 'File' and 'New File'. This will open a new window where you can type your code.

To save a program, click on 'File' and 'Save As …', give the file a .py extension and then click 'Save'.

When you want to run your code, click on 'Run' and 'Run Module'.

Key points

The key points to remember for this project are summarised below.

Outputting messages and inputting variables

The basic print command: `print('Hello World')`.

Printing variables: `print(name)`.

Combining strings and variables: `print('Hello', name)`.

Assigning a value to a variable: `name = 'John'`.

Asking the user to input data using a prompt and assigning the data input to a variable: `name = input('What is your name? ')`.

Specifying that a whole number will be input: `stock = int(input('How many items in stock? '))`.

When using a variable to keep track of a value, such as a score, the variable needs to be initialised to zero before the main body of the program, for example: `score = 0`.

The random module

The random module is imported using `import random` at the top of the program.

Random numbers are generated using `random.randint`. For example, to generate a random number between 1 and 10: `number = random.randint(1, 10)`.

The structure of a for loop

```
for <<index>> in range(<<start>>, <<end>>):
    <<code to be executed>>
```

For example, to output the number **1** to **10**:

```
for i in range(1, 11):
    print(i)
```

if, elif and else statements

Every condition must be a question that can be answered with true (yes) or false (no).

Use if for the first condition to be checked. Use elif for each additional condition to be checked. The else code runs if none of the preceding conditions have been met.

Indent the block of code to be run when a condition is met. Stop indenting the code to return to the main program.

Boolean operators

Conditions are written using Boolean operators:

Operator	Meaning
>	greater than
>=	greater than or equal to
<	less than
<=	less than or equal to
==	equal to
!=	not equal to

For example: **if age >= 18** will check whether the value stored in the variable **age** is greater than or equal to **18**.

String handling

To find the length of a string: **len(myString)**

To look at each letter in a string we can use a for loop to return each letter in the word:

```
word = 'computer'
for i in range(0, len(word)):
    letter = word[i]
```

We can then process each letter in turn.

However, there is a much simpler and tidier method, which will return each letter in the word in turn:

```
for <<letter>> in <<identifier for string>>:
```

For example, the code above written using this method would be:

```
word = 'computer'
for letter in word:
```

Boolean variables and the logical operator and

A Boolean variable is a variable that is only **True** or **False**.

and is a logical operator that allows for two conditions to be checked; for it to return True, both conditions must be true.

You can use Boolean variables in an if statement containing two conditions to be checked using **and** as follows:

```
one = True
two = True
if one and two:                    # 1
    print('Both conditions are
true.')
```

1 we could say if one == True and two == True but we don't need to

Arithmetic quiz

Part 1

Write a program that:

▶ generates two random whole numbers between 1 and 10

▶ creates an arithmetic question using the two random numbers and the **+** operator

▶ asks the user to enter the answer to the question

▶ decides whether the answer is correct or not and outputs **Well done.** if the answer is correct and **That is not right.** if the answer is incorrect

▶ asks 10 questions

▶ counts the number of correct responses and outputs **You scored X**, with **X** being the number of correct responses.

Save your program as 'Version 1' debug and test it. Check that your program outputs the expected response when you enter a correct answer and when you enter an incorrect answer. Remember to record what you do in a test table and provide evidence of your testing.

Part 2

Save a new version of your program that asks 10 addition questions and call it 'Version 2'.

Modify Version 2 so that it asks 10 subtraction questions. The questions should not have a negative answer so you will need to work out which of the two random numbers is larger and use if else to ensure you always subtract the smaller number from the larger number.

Debug the program and then check that it outputs the expected response when you enter correct answers and when you enter incorrect answers. Remember to record what you do in a test table and provide evidence of your testing.

Part 3

Combine your addition and subtraction programs into one program that randomly generates 10 questions that are addition, subtraction or multiplication questions. The third version of your program should:

▶ generate a random number between 1 and 3 to select the operator, **+**, **-** or *****

▶ combine the first two programs with a third segment asking multiplication questions, and run the appropriate segment of code when the corresponding operator is randomly generated.

Debug your program and then check that it outputs the expected response when you enter correct answers and when you enter incorrect answers. Remember to record what you do in a test table and provide evidence of your testing.

Password strength program

Part 1

Your task is to write a program that checks a password entered by the user. It must:

▶ be at least eight characters long.

▶ contain at least one upper case character.

▶ contain at least one lower case character.

▶ contain at least one number.

Analyse how these characteristics can be checked and design an algorithm for your program using a flow diagram.

> **HINTS** Once you have checked if the password contains eight or more characters, use Boolean variables as flags for each of the other requirements. The value stored in each variable should be False initially, changing to True when the requirement is met. When all the flags are True, the password meets all the requirements. To do this you will need to check multiple conditions using the logical operator **and**.
>
> Use **for letter in word:** to look at each letter of the password in turn.
>
> Use the logical operator **and** in an if statement to check that two conditions are true.

Part 2

When you have designed your program, code it section by section using the iterative approach to project development. Remember to debug and test each version, record what you do in a test table and provide evidence of your testing.

➡ Project 2

The finance system

You will be using your spreadsheet skills to develop a finance system for a small hotel. The finance system contains a number of different features and you should use an iterative approach to project development to build and test each feature to make sure it is working as it should before moving on to add the next feature. You should also save a new version of the spreadsheet each time you begin to add a new feature, so you can return to a working version if something goes wrong.

As a starting point, you will be provided with a workbook containing two spreadsheets (also known as 'tabs'). One tab contains data about guests and one tab contains data about services and how much they cost. Among the tasks you will need to complete to build the finance system, you will need to create an invoice and the hotel's accounts.

The invoice

When a guest checks out of the hotel, they must be given an invoice. This sets out the goods and services they purchased and tells them how much they need to pay. The invoice must be easy to read and understand, and it must contain:

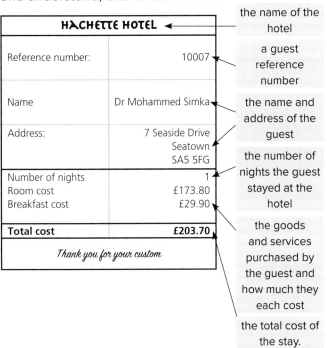

the name of the hotel

a guest reference number

the name and address of the guest

the number of nights the guest stayed at the hotel

the goods and services purchased by the guest and how much they each cost

the total cost of the stay.

The accounts

All businesses need to keep accounts. These are a record of:

▶ income: the money received from guests

▶ costs: the money spent on paying staff and other fixed costs

▶ profit/loss: the money left over when costs have been paid; this can be a positive sum (profit) or a negative sum (loss).

Total number of guests		19	

Staff	Number	Salary	Cost
Manager	1	£520.00	£520.00
Deputy manager	1	£440.00	£440.00
Night manager	1	£360.00	£360.00
Receptionist	2	£370.00	£740.00
Cleaner	3	£350.00	£1,050.00
Chef	2	£400.00	£800.00

Fixed costs		£1,200.00
Total running costs		£5,110.00
Total income		£5,501.75
Profit/Loss		£391.75

Additional skills

In addition to the spreadsheet skills you have already developed, you will also need to work with multiple spreadsheets in a workbook and use the **CONCATENATE** and **ROUNDUP** functions.

Working with multiple spreadsheets

The finance system you will be building requires you to work with multiple spreadsheets in a workbook. The spreadsheets can be accessed by clicking on the tabs at the bottom. To add a new spreadsheet, click on the plus sign. Right click on a tab and select 'Rename' to give the new tab an appropriate name.

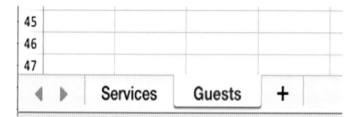

You can link to data on another spreadsheet in the same workbook. First, select the target cell (the cell in which you would like the data to appear) and type **=.** Then select the spreadsheet containing the source data, select the relevant cell and press 'Enter'.

You can also use a **VLOOKUP** function to look up values on another spreadsheet in the same workbook.

Select the target cell, type **=VLOOKUP (** and select the cell containing the look up value. In the example below, it is **Calculator** in cell A7. Type a comma. Then select the spreadsheet containing the table of values and select the area that contains the data to enter the range. In this example, the range is **A2:D5** on the 'Stock sold' spreadsheet. Type a comma. In this example, we want to return the value in the fourth column so we type **4**, close the parentheses and press 'Enter'.

Remember to use absolute cell references for the range if you want to replicate the function.

The CONCATENATE function

The **CONCANTENATE** function joins together strings in multiple cells to form one longer string.

In this example we are joining **3** from cell B2, a space, **Calculator** from cell A2, and an **s** to form the string **3 Calculators**.

	A	B	C	D	E	F	G
1	Item	Number sold	Cost per item	Total cost			
2	Calculator	3	£5.99	£17.97		=CONCATENATE(B2, " ", A2, "s")	
3	Pen	4	£2.99	£11.96			
4	Pencil	5	£0.50	£2.50			
5	Ruler	3	£1.25	£3.75			
6							
7				£36.18			

The ROUNDUP function

The **ROUNDUP** function is used to round a value up.

In this example, we are rounding the result of **B2*C2** to **0** decimal places.

	A	B	C	D
1	Item	Number sold	Cost per item	Total cost
2	Calculator	3	£5.99	=ROUNDUP(B2*C2, 0)
3	Pen	4	£2.99	£11.96
4	Pencil	5	£0.50	£2.50
5	Ruler	3	£1.25	£3.75
6				
7				£36.21

You may need to adjust the cell formatting to ensure that no trailing zeros are displayed. Use the 'Decrease Decimal' button to do this.

Finance system

You will be using your spreadsheet skills to develop a finance system for a small hotel.

Open 'Excel workbook 2.1', which contains two spreadsheets.

▶ The 'Guests' spreadsheet includes data for 19 guests and contains drop-down lists showing the room type, room rate and type of breakfast for each guest.

▶ The 'Services' spreadsheet contains details of the cost of each room type, the discount or supplement that applies to each room rate and the cost of each breakfast choice. It also contains details of staff costs and fixed costs.

Data for one week of bookings has already been entered on the 'Guests' spreadsheet.

Part 1

1 Save a new version of the spreadsheet, as 'Version 1', and complete the tasks below.

Add the following seven column headings to the 'Guests' spreadsheet:

● Cost of room per night

● Discount or supplement applied via the room rate

● Total cost of room per night, with discount or supplement applied

● Total cost of room for duration of stay

● Total cost of breakfast for duration of stay

● Total cost of stay

● Guest's full name

These columns should be wide enough to display the headings without breaking any words. Use the formatting options to set the alignment and wrap text onto multiple lines.

2 Use a **VLOOKUP** function to calculate the cost of the room per night for the type of room selected. Use absolute references as necessary and replicate this formula for all the guests. Make sure the data is shown as currency.

3 Use a **VLOOKUP** to find the discount or supplement applied based on the room rate and replicate this formula for all the guests. Make sure that this data is shown as a percentage with no decimal places.

4 Use the cost of the room per night and the discount or supplement applied to create a formula to calculate the total cost of the room per night with discount or supplement applied. Replicate this formula for all guests. Make sure the data is shown as currency.

Part 2

Save a new version of the spreadsheet, as 'Version 2', and complete the tasks below.

5 Create a formula using the total cost of the room per night and the number of nights to calculate the total cost of the room for the duration of the stay for each guest.

6 Use a **VLOOKUP** function to find the cost of the breakfast chosen and multiply this by the number of nights to calculate the cost of breakfast for the duration of the stay for each guest.

7 Use the data to calculate the total cost for each guest. This will be the total cost of the room for the duration of the stay plus the cost of breakfast for the duration of the stay.

8 Use a **CONCATENATE** function to join together each guest's title, first name and surname into one string. You will need to add a space between each part of their name.

Add more information below the guest details.

9 Use a **COUNTA** function to calculate the total number of guests staying at the hotel for the week.

10 Use a **COUNTIF** function to calculate the number of guests opting for each room rate.

11 Calculate the total income generated for the week.

Part 3

Save a new version of the spreadsheet, as 'Version 3', and complete the tasks below.

12 Create another spreadsheet in your workbook and name it 'Invoice'.

13 Add a suitable hotel name to fit across the top of your invoice. Use text formatting, borders and fills to make this a feature of the invoice.

14 Below this, in column A, add a label called 'Reference number' and, in the adjacent cell in column B, create a drop-down list using the data in the 'Ref' column on the 'Guests' spreadsheet.

15 Add further labels in column A, as follows:
  - Name
  - Address
  - Number of nights
  - Room cost
  - Breakfast cost
  - Total cost

16 Write **VLOOKUP** functions that use the reference number selected from the drop-down list to fill in the guest's full name and address using the data in the 'Guests' spreadsheet.

17 Write **VLOOKUP** functions that use the reference number selected from the drop-down list to fill in the number of nights, the total cost of the room for the duration of the stay, the cost of breakfast for the duration of the stay and the total cost of the stay using the data in the 'Guests' spreadsheet.

18 Format the invoice using suitable fonts, colours and borders to make a well-presented document that can be printed on an A4 sheet of paper and given to the guest when they check out.

Part 4

Save a new version of the spreadsheet, as 'Version 4', and complete the tasks below.

19 Add another spreadsheet to your workbook and name it 'Accounts'.

20 In cell A1 add a label 'Total number of guests' and, in the adjacent cell in column B, use a cell reference to link to this value in the 'Guests' spreadsheet.

21 Leave an empty row, then add the following headings to the columns in row 3:
  - Staff
  - Number
  - Salary per week
  - Cost

22 Below this, in column A, add the following staff titles:
  - Manager
  - Deputy manager
  - Night manager
  - Receptionist
  - Cleaner
  - Chef

23 In the adjacent cells in column B add numbers to show that there is one manager, one deputy manager, one night manager and two receptionists.

24 One cleaner is required for every seven rooms occupied. Write a formula to calculate the number of cleaners required based on the total number of guests. This must be rounded up to a whole number.

25 One chef is required for every 10 guests. Write a formula to calculate the number of chefs required based on the total number of guests. This must be rounded up to a whole number.

26 Use a **VLOOKUP** function to show the weekly salary for each staff position using the data in the 'Services' spreadsheet. Then use these values to calculate the total cost of each staff position.

27 Add another label, 'Fixed costs', below the staff and use a cell reference to link to this value in the 'Services spreadsheet'.

28 Add a suitable label and calculate the total running costs for the week. The total running costs are the staff costs plus the fixed costs.

29 Add a suitable label and use a cell reference to link to the total income value in the 'Guests' spreadsheet.

30 Add a suitable label and calculate the total profit/loss for the week.

Part 5

Save a new version of the spreadsheet, as 'Version 5', and complete the tasks below.

31 Use the spreadsheet to model the effects of the following scenarios on the profit/loss for the week. Apply the changes in sequence, with the changes made for part a applying to part b and the changes made for parts a and b applying to part c and so on.

  a Increase the number of guests to the maximum of 25. All of the new guests should be staying in a 'Standard' room type for three nights at the 'Special' room rate, with 'English breakfast'.

  b Change all 'Last minute' and 'Peak' room rates to 'Standard' and change the 'Special' discount to 15%.

  c Use the 'Standard' room rate for all guests.

  d Use Goal Seek to calculate how much the 'Standard' room rate should be for the hotel to make a profit of £1000 if all 25 guests are staying in a 'Standard' room type.

  e Experiment, applying your own changes to the room rates and breakfasts to see how you can maximise profits.

32 Write a brief report for the owners of the hotel to show how profits will alter with each scenario and to advise them on how they can increase their profits. Include evidence from the spreadsheet to justify any recommendations.

→ Project 3

You will be using your skills with graphics, audio and video editing software to create a 30-second advert for a theme park.

You will need to:
- ▶ design and develop a logo
- ▶ plan how you will use video and audio to create your advert

- ▶ create a soundtrack
- ▶ edit together the sound track, video clips and logo to create the final advert.

You will need to use an **iterative approach to project development** to create each element before moving on to the next element and you will need to be prepared to tweak elements when you combine them together to create the final advert.

Theme park advert

You will be using your skills with graphics, audio and video editing software to create an advert for a theme park. The advert must be 30 seconds long and include:

- ▶ background music
- ▶ a voiceover
- ▶ at least three background sounds
- ▶ at least five video clips
- ▶ transitions between the video clips
- ▶ a logo, which could be on the screen throughout or shown at the end.

The images, videos and sounds must be mixed together to create a watchable advert.

Part 1

1 Design a simple logo for your theme park. If you choose to give your theme park a name other than 'The Theme Park', this should be included in your logo.

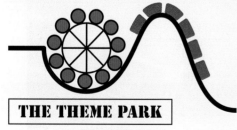

THE THEME PARK

➡ An example of a logo for a theme park

2 Use the vector drawing tools in Microsoft Word to create your logo.

3 Take a screenshot of your logo and then open it in GIMP to make any final edits. If you wish to display your logo over the video clips, you will need to edit the background so that it is transparent. Ensure that your finished logo is exported from GIMP as a .png file.

Part 2

4 Download audio and video clips to use in your advert. You can find background sounds at http://bbcsfx.acropolis.org.uk/ (try searching for 'fairgrounds'), background music at www.bensound.com and video clips at www.pexels.com or https://pixabay.com/.

5 Write a voiceover to be recorded and used in the advert. It should include a minimum of the following two phrases:
- ● 'Welcome to <the name of your theme park>'
- ● 'Thrills and excitement for everyone!'

6 Decide which sounds and visuals you want to use in your advert and plan your advert using a timeline like the one below. Create a labelled block for each audio and video clip, and for the logo and transitions, and position them carefully on the timeline.

Part 3

7 Use Audacity to create the sound track for your advert, following the plan that you have drawn up. Once you have finished creating your soundtrack, save it as an Audacity project and export it as an .mp3 file and save it to your project folder.

Part 4

8 Use OpenShot to import and edit your video files. Order and layer the clips, following the plan that

you have drawn up, remembering to add suitable transitions between the video clips and to include your logo. Then add your soundtrack and make any necessary adjustments to ensure that the images and sound are synced together correctly. Use titles to add text over your video if desired. Export your finished video advert as an .mp4 file.

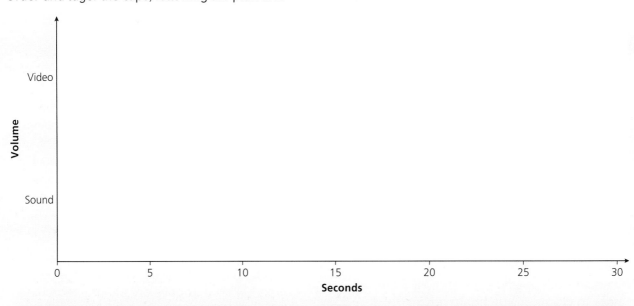

Glossary

absolute cell reference a cell reference that does not change when it is replicated to several columns or rows of data in a spreadsheet, for example, `=$A$1+$B$1`

abstraction removing unnecessary and unhelpful detail; one of the cornerstones of computational thinking

acceptable use policy the rules that govern how a computer network should be used

action the output if the condition is met

algorithm a series of simple, logical, step-by-step instructions that must be followed in a strict sequence

algorithm design planning a solution based on your understanding of the problem; one of the cornerstones of computational thinking

AND a logical operator that allows for two conditions to be checked; for it to return True, both conditions must be true

AND in spreadsheets, the AND logical operator can be used in IF functions to check that more than one condition is True

AND gate a logic gate that requires both condition 1 AND condition 2 to be met for the gate to open

anti-malware software scans computer programs and emails for malicious code and puts anything suspicious in quarantine; also referred to as anti-virus software

app a computer program/piece of software; short for 'application'

arrange to organise sounds according to your audio timeline

ASCII The American Standard Code for Information Interchange was invented to standardise the denary numbers assigned to each character on a keyboard

attribute a characteristic. The attributes of a vector graphic include its height, width, outline colour and fill colour. An attribute is also the information that is included inside an HTML tag, for example, the src and alt attributes must be included inside the <img> tag

Audacity a free Digital Audio Workstation (DAW)

audio effect something that is used to enhance or process audio, to make it sound different; there are four main audio effects: fade in/fade out, reverb, compression and envelope

avatar a profile picture on social media

AVERAGE in spreadsheets, this function calculates the mean of the values in a range of cells

bar charts allow you to compare categories of data that are not directly related in order to identify similarities and differences

base 10 the number system that uses ten digits: 0, 1, 2, 3, 4, 5, 6, 7, 8 and 9; also known as the decimal system or the denary system

base 2 the number system that uses just two digits: 0 and 1; also known as the binary system

binary system the number system that uses just two digits: 0 and 1; also known as base 2

bit each 1 and 0 in a binary number is known as a bit

bitmap graphic data about an image is stored by a computer as pixels; also known as a raster graphic

Boolean operators logical tests in Python use the following Boolean operators:

<	less than
<=	less than or equal to
!=	not equal to
==	equal to
>	greater than
>=	greater than or equal to

Boolean value a value that can be only True or False

Boolean variable a variable that is only True or False

border a line around the outside of an element creating a box

brute force attack using a program that tries every possible combination of letters, numbers and special characters to identify your password

bug an error in a computer program

button in spreadsheets, macros are assigned to buttons

byte unit of storage; other units of storage include bit (there are 8 bits in a byte), kilobyte (1000 bytes), megabyte (1,000,000 bytes), gigabyte (1,000,000,000 bytes), terabyte (1,000,000,000,000 bytes) and petabyte (1,000,000,000,000,000 bytes)

casting declaring what data type a variable will be

cell a box on the spreadsheet, into which you can place numbers, text or calculations

cell range two or more cells next to each other in a row or a column in a spreadsheet, for example, `A1:A10`

cell reference a unique reference used to identify a cell in a spreadsheet. Cell references can be relative, for example, `=A1+B1`, or absolute, for example, `=$A$1+$B$1`

check box a type of form control that allows the user to select one or more items from a range of options; also known as a tick box

cipher an encryption algorithm

ciphertext in encryption, the encrypted message is in ciphertext

clock speed how many fetch–decode–execute cycles a CPU can process per second; often referred to as just 'speed'

cloud computing data is stored online and software is used via an internet browser, rather than being stored locally on a computer's hard drive

column a spreadsheet is divided into rows and columns

column charts allow you to compare categories of data that are not directly related in order to identify similarities and differences

compression an audio effect that is used to make sure that no parts of a sound are too quiet or loud; it makes the quiet sounds louder, and the loud sounds slightly quieter

computational thinking a logical, strategic approach to problem solving involving four cornerstones: decomposition, abstraction, pattern recognition and algorithm design to formulate an efficient and effective algorithm

computer network a collection of computers and other digital devices that are connected together

computer program a set of instructions that a computer follows precisely

concatenation in Scratch, it is using the 'join' block to join text together with variables; in Python, it is using + to join more than one piece of data into a single print statement

condition what the data has to be for an action to be performed; the condition in an if statement must be a question that can be answered with true or false

conditional formatting allows you to alter the appearance of a cell depending on the value it contains

constant a value stored by the computer that cannot be changed by the program

copyright the person who creates content (text, images, videos and sounds, etc.) owns the copyright in that content and this protects them from other people copying it without their permission

COUNT in spreadsheets, this function counts the number of cells in a selected range that contain a number

COUNTA in spreadsheets, this function counts the number of cells in a selected range that contain a value (text or a number)

COUNTIF in spreadsheets, this function counts the number of cells in a selected range that meet a specific criterion

CPU the Central Processing Unit carries out all the processing in a computer by completing the fetch–decode–execute cycle

Creative Commons licence a person can release their content – text, images, videos and sounds and so on – with a Creative Commons license, which explains how they allow it to be used by other people

credit acknowledging who created content – text, images, videos and sounds and so on – that you are making use of

criterion in a spreadsheet, the condition that determines which cells will be counted in a COUNTIF function. It can be a number, a mathematical expression or text

CSS (Cascading Style Sheet) the properties in a CSS style sheet are used to format the layout of a web page

CSS class it is possible to apply different styling to specific HTML elements using the CSS class selector; the styling is defined in the style sheet with a full stop followed by your chosen class name

CSS properties the properties in a CSS style sheet are used to format the layout of a web page

data the numbers and characters stored and processed by a computer

Data Protection Act 2018 one of the two main laws that protect personal data from exploitation in the UK

data representation converting text, images and sound into binary, so they can be processed by a computer

debugging the activity of finding and correcting errors in a computer program

decimal system the number system that uses ten digits: 0, 1, 2, 3, 4, 5, 6, 7, 8 and 9; also known as the denary system or base 10

decision a choice has to be made; the standard symbol for a decision in a flow diagram is a diamond

declaration a CSS style rule contains a declaration block, which includes the CSS property name and value, separated by a colon; each declaration block is surrounded by curly brackets

decomposition breaking down a complex and seemingly impossible problem into smaller problems to gain a better understanding of it; one of the cornerstones of computational thinking

decryption unscrambling an encrypted message so that it makes sense again

denary system the number system that uses ten digits: 0, 1, 2, 3, 4, 5, 6, 7, 8 and 9; also known as the decimal system or base 10

design cycle a process describing an iterative (repeating) approach to design

digital footprint the information about a person on the internet

digital wellbeing having a healthy relationship with technology

DNS the system that lets a web browser look up the IP address for a website

document the name often given to a file that contains text

domain name the part of a web address that indicates the organisation that runs the site, for example, hoddereducation.co.uk

drop-down list a type of validation that limits the values that can be entered into a cell in a spreadsheet

e-waste electrical devices that have been thrown away

element a data item in a list. Also, an .html document consists of a series of elements, for example, headings, paragraphs, images or hyperlinks

elif statement short for 'else if' and used with if statements and else statements to check several different conditions in a row

else statement used with if statements to tell a computer program what to do if the condition is false

email electronic messages sent via a computer network

encryption a method of scrambling a message so that it cannot be understood if someone else reads it

envelope an audio effect that allows you to make a track quieter and louder at certain points

escape characters used to add punctuation and formatting to an output

Ethernet cables are used to create a wired network connection

export saving a file in a format that can be imported into a different software program

external storage device saves data, for example, a memory stick

external style sheet a single document, saved with a .css extension, that sets out the styling to be used for all the main elements on every page of a website

fade in/fade out an audio effect added to the beginning and/or end of a track so that it starts and stops playing smoothly, without pops or crackles

file all data stored on a computer is saved to a file

file extension the characters software adds to a file name to tell the computer what type of file it is, for example: .doc and .png

fill handle the spreadsheet tool that enables you to replicate information from one cell to another

floating point number (also known as real number) a data type consisting of numbers with decimal points; 2.3, 5.44 and 10.9 are all floating point numbers

flow diagram a graphic representation of the flow of something through a system; flow diagrams are often used to illustrate the sequence of instructions in an algorithm

folder a selection of files can be stored in a folder

for loop a type of loop used when we know how many times we want to do something

form control a form control is an object that can be placed onto a spreadsheet to help the user interact with the data and select items from lists

formatting cells helps to make a spreadsheet easier to read. You can change the font, text size, text colour, fill colour, number format, text alignment and borders

formula a calculation; most formulae in spreadsheets use cell references so you can change a value in a cell and the formula automatically recalculates the answer

function in spreadsheets, functions are pre-programmed calculations that can be used to simplify formulae, for example, `=SUM(A3:G3)`

function name the name of a function

GDPR the common name for the General Data Protection Regulation (EU) 2016/679, one of the two main laws that protect personal data from exploitation in the UK

generalisation when a solution to a problem is applied to many similar types of problems; generalisation makes coding much more efficient and improves productivity

Goal Seek is a built-in spreadsheet tool that enables you to ask 'what if' questions to achieve a specific goal

GPS an input device that collects data on the location of a device

graphics card an additional component of a computer that plugs directly into the motherboard; used to output and display graphics on a screen

hacking gaining unauthorised access to a computer system

hard drive the permanent storage in a computer; there are two main types: magnetic hard drives and solid-state hard drives

hardware the physical parts of a computer that you can touch

header data added to a packet that includes the packet number, the IP address of recipient and the IP address of sender

hertz unit of speed; other units of speed include kilohertz (1000 hertz), megahertz (1,000,000 hertz) and gigahertz (1,000,000,000 hertz)

HTML (Hypertext Markup Language) used to describe the structure of a web page

hyperlink allows users to move from page to page within a website, or to move to a page on another website

hyperlink reference the attribute href is short for 'hyperlink reference' and is used to identify the destination that the hyperlink will take you to; included inside the anchor tag <a> when defining a hyperlink

`IF` in spreadsheets, this function is used to make choices

if-else statement performs one action if the condition is True and another if it is False; it will not perform both actions

if statement the most common way of implementing selection in a computer program, if statements are used to decide what to do next if a condition is True

illegal against the law

image editing software software that enables you to edit a bitmap image, for example, GIMP

immoral against acceptable standards of behaviour

import bringing a file into the software program you are using

index value the elements in a list are identified by an index value; in Python the first element in a list has the index value 0

input device a device that allow the user to enter data into a computer, for example, keyboard and mouse

input when data is sent into a system; the standard symbol for input in a flow diagram is a parallelogram

integer a data type consisting of whole numbers; 1, 10 and -100 are all integers

internet a global network that connects computers across the world so that they can communicate with one another

Internet of Things (IoT) an IoT device is a device that connects to the internet so that it can 'talk' to other devices; often referred to as 'smart' devices

inverter a logic gate that inverts the input from a sensor or the output from a logic gate so that 1 becomes 0 and 0 becomes 1; also called a NOT gate

IP address each device on a network has a unique IP address so that data can be sent to the correct place; 'IP' stands for 'Internet Protocol'

iteration when a set of instructions is repeated; also referred to as using a loop

key in encryption, the number of letters the Caesar Cipher is shifted left

keyboard an input device that collects data when text or numbers are typed in

layer when creating vector graphics, objects can be placed on top of each other to create a sense of depth or more complex shapes; when creating bitmap graphics, images can be placed on top of each other to create complex images

level the volume of an audio track

light sensor an input device that collects data on how much light there is in an area

line graphs are used when you want to show how something has changed over time. They are useful for plotting the results of experiments

linear search a type of search that looks at each element of the list and compares it to what is being searched for

link text the text that is shown on the screen to indicate a hyperlink; included inside the anchor tag <a> when defining a hyperlink

linked cell when a check box is ticked on a spreadsheet, the linked cell returns TRUE and when it is not selected it returns FALSE

list a data container that uses a single identifier to store several data items

log in the process you have to go through to gain access to a computer network, an email system and a VLE; you will usually have to enter a username and password

logic gate two or more switches combine to create a logic gate; logic gates make decisions by processing two or more inputs and producing the correct output

logical operators return a Boolean value, a value that can be only True or False; there are three that can be used in programming: AND, OR and NOT. In spreadsheets, logical operators can be used in IF functions to check more than one condition

logical test (also logical expression) a question to which the answer can be either true or false

look-up table in spreadsheets, a look-up table is the table of data used in a VLOOKUP function

loop when a set of instructions is repeated; also referred to as iteration

macro a small program that records your mouse clicks and key strokes as you complete a task, automating routine tasks

magnetic storage a type of secondary storage that uses magnetic platters and a write/read head to write to and read from the disc; examples include hard drives and data tapes

malware software designed to do harm to a computer

MAX in spreadsheets, this function finds the largest value in a range

metadata data about data

microchip many transistors can be etched onto a microchip, bringing about the second big reduction in the size of electronic computers

microphones an input device that collects data when speech or other sounds are detected

MIN in spreadsheets, this function finds the smallest value in a range

mobile data using a SIM card to connect to the internet using the mobile phone network of cell towers; 2G, 3G, 4G and 5G are all types of mobile data

modelling allows us to predict what is likely to happen when something changes

Moore's Law the number of transistors on a single microchip will double every two years

moral dilemma a situation that requires a choice between two options, both of which can be viewed as immoral

motherboard the main circuit board found in a computer, which connects all the components together so they can communicate

motion sensor an input device that collects data on movements in an area

navigation bar a set of hyperlinks used to move between the pages of a website

NOT a logical operator; for it to return True, the value being checked has to be anything but the value being asked for

NOT gate a logic gate that inverts the input from a sensor or the output from a logic gate so that 1 becomes 0 and 0 becomes 1; also called an inverter

object larger vector graphics are made up of shapes called objects

OpenShot Video Editor free video-editing software

optical drives use a laser to read from or write to optical discs

optical storage a type of secondary storage that uses a laser to write data to and read data from a disc; examples include CD drives/CDs, DVD drives/DVDs and Blu-ray Disc drives/Blu-ray Discs

OR logical operator that can be used in IF functions to check that one or more conditions are True

OR gate a logic gate that requires either condition 1 OR condition 2 to be met for the gate to open

ordered lists numbered lists, used when the items need to be presented in a particular order

output data generated by a computer and sent out of a system; the standard symbol for output in a flow diagram is a parallelogram

output device a device that allows the user to display the results after a computer has processed data, for example, monitor and speakers

packet a small chunk of data; when a file or an email message is sent over a network, it is split into small packets

packet switching when travelling over a network, packets of data can take different routes to their destination to avoid traffic jams

padding adds space between the border and the contents of the box it defines

parameters the rules we give a for loop; the first parameter tells the program when to start counting, the second tells the program when to stop counting and the third – the step value – tells the program how many values to jump

parentheses ( ) in spreadsheets, the individual cell references or range of cells used by a function are enclosed in parentheses

password a string of characters a user needs to enter to enable them to log in to a computer network, an email system and a VLE

password policy a set of rules for passwords that tries to keep them as secure as possible

pattern recognition identifying patterns in data; one of the cornerstones of computational thinking

peripheral a device that allows information to be entered into or retrieved from a computer; peripherals are normally divided into input devices, output devices and external storage devices

phishing tricking someone into giving away their password, usually by sending them an email asking them to click on a link to a fake website and enter their login details

pie charts show the individual parts that make up a whole; they are useful to show percentages

pixel data about a bitmap image is stored as pixels, which is short for 'picture element'; the colour of every pixel is stored and every different colour has its own unique binary code

pixelated when we can see the pixels in an image, we say it is pixelated

placeholder a string of characters that temporarily takes the place of the final data

place value the value of each digit in a number. In base 10, it increases in multiples of 10 (units followed by 10s, 10s followed by 100s, 100s followed by 1000s, etc.). In base 2, it increases in multiples of 2 (units followed by 2s, 2s followed by 4s, 4s followed by 8s, 8s followed by 16s, etc.)

plaintext in encryption, the original message is in plaintext

power supply provides the power to all the components in a computer that need it

pressure sensor an input device that collects data on the force being applied to a device

primary storage accessed directly by the CPU and normally the fastest memory in a computer; RAM is an example

privacy settings the settings that control who can see your social media posts

private IP address allows a device to connect to a local network, which then connects to the internet

programming constructs there are three key programming constructs: sequence, selection and iteration

prompt an instruction or question that tells the user what data to input

property name the CSS property name is included in the declaration block; property names include 'color' to set the colour of the text and 'font-family' to set the font

protocol a set of rules; the Internet Protocol is a specific set of rules for how to transmit data from one device to another: all IP addresses must contain four numbers between 0 and 255, separated by full stops

public hotspot a method of connecting to the internet wirelessly; everyone has access to a public hotspot and access is usually free

public IP address allows a device to access the internet directly; they are unique

RAM (Random Access Memory) is storage connected directly to the motherboard of a computer; data stored in RAM can be accessed more quickly than data stored on the hard drive

ransomware a type of malware that encrypts a user's files and demands a payment to unlock them

raster graphic data about an image is stored by a computer as pixels; also known as a bitmap graphic

real number (also known as floating point number) a data type consisting of numbers with decimal points; 2.3, 5.44 and 10.9 are all real numbers

relative cell reference a cell reference that needs to change to match the row or column it applies to when it is replicated to several columns or rows of data in a spreadsheet, for example, =A1+B1

replication copying information from one cell to another in a spreadsheet using the fill handle

REPT in spreadsheets, this function is used to repeat a string of characters a given number of times

resolution the quality of a bitmap image depends on its resolution, the number of pixels in the image; the higher the resolution, the better quality and more realistic the image

reverb an audio effect that is used to make a sound feel like it is in a different space

row a spreadsheet is divided into rows and columns

scalable can be enlarged without any loss in quality; vector graphics are scalable

secondary storage not accessed constantly by the computer; there are three types: optical storage, magnetic storage and Solid State storage

selection used when we want to make a decision in a program; involves asking a question to which the answer is either true (yes) or false (no) and, depending on the answer, the program will follow certain steps and ignore others

selector a CSS style rule contains a selector to indicate the HTML element the styling refers to

semantic elements used within the <body> element; each one is like a box and its name describes its purpose and content

sequencing when a set of instructions is carried out in order

server computer hardware or software that provides a service to digital devices; data and software in the cloud is stored on servers

shoulder surfing looking over someone's shoulder as they enter their password so that you know what their password is

site plan a plan that shows what information will go on each page of a website

social media profiles a description of a person's characteristics that is used to identify them on social media sites

software programs that use computer hardware to run

Solid State storage a type of secondary storage that uses miniature electronic switches to store data, has no moving parts and provides very fast access to data; examples include memory sticks, memory cards and Solid State drives

sort in spreadsheets, you can sort the whole spreadsheet, or just a selected range of cells, into alphabetical (A–Z) or numerical (0–100) order using the sort facility

soundtrack the sounds that accompany the visuals in a video

spreadsheet a grid of cells used to store data; Microsoft Excel and Google Sheets are spreadsheet programs

spyware a type of malware that watches and records a user's actions and sends them back to the creator

storage device hardware or computer peripheral that stores data or saves data to a storage medium, for example, magnetic hard drives and CD drives

storage medium the thing that stores the data for a storage device that cannot store it itself, for example, CDs and DVDs; the plural is storage media

string a data type consisting of alphanumeric characters; 'Hello', '%^$&*' and '12345' are all strings

substring a string contained within a string; part of a string

SUM in spreadsheets, this function adds up the values in a range of cells

switch inputs are like switches; If the switch is turned on, the input is YES and this is represented by a 1 but, if the switch is turned off, the input is NO and this is represented by a 0

switch a piece of network hardware that connects devices on a network so they can send data to each other

tags the elements in a .html document are labelled using opening and closing tags, for example, <p> and </p>

temperature sensor an input device that collects data on how warm or cold an area is

template a blank document with a pre-set format

tick box a type of form control that allows the user to select one or more items from a range of options; also known as a check box

timeline shows how the individual sounds that make up an audio track or the sounds and visuals that make up a video are organised

titles (extra words) added to a video to tell the viewer something important; titles are a visual effect

transistors replaced valves as the switches to process data and brought about the first big reduction in the size of electronic computers

transition a visual effect added between video clips to add some excitement when the video changes from one scene to the next and smooth the passage between clips

trigger the data collected by an input device used by the IoT device in order to make a decision

trojan a type of malware where a whole program pretends to do something that people will want to trick them into installing it

truth table describes how a computer processes data; the operation of AND, OR and NOT gates can be summarised in a truth table

Unicode an international standard invented to standardise the denary numbers assigned to each character on a keyboard; can represent many more characters than ASCII

unordered lists bullet point lists, used when the order of the items is not important

user interface (UI) the mechanism a person uses to interact with a digital device or an application

username a unique ID given to a user to enable them to log in to a computer network, an email system and a VLE

validation tools that limit the values that can be entered into a cell in a spreadsheet

valves the switches used to process data in early computers

variable a storage location in a computer

vector graphic data about an image is stored by a computer as a list of attributes

virus a type of malware where a piece of malicious code is inserted into an existing file or program or game

Visual Basic the programming language used to record and save macros in Microsoft Excel

visual effect something that is used to enhance or process video, to make it look different; visual effects include transitions and titles

VLE (Virtual Learning Environment) an online system that stores learning resources such as documents, presentations and video and audio files

VLOOKUP in spreadsheets, this function takes the value in a cell, searches for it in a table of data elsewhere on the spreadsheet and returns a value from an adjacent cell

voiceover the words that provide a commentary on what is happening

web browser the software used to view and interact with web pages

while loop a type of loop used when we are unsure how many times we wish to carry out a repeated task

Wi-Fi uses radio waves transmitted to and from a wireless access point to create a wireless network connection

word-processing software is used to create and manipulate a text-based document, for example, Microsoft Word and Google Docs

worm a type of malware that doesn't need to be run by the user; it can copy itself from one machine to another automatically

Getting started

1 Logging in

1 To prove our identity and allow access to our own files

2 The rules that need to be followed when using a computer network

3 A password that cannot easily be guessed or discovered by someone else. A strong password is long, includes a range of characters and is random and unpredictable.

2 File management, cloud computing and VLEs

1 A file

2 A selection of files

3 Characters added to the end of a file name that tell the computer what sort of file it is

3 The Internet and digital wellbeing

1 A worldwide network of computers that can communicate with one another

2 Complete and hand in work, research, email teachers

3 Play games, message friends, watch videos, listen to music

4 Having a healthy relationship with technology

4 Vector graphics

1 A vector graphic

2 As a set of points that are joined together by lines

3 They can be enlarged without losing any quality

4 .eps, .svg

5 Bitmap graphics

1 As a matrix of coloured pixels

2 The resolution of the image

3 The quality decreases. The individual pixels can be seen

4 .png, .jpg, .gif, .bmp, .tif

6 Impossible photographs

1 Using layers, so that one image is superimposed over the top of another one

2 The background needs to be transparent

3 Re-sizing the images so that they are a suitable size for the background and feathering the edges so that they blend into the new image

Introducing spreadsheets

1 Formulae, replication and referencing

1 Replication is where you copy information from one place to another using the fill handle. You select the cells containing the first few numbers in a series, and move the pointer to the fill handle which you drag down over the cells where the rest of the series is needed

2 It is a cell reference that adjusts automatically when it is replicated to different cells

3 It is a cell reference that does not change when it is replicated.

2 Functions using SUM, AVERAGE, MAX and MIN

1 For example: C1:C5

2 It is much quicker and easier to use a function, and you are more likely to make a mistake when writing a formula.

3 MAX

3 Boolean operators and the IF and COUNT functions

1 The question or logical test, the value to be returned if the condition is True and the value to be returned if the condition is False.

2 The COUNT function tells you how many cells in a selected range contain a number.

3 The COUNTIF function

4 Formatting, graphs and charts

1 Change the type and size of font, change the text colour, change the number format, add a background fill, change the text alignment.

2 For example: we could use conditional formatting when we want to quickly see which students have scored more than the pass mark and which students have scored less than the pass mark.

3 A pie chart

5 Modelling

1 It is a process that allows us to predict what is likely to happen when something changes.

2 Spreadsheets are good to use for modelling because they are easy to set up, then perform calculations on data and you can try out lots of different scenarios to find the best result.

3 Goal Seek enables you to ask 'what-if' questions to achieve a specific goal.

6 Theme park challenges

Student's own answers

Computing: past, present and future

1 The history of word processing

1 Documents were handwritten or typewritten.

2 A mind map is diagram that organises information around a central concept or topic. Pieces of information are linked together, with more important information closer to the centre.

3 You should review it, to make sure you've done everything you set out to do. You should reflect on it to see how you could make it better. And you should edit it, making the changes you have identified.

2 Designing a leaflet

1 You experiment, use the application's built in 'Help' feature, or, if you're really stuck, find an online tutorial.

2 The highlighted text becomes *italic*.

3 False, the design cycle should be repeated until the design is fit for purpose and no more improvements are required.

3 Moore's Law

1 Gordon Moore

2 Valves

3 They contain transistors etched onto microchips.

4 The history of computing

1 Student's own answers

2 False, it includes early methods and devices for carrying out calculations, such as the abacus.

3 Tim Berners-Lee

5 Learning to present

Student's own answers

6 The future of computing

We can only guess how computers might impact our lives in the future because new discoveries frequently take technological developments in unforeseeable directions.

Programming in Scratch

1 Introduction to the Scratch environment and sequencing

1 When a set of instructions is carried out in order

2 It would draw the letter 'L'.

2 Sequencing

It would make the cat turn 360 degrees, so it does a full circle

3 Using variables

1 A variable is a container that temporarily holds a value (a number or a piece of text). The value can be retrieved within the program using its variable name.

2 There are three variables: **name**, **age** and **favsport**.

4 Selection

1 Selection is used to check a condition and then do one thing if the condition is True and one thing if it is False.

2 `You are not old enough to drive yet`

5 Selection and logical operators

1 Two

2 At least one

3 The program will always return **FALSE** because there is no value that can meet both conditions. A number cannot be simultaneously more than 50 and less than 50.

6 Iteration

1 Iteration is when a set of instructions is repeated.

2 4

Computing components

1 Computer hardware

1 CPU

2 Motherboard

3 Hard drive

2 Measuring computer performance

1 No. There are 1000 kilobytes in a megabyte.

2 1600 MHz. 1.5 GHz = 1500 MHz

3 They will be taking a large number of high-resolution photographs, which require a large amount of storage space.

3 Computer peripherals

1 For example: keyboard and mouse

2 For example: speakers, headphones and monitor

3 For example: a keyboard for typing emails, a mouse for navigating around the computer and opening lesson resources, a projector for displaying presentations on the board, a memory stick for storing documents and a printer for printing out worksheets

4 Storage devices and media

1 RAM

2 Optical storage, magnetic storage, Solid State storage

5 The Internet of Things

1 An IoT device connects to the internet so that it can 'talk' to other devices.

2 An IoT device collects data, analyses it and, if appropriate, automates a process by talking to another IoT device.

3 Trigger (the data collected by input device), condition (what the data has to be for the action to be performed) and action (the output if the condition is met).

Programming in Python: sequence

1 Computer programs

1 A variable is a storage location in a computer, where we store the data we are using in the program.

2 We should use a variable name that describes the data the variable contains so that, when we come back to a program, we know what type of data it stores.

3 Variable names cannot start with a number. They must start with an alphabetic character.

2 Getting data from the user

1 The input data needs to be assigned to a variable, for example: `name = input('What is your name?')`.

2 It will output `name` because `name` is inside quotes and is, therefore, a string and not the name of a variable.

3 Data types

1 It is a string.

2 It is an integer.

3 It is a real or floating point number.

4 We enclose the string in quotation marks.

5 Python requires variables that contain integers to be cast using `int`.

6 Python requires variables that contain real numbers to be cast using `float`.

4 Placeholders and lists

1 `onion`

2 `veg[6]`

5 Working with lists

1 `coat` is output.

2 A element containing `socks` is added to the end of the list, so the list becomes `['hat', 'coat', 'shoes', 'gloves', 'socks']`

3 A new value, `scarf`, is inserted into the list at the location with index value 2, so the list becomes: `['hat', 'coat', 'scarf', 'shoes', 'gloves', 'socks']`

4 6 is output. Two new elements have been added to the original list so it now contains 6 elements.

5 `tie` is inserted into the list at the location with index value 3, so the list becomes: `['hat', 'coat', 'scarf', 'tie', 'shoes', 'gloves', 'socks']`

6 Working with strings

1 9

2 `PHONE APP`

3 `pen`

4 `hone`

Advanced spreadsheets

1 Drop-down lists, VLOOKUP and sorting data

1 We can use a drop-down list.

2 To help eliminate input errors

3 Find the value of a cell in a table and return the data in an adjacent cell

2 Check boxes

1 One

2 Check boxes

3 `TRUE`

4 In a cell linked to the check box

3 Macros

1 To automate frequently performed tasks

2 Visual Basic

3 You assign it to a button which can be clicked to run the macro.

4 Logical operators and the `REPT` function

1 `OR`

2 `AND`

3 The `REPT` (repeat) function

5 and 6 Quiz

1 The 'Data' tab

2 The 'Data validation' tools

3 The `VLOOKUP` function

Algorithms

1 Using computational thinking to solve problems

1 Computers can only follow instructions and so, for a computer to implement the solution to a problem, the problem must be written as a series of instructions.

2 Abstraction

3 Breaking down a complex and seemingly impossible problem into smaller problems to gain a better understanding of it

2 Pattern recognition

1 An algorithm

2 Pattern recognition

3 c only has 4 lines, the others have 5

3 Using flow diagrams to solve computational problems

1 Three: flow diagrams, a sequence of pictures and text

2 One

3 Two

4 Cholera in Soho

1 Dr Snow's map enabled him to break down, or decompose the problem, in order to recognise patterns in the distribution of the deaths from cholera.

2 The map simplified the real world in such a way as to make the patterns visible.

3 The cluster of deaths around the Broad Street pump and the brewery workers and workhouse inmates who did not die and did not drink water from the Broad Street pump.

5 Malaria in Kitanga

1 Deconstructing a model helicopter, breaking down how to brush your teeth, breaking down an everyday activity, taking apart a paper aeroplane, analysing flower designs, thinking about the traffic light algorithm, investigating the Soho cholera outbreak, investigating malaria in Kitanga.

2 Removing unnecessary detail from an algorithm to brush your teeth, simplifying your algorithm to construct a paper aeroplane, analysing flower designs, thinking about the traffic light algorithm, investigating the Soho cholera outbreak, investigating malaria in Kitanga.

3 Analysing flower designs, thinking about the traffic light algorithm, investigating the Soho cholera outbreak, investigating malaria in Kitanga.

4 Algorithm to construct a paper aeroplane, algorithm to draw a flower, algorithm to program a lighthouse, algorithm to manage traffic lights, Dr Snow's algorithm.

Programming in Python: selection

1 Selection

1 It must be a question that can be answered with either True or False.

2 There must be a colon at the end of an if statement.

3 The code that runs if the condition is true is indented

4 They are used to create a logical test and we can use them to create a condition in an if statement.

2 Decisions based on calculations

1 The lines of code the program needs to execute are indented.

2 The lines of code the program executes are not indented. These lines will be executed if the statement returns False. They will also be executed after the code that is executed when the statement returns True.

3 a 2 because 2 is not greater than or equal to 3 and so the third line of code is not run.

   b 8

     4

     4 is greater than 3 and so the third line of code runs. Then, once the if statement is complete, the program carries on and runs the fourth line of code.

   c 6

     3

     3 is equal to 3 and so the third line of code runs. Then, once the if statement is complete, the program carries on and runs the fourth line of code.

3 If else

```
num = int(input('Enter a number between 5
and 10: '))
if num < 5:                            # 1
    print('Too small')
if num > 10:                           # 2
    print('Too big')                   # 3
else:                                  # 4
    print('You chose', num)            # 5
# 1 less than
# 2 the number 10
# 3 a statement about the number being
    too big
# 4 don't forget the colon
# 5 the variable num
```

4 Comparing strings and numbers

1
```
import random
random.randint(20, 30)
```

2
```
num = int(input('Enter a number: '))   # 1
if num % 5 == 0:                        # 2
    print('Number is divisible by 5')
else:                                   # 3
    print('Number is not divisible
 by 5')                                 # 4
# 1 num is an integer
# 2 we need to check if the remainder
    after whole number division is 0,
    so we use the % operator and the ==
    Boolean operator
# 3 don't forget the colon
# 4 a statement if the number is not
    divisible by 5
```

5 Elif

```
import random                           # 1
num = random.randint(1,10)
guess = int(input('What number am I
thinking of? '))                        # 2
if guess > num:                         # 3
    print('My number is smaller.')
elif guess < num:                       # 4
    print('My number is bigger.')       # 5
else:                                   # 6
    print('Well done!')                 # 7
# 1 the random module is imported
# 2 guess is an integer
# 3 use > to compare guess and num
# 4 what to do if guess is not > than num
# 5 output if guess < num
# 6 don't forget the colon
# 7 a statement if the number is guessed
    correctly
```

6 Multiple elifs

1 `if`

2 `elif`

3

```
age = int(input('Enter age: '))          # 1
height = float(input('Enter height: '))  # 2
if age >= 15:                             # 3
    print('Old enough to ride.')
elif height >= 1.5:                       # 4
    print('Tall enough to ride.')         # 5
else:                                     # 6
    print('Sorry not old enough and not
tall enough to ride.')
# 1 age is an integer
# 2 height is real or floating point
    number
# 3 age is 15 or greater
# 4 check the other condition: height is
    1.5 or greater
# 5 a statement if they are 1.5 m or
    taller
# 6 don't forget the colon
```

Internet safety, cyber security and encryption

1 Digital footprint

1 Social media posts that refer to something illegal or show stupid, irresponsible or mean actions could get the person posting them into trouble.

2 Don't get into an argument online, make use of privacy settings, don't include personal information in your profile, don't use a photo of yourself as your avatar, do block people and report offensive posts, and check with people before you post photos of them online.

2 Passwords and phishing

1 It is quite long. It contains a mixture of upper-case and lower-case letters, digits and special characters. It is changed regularly. It does not contain real words or names. It is not used for lots of other accounts.

2 It is a piece of software that stores passwords securely so that the user doesn't have to remember them all.

3 It has a generic greeting. It contains spelling mistakes. It uses an email address that has not come from the real company. It contains a hyperlink to a suspicious website. It is offering you something that is too good to be true and you have to act quickly.

3 Malware

1 People use the word 'virus' to describe a range of different malware. They might have an actual virus, or they might have been targeted with a trojan, a worm, ransomware or spyware.

2 Anti-malware software scans computer programs and emails for malicious code and stops the program running or the email from being opened.

3 Always install the latest software updates when they become available.

4 Encryption

1 The Atbash Cipher is the easiest to crack because the method never changes.

2 The Keyed Caesar Cipher is the hardest to crack because it is hard to use brute force to crack a cipher that has 26 possible number keys and an infinite number of possible word keys.

5 Automating encryption

1 26, because 26 is the same as 0, 27 is the same as 1 etc.

2 Once it has been set up, it can convert messages much more quickly than you can manually.

3 Writing a program might take longer than decoding a small number of messages message manually.

Binary and computer logic

1 Logic gates

1 Data is input as 1s and 0s.

2 Data is output as 1s and 0s.

3 0

4 1

2 Introducing binary

1 Base 2

2 Decimal system or base 10

3 77

3 Creating an app

1 Logic gates

2 1

3 42

4 Testing and reviewing an app

a = 1, b = 0, c = 1, d = 0

A	B	Out
1	1	1
1	0	0
0	1	0
0	0	0

5 Representing text

1 Binary digits (1s and 0s)

2 67 97 98

3 1000000 or 01000000

Sound and video editing

1 Introduction to sound editing and Audacity®

1 False

2 False

3 True

2 Audio effects

1 Adding the fade in/fade out audio effect makes a sound start and stop smoothly, without pops and crackles.

2 Adding the reverb audio effect makes a sound feel like it was recorded in a different space, with a different echo.

3 Adding the envelope audio effect enables you to make a sound quieter or louder at specific points.

3 Planning a video advert

1 True

2 True

3 False

4 Creating a soundtrack for a video advert

1 Fade out

2 Fade out

3 Fade in

4 Fade in

5 Fade out

6 Fade out

7 Fade in

8 Fade in

5 Introduction to video editing and OpenShot

1 True

2 False

3 True

6 Visual effects

1 Visual effects enhance or process video to make it look different.

2 Transitions add some excitement when the video changes from one scene to the next and smooth the passage between clips.

3 Titles tell the viewer something important.

Designing websites

1 Basic styling using CSS

1 To format the styling of a web page

2 To describe the structure and content of a web page

3 A style that is applied to specific elements on a web page

2 Images and lists

1 `<img>`

2 The link to the source image and the alternative text that describes the image

3 The image's width and height

3 Hyperlinks and navigation

1 The anchor tag `<a>`

2 Hyperlink reference

3 The link text

4 It creates a block around the link, with the whole block clickable, not just the text

4 Layout elements and web page design

1 `<!DOCTYPE html>` so that the browser knows that it is an HTML5 document and it is displayed correctly.

5 and 6 Web page design (parts 1 and 2)

You cannot tell if the first rule has been broken, because you cannot see more than the home page. The second rule has definitely been broken: the home page contains lots of different colours. The text is in both black and white and four different colours – blue, yellow, white and orange – are used for the background. The third rule has been broken: the background is very busy, with the same image repeated several times and the text appearing in lots of different boxes. The text generally stands out from the backgrounds, but it's hard to know what to focus on with so many different things to look at. It looks like only one font has been used, so the fourth rule has been followed. It looks like the most important information has been placed at the top of the screen (the fifth rule), the text is all left-aligned (the sixth rule), it has been divided into logical bite-size blocks (the seventh rule) and the lines are short (the eighth rule). Breaking just two rules can have a big impact on the look and feel of a website!

Networking and the internet

1 IP addressing and switches

1 Four numbers, separated by full stops, with each number between 0 and 255.
2 An IP address is used to send data between devices. A public IP address identifies a network and a private IP address identifies a device on a network.
3 A switch directs data packets between devices on a local network.
4 IP addresses on the local network start with 192.168.x.x, 172.x.x.x or 10.x.x.x.

2 Domain names and DNS

1 Domain names are much easier to remember and are more meaningful.
2 Domain Name System
3 The web browser uses a DNS server to look up the IP address of the domain name and then uses the IP address to communicate with the website.

3 Packets and packet switching

1 A file is split up into small chunks. The chunks are sent one at a time and put back in order at their destination.

2 The IP address of the sender, the IP address of the recipient and the packet number.
3 Advantage: If one packet is lost, then only that packet needs to be re-sent not the whole message or file. Disadvantage: The extra data that must be added to each packet means more data must be sent overall.
4 A packet can find its own route around a bottleneck or take a completely different route if there is heavy traffic.

4 The internet

1 Existing phone lines and submarine cables allow messages to be sent all over the world.
2 For example: online shopping lets you view products from shops anywhere in the world and get them delivered to your home.
3 Storing files online rather than on a device or using software online rather than downloading it to a computer.

5 Connecting to the Internet

1 Connection is likely to be faster and more reliable.
2 You can move around and remain connected to a Wi-Fi network, and don't need to install cables.
3 Mobile data is generally expensive, especially if you go over your monthly allowance. Connection speeds can slow considerably if lots of people use mobile data in a small area.

6 A community guide to the internet

1 Web browser
2 DNS
3 Packet
4 Cloud computing

Programming in Python: iteration

1 Repeating instructions

```
2
5
8
11
```

2 User-defined for loops

```
step = int(input('Enter number to be
multiplied: ')                             # 1
upper = int(input('Enter upper
number: ')                                 # 2
for index in range(step, upper + 1,
step):                                     # 3
    print(index)
# 1 the input must be cast as an integer
# 2 again the input must be cast as an
    integer
# 3 we need to start counting at the
    value of 'step', stop counting at the
    upper limit using 'upper + 1' and
    count in increments of the value of
    'step'
```

3 For loops and strings

1 **8.** **+=** adds a value to the original variable.

2 **catdogdog.** 'dog' is printed just twice because the last number in the range is one more than the number of loops required.

4 For loops and lists

Kiwi. The index value of the last element in the list is one less than the number of elements in the list.

5 Searching using for loops

```
fruits = ['Damson', 'Pear', 'Orange',
'Apple', 'Kiwi']
for i in range(0, len(fruits)):           # 1
if fruits[i] == 'Orange':                 # 2
print('Orange is found at index
value', i)                                # 3
# 1 the second parameter is set to
    len(fruits)
# 2 each element is checked in turn to
    see if it is Orange using ==
# 3 the index value of Orange is output
    if it is found
```

6 While loops

1 When you know how many times to repeat the code

2 When you don't know how many times to repeat the code, but have a condition that can be met to end the loop

3 A while loop

4 You could ask the user to enter a specific value, for example −1, when they have finished entering values and use that input in a while loop condition. The specific value must not be a value that the user is likely to want to input otherwise.

The ethics of computing

1 Sourcing content responsibly

1 To credit a source, you must state who created it (author and/or company), the title of the article or page it came from, the date it was published, the web address of the page you found it on and the date you accessed the web page.

2 It can be good publicity if your work is shared widely, and it can lead to paid work.

3 Companies spend a lot of money creating content and they do not want to give it away for free. They also want to control the way it is used.

2 Using technology responsibly

1 False, something can be immoral without being illegal. For example, using CCTV cameras to spy on your staff could be considered immoral, but it is not illegal.

2 True, something that is immoral can also be illegal but, when commenting on behaviour, we tend to focus on the fact that it is illegal because illegal acts can be formally punished.

3 False, there are situations in which you might have to break the law to do what is morally right. For example, Dr Martin Luther King Jr was imprisoned five times in his life, as he fought for civil rights in the US.

3 Technology and the environment

Examples of reasons why it is right include phones becoming more energy-efficient with each new model and people buying a new phone after using their old one for a long time wanting to buy the latest model. Examples of reasons why it is not right include people feeling pressured into buying a new phone every year to keep up with the latest trends and mobile phone manufacturers failing to take responsibility for the e-waste generated by their products.

4 Technology and the law

1 Decisions based on inaccurate or out-of-date information can be harmful to the organisation making the decision and the person the decision is being made about. For example, inaccurate data held by a credit referencing agency might stop someone from buying or renting somewhere to live.

3 Yes. According to Article 5(1)(c) of GDPR, the data stored should be relevant and limited to what is necessary. This information is all relevant to dog walking.

5 Moral dilemmas (Part 1)

There are a lot of answers to this question. For example, tech companies are struggling with the moral dilemma of how far they should protect their customers' data from government requests to see it. For example, algorithms are used to make serious decisions that affect the lives of real people, but do these algorithms have the unconscious biases of the people who develop them embedded into them?

6 Moral dilemmas (Part 2)

Student's own answers

Acknowledgements

Photo credits

p. 7 *t* © Andrey Kuzmin/stock.adobe.com, *b* © Nikolai Titov/stock.adobe.com; **p. 9** © CarryLove/stock.adobe.com; **p. 14** *background* © yaalan/stock.adobe.com, *runner* © Ljupco Smokovski/stock.adobe.com; **p. 17** *duck* © shishiga - stock.adobe.com, *lion* © Anek Suwannaphoom – 123RF, *background* Shutterstock / Graeme Shannon; **p. 26** © Bastos - Fotolia.com; **p. 30** © Andriy Bezuglov/stock.adobe.com; **p. 32** *tr* Google Workspace **p. 34** *tl* © Nneirda/stock.adobe.com, *ml* U. S. Army Photo, *bl* © Geza Farkas/stock.adobe.com, *mr* © borissos/stock.adobe.com, © TRAVELARIUM/stock.adobe.com; **p. 39** © Yael Weiss/stock.adobe.com; **p. 40** *tl* © Alexander Potashev/stock.adobe.com, *ml* © Elnur/stock.adobe.com, *bl* © Vladislav Ociacia/stock.adobe.com, *tr* © viperagp/stock.adobe.com, *mr* © Andrey Popov/stock.adobe.com; **p. 41** © MclittleStock/stock.adobe.com; **p. 54** *motherboard* © Andrei/stock.adobe.com, *CPU* © Maxim_Kazmin/stock.adobe.com, *RAM* © Evgeniia/stock.adobe.com, *graphics card* © Dan74/stock.adobe.com, *power supply* © Coprid/stock.adobe.com, *optical drive* © littlej78/stock.adobe.com, *hard drive* © Destina/stock.adobe.com; **p. 55** *t* © 300_librarians/stock.adobe.com, *b* © Elegant Solution/stock.adobe.com; **p. 58** *headphones* © Ivan/stock.adobe.com, *keyboard* © Gresei/stock.adobe.com, *monitor* © Ruslan Ivantsov/stock.adobe.com, *mouse* © New Africa/stock.adobe.com, *laptop* © Sergey Peterman/stock.adobe.com, *scanner* © Destina/stock.adobe.com, *microphone* © goir/stock.adobe.com, *printer* © tankist276/stock.adobe.com, *self checkout* © photosvac/stock.adobe.com; **p. 61** *tape drive* © Roman Ivaschenko/stock.adobe.com, *hard drive* © homydesign/stock.adobe.com, *CD drive* © littlej78/stock.adobe.com, *Blu-ray* © Peter de Kievith/stock.adobe.com, *DVD drive* © Alexey Rotanov/stock.adobe.com, *memory stick* © murat/stock.adobe.com, *Solid State drive* © trongnguyen/stock.adobe.com; **p. 64** *t* © Unkas Photo/stock.adobe.com, *m* © Gudellaphoto/stock.adobe.com, *b* © Jiggo_Putter/stock.adobe.com; **p. 66** *tl* © canbedone/stock.adobe.com, *bl* © fotofabrika/stock.adobe.com, *tr* © monshtadoid/stock.adobe.com, *br* © Oleg/stock.adobe.com; **p. 92** © Simon/stock.adobe.com; **p. 94** *ml* © World History Archive/Alamy Stock Photo, *bl* NATIONAL LIBRARY OF MEDICINE/SCIENCE PHOTO LIBRARY, *mr* Compliments of Ralph R. Frerichs, Department of Epidemiology, UCLA Fielding School of Public Health, Los Angeles, CA USA; **p. 96** © Kletr/stock.adobe.com; **p. 112** © korkeng/stock.adobe.com; **p. 113** *'Harry Iqbal'* © Prostock-studio/stock.adobe.com, *'HenryIqbal'* © DM7/stock.adobe.com, *'LC Johnson'* © alexei_tm/stock.adobe.com, *scientist* © Jeanne McRight/stock.adobe.com, *monopoly* © Lynne Sutherland/Alamy Stock Photo; **p. 116** © pandavector/stock.adobe.com; **p. 117** © byjeng/stock.adobe.com; **p. 134** © gicku91/stock.adobe.com; **p. 138** © Audacity®; **p. 142** © icemanphotos/stock.adobe.com; **p. 146** OpenShot™ Video Editor. Copyright © 2008-2021 OpenShot Studios, LLC. All Rights Reserved. Reproduced with permission of OpenShot Studios, LLC.; **p. 153** © _aine__stock.adobe.com; **p. 161** © Yale School of Art, www.art.yale.edu; **p. 168** *t* © alexlmx/stock.adobe.com, *b* © jonathan tennant/Alamy Stock Photo; **p. 170** *ethernet cable* © Roman Ivaschenko/stock.adobe.com, *Wi-Fi* © faraktinov/stock.adobe.com; **p. 171** © CoolVectorStock/stock.adobe.com; **p. 172** © Julia Tim/stock.adobe.com; **p. 188** *tl* © chokniti/stock.adobe.com, *bl* © stnazkul/stock.adobe.com, *tr* © Oleg Breslavtsev/stock.adobe.com; **p. 189** *'Paul Derrick'* © BillionPhotos.com/stock.adobe.com, *celebration* © lorabarra/stock.adobe.com, *'FishBandit'* © NITIKAN T./stock.adobe.com, *graduation* © Sc Stockraphy/stock.adobe.com; **p. 190** *t* © maru54/stock.adobe.com, *b* © slowmotiongli/stock.adobe.com; **p. 191** © VanderWolf Images/stock.adobe.com; **p. 194** © zapp2photo/stock.adobe.com; **p. 200** © vectorfusionart/stock.adobe.com; **p. 206** © urbanbuzz/Alamy Stock Photo; **p. 208** © pixel78.de/stock.adobe.com

Index